In the *Fiery Furnace*

"Hitherto hath the LORD helped us."

Life in Ukraine, Siberia, Kazakhstan, and Germany:

*The Autobiography of
Johann and Elfriede Steffen*

Translated by Edward Kline from the German book
Im Schmelztiegel:
Bis hierher hat uns der Herr geholfen

read — April 2023

In the Fiery Furnace was translated from the German book
Im Schmelztiegel
Bis hierher hat uns der Herr geholfen
by permission of the authors,
Johann and Elfriede Steffen.

Publishing information for German book:
Christliche Schriftenverbreitung
Postfach 100153, D-42490 Hückeswagen
© 1996 by Christliche Schriftenverbreitung, 42499 Hückeswagen
Farbbilder: Missionswerk Friedensbote, 51603 Gummersbach
SchwarzweißBßbilder: Johann und Elfriede Steffen
Zeichnungen: Birgit Winterhoff
ISBN 3-89287-771-8

Notes about English edition:

Johann Steffen sent some additional details to be inserted in the English text, which is not in the original German. This material is included on pages 14, 36, 44, 46, 48 (footnote), 56, 58, 61, 68, 69, 72–73, 92, 95–100, 107, 130–132, 144–144, 148–150, 189–189. Appropriate headings were added at some places.

The following items were also added to the English translation: the introduction to the English edition, the chapter introductions, most of the footnotes, the appendices, some main headings, and all the subheadings in smaller font. We respected the way the book was originally written in German and basically followed their style of writing in the translation.

Persons involved in various phases of the project: Frank Weaver, John B. Martin (translator), Alta Hoover, Dorothy Witmer, Ed Kline (translator), Alvin Hoover, James K. Nolt.

English edition © Frank Weaver, 2022
Color pictures (pages 121–124):
© Missionswerk Friedensbote e.V., Volmestr. 51, D-58540 Meinerzhagen
www.friedensbote.org

ISBN: 978-1-7333266-6-7

Available from your Christian bookstore or order from
Fiery Furnace
2233 Little Hill Rd.
Narvon, PA 17555-9389
inthefieryfurnace2022@gmail.com

Table of Contents

Appendices

Introduction to the
English Edition

Welcome to this first-hand account of Christians who bravely suffered for their faith under Soviet communism. We who lived during the twentieth century remember hearing the distant rumblings of persecution in communist countries while we were enjoying the blessings of freedom of religion. Now we can learn more details about those stories and pass them on to a younger generation who has no personal memory of that era. *"Remember them that are in bonds, as bound with them; and them which suffer adversity, as being yourselves also in the body"* (Hebrews 13:3). Our memory of Christians faithfully suffering both in the past and present inspires us and helps us to avoid the complacency, lukewarmness, and ingratitude that come so easily.

Johann and Elfriede Steffen's Mennonite ancestors moved to Ukraine and then to other areas that were later controlled by communism. They wrote about their persecution with the intent to honor Jesus Christ, refraining from complaint, fanfare, and self-exultation. They lived according to 1 Peter 4:12: *"Beloved, think it not strange concerning the fiery trial which is to try you, as though some strange thing happened unto you."* The Russians confined Johann six times, about eighteen years total. They punished him with forced labor and then imprisonment for helping the Germans during World War II. Later they imprisoned him four more times for his Christian work, about eleven years and two months.

The Steffens wrote their autobiography in German, and this English translation developed through Johann and Elfriede's visit to the United States. Frank Weaver, Narvon, Pennsylvania, traveled with the Steffens and translated from German into English as Johann shared about his life experiences at a Christian Aid Ministries Open House in 1992 and at various speaking engagements afterward. Johann of Russian Mennonite roots and Frank of Swiss Mennonite roots developed a special friendship, and Frank persevered and pursued his labor of love in getting the Steffens' story translated and published in English.

This account serves as primary source material for the historian who wants to understand this Russian experience, and it also provides inspirational reading for those who want to follow the writers' lives without being overwhelmed with details of time and place.

We added several appendices to this translation to facilitate the reader's understanding. Ed Kline introduced the Mennonite experience in Russia, including how Mennonites were absorbed into the Baptist Church. Since both Johann and Elfriede wrote about the same events from their unique perspectives, the timeline helps to clarify the sequence and context of these events. Other appendices describe special travels after the Steffens emigrated to Germany. Hopefully, the maps inside the back cover and the geographical footnotes will solve at least some of the mysteries of Eurasian geography.

We hope this book will inform and inspire Mennonite readers of both Swiss and "Russian" descent as they read how their spiritual kinsmen suffered for their faith. We likewise recommend it to immigrants from the former Soviet Union, who want to better understand what their spiritual fathers suffered under communism. *"Hitherto hath the LORD helped us"* (1 Samuel 7:12). May He be glorified through this work and may His people be encouraged to be "more than conquerors" through Jesus Christ in all of life's challenges.

—*James K. Nolt*

Publisher's Foreword

(Translated from German)

We are grateful to God for the publication of the autobiographies of Johann and Elfriede Steffen.

All too soon, we in the "West" have become accustomed to the current political situation in the countries of the former Soviet Union. In the Epilogue, the authors express their joy at the change that took place, that the decades of persecution of Christians under Communist rule has ended.

Johann and Elfriede Steffen each describe their childhood and adolescence, then the seemingly endless time of fear, need, separation, and deprivations that ended only with their departure to Germany in 1988.

The publishers have avoided an extensive revision of the author's manuscripts, so the originality and authenticity of their reports would not be hindered.

Our sincere wish for all readers of this autobiography is that they would be amazed at the ways of God with this family, who was not disappointed by their trust in Him, and that the readers would reverence this God themselves.

—The Publisher

Introduction

(Translation from German)

We knew Johann Steffen already since 1953 because he also was on the Middle Asian Council of Brothers. He was in prison four times because of his faith. Who in those churches would not have known him because of that? From the beginning of the sixties he assumed responsibility of the local church in Issyk. If Johann and Elfriede had not been such committed Christians, they would not have needed to spend so many years of their lives in prisons and concentration camps. Johann's wife did not have it easy. She had to stay alone with the children so often that one would hear others say, "How can she endure everything?"

This book gives a description again of the facts, that no one can contradict. It shows what a source of strength comes from trusting in God. May this book be a blessing to many, that by it many of God's children may unconditionally trust in the Lord Jesus as this couple did.

—*Jakob Tissen*

1. Childhood and Youth

(1932–1950) This chapter covers Johann's life from 1932, when he was a young boy and living in Ukraine, to 1950, when he was sent to a prison camp in Siberia.

During this time, his family left the fertile lands of southern Ukraine and moved to Poland. The almost utopian life that the Russian Mennonites had enjoyed before the war had been virtually destroyed by World War I and the raids by the anarchists that followed. By 1929, thousands had emigrated to Canada and the United States to escape the terror and famine in the Ukraine.

When Hitler's armies occupied Ukraine, the German-speaking Mennonites were protected and watched over by the Germans. After two years of advancing into the Russian interior, the German army was defeated at the battle of Stalingrad, and what was left began retreating. When the German armies were forced to retreat from Ukraine in 1943, they took around 25,000 Mennonites along to Poland, among them Johann's family.

As the German armies retreated through Poland, many Mennonites tried to escape the coming Russians by escaping to Germany. While some were successful in escaping to America, many were forcibly deported to Russia. Those who remained in Poland, such as Johann's family, were subject to relocation and exile, and many were sent to Siberia by the Russians.

Famine conditions existed from World War I through World War II. The military trenches Johann helped dig in Schretersburg were to deter the Russian tanks from following the retreating German armies. These activities for the German army later brought Johann much persecution from the Russians.

Visitors

Johann Steffen

It was the winter of 1932. My mother cast a furtive glance through the kitchen window, and she saw several activists coming into the courtyard. These men, including one of our neighbors, had earlier brought misfortune to a number of families.

Mother and my sister Anna were washing clothes, and several pails and pots of snow were melting into water on the long bench behind the stove. Both of them immediately stopped washing. They grabbed bags of peas, beans, and grits from the wall shelf, and stuffed them into the pails and pots of melting snow. They packed the snow back into the pails, covering up the bags. Mother wanted to hide whatever possible from those men, who could already be heard in the next room.

Six years old at the time and naturally curious, I followed the strangers to see what they would do. The men searched the entire house and took whatever they could find. Then they took crowbars and shovels and began digging through the barnyard and the dirt barn floor. Finding nothing new, they gave up and left the house with their loot.

Minutes later Mother and Anna fished the bags of food out of the water and spread the contents on the kitchen table to dry. There was nothing else edible left in the house. The men had stripped our larder.

Several days earlier these activists had made an unexpected visit and had taken Father away. They came early in the morning when I was still in bed. In parting, Father gave me a handful of sunflower seeds and said to Mother, "Take especially good care of him so that he survives!" He probably said this because I was frequently sick.

Famine

Russia was afflicted by a severe famine that year, and without Father everything was much more difficult. Our hunger was real, and in such difficult times, it was extremely hard for Mother to keep five hungry children fed. My oldest brother Abram already worked elsewhere, and my fourteen-year-old sister Anna often had to go begging.

By the following spring, only a small box of seed potatoes was left. That was only because Mother had hidden it well. The potatoes weren't much bigger than beans, yet after Mother prayerfully stuck them into the ground, it began to rain. By the grace of God, we were able to harvest nice, big potatoes—it was a fruitful year.

Johann Steffen (first row, first from right) in fourth grade with his class in front of the school at Wernersdorf. Teacher is in the middle of the photo.

Severe persecution was directed at the Christians at this time. Nevertheless, Mother continued to read to us from the Bible, especially during the winter when she had more free time. As a precaution, we draped the windows so nobody could look in and observe us.

We received the sad news from prison that Father had died. As Mother was building a fire in the stove one evening, I saw tears in her eyes. "Are you crying because Father is dead?" I wondered.

She replied, "No, I'm crying for you children because I worry that you aren't receiving enough instruction from the Word of God." She simply didn't have enough time to instruct us since she had to work from morning to evening every day. Church services were now nonexistent, and at school we learned there was no God. Still Mother persisted in much praying, often with tears. God heard those sincere prayers of my weeping mother.

War

Finally, the famine ended. By the grace of God our family had managed to survive. However, before many years passed, these trying times were to be replaced by still harder times. War began in the fall of 1941.[1] Irresistibly, the front advanced.

We Germans were to be relocated to eastern Russia near Kazakhstan. By order of the authorities, we waited at the train station for a whole week. When the front came pressing closer, we were forced to return to our village.

Finally, at the Stulnewa station, we boarded the train with all our luggage. During the night the order was given to disembark again with all our luggage and wait in an adjoining field. As we camped in the field, we saw the Russian soldiers go about with torches and set the entire train station on fire. Here and there they blew up parts of the track.

We discussed among ourselves whether the Germans were coming. In the morning some of our fellow villagers went to Wernersdorf,[2] seven kilometers away. They wanted to see what was going on and bring wagons and horses.

When we returned to our village, the German soldiers were already there. As Mother was kindling a fire in the stove using straw to heat coffee for the evening meal, a German soldier came in (they had already taken up lodging at our house), and asked, "Do you heat with straw? In Germany there is no straw to be found in the streets. We have liberated you!" Haughtily he added, "Now it will be easier for you!"

I stood beside Mother, who answered, "Hopefully it won't go with us as it did after World War I when at first the German army was pushing forward, but then it was utterly routed." Then she added pointedly, "After that, it became very difficult for our husbands."

"Wherever the Germans set foot, they don't retreat!" he retorted in a sharp tone that frightened me.

I pleaded with Mother to be quiet so he wouldn't hurt us. After that, we spoke Low German, which he couldn't understand.

Migration to Poland

Two years later, on September 11, 1943, conditions forced us to leave our village because of the German troops' retreat. Like many

---

1. World War II began in 1939 and entered Ukraine in 1941.
2. A Mennonite village in Ukraine; also called Rosental. Its current name is Ostrykivka.

Johann's mother in Poland, 1944.

others, we migrated to Poland, and under great hardship, reached Warthegau[3] in February 1944.

In Warthegau we had to linger in a camp for several weeks, after which we were separated and placed on various estates. Our family was sent to the estate of Hinschfelde, near the city of Krutschwitz. For some time we worked on this estate.

Later, some inhabitants of our village, myself included, were taken to Schretersburg to dig military trenches. During this entire time, I worked with our neighbor, the one who had helped raid our house after Father was taken prisoner.

Irresistibly the front advanced nearer. One day we received the command to return to the Hinschfelde estate. A few days later, a wagon was provided for us to travel farther west, but we didn't make speedy enough progress. By the fourth day, Russian soldiers had already caught up with us. They thoroughly searched our wagon, expecting to find weapons.

In the course of their search, one soldier saw my sister-in-law's clock and was going to take it. But at just that moment, another man

---

3. *Wartheland* (English).

came along and restrained him. "These are Russian Germans," he commented. Thereupon both men left. However, several minutes later the second man was back. He gave my sister-in-law a nice piece of sausage and tried to cajole her into giving him the clock. In the end, he got her clock.

We waited until noon, after the Russian army had moved on, and then returned to our old estate. There we all crowded into one building because each was afraid to stay alone.

A few evenings later, three Russian soldiers came to our barracks. This was terrible for the women, as the soldiers stayed all night. The next morning, they cleaned their guns and counted the cartridges. *Are there enough cartridges to shoot us all?* my mother thought.

Later, they left. They were the kind of soldiers who came along behind the front and committed shameful deeds.

Imprisoned in the Camp at Minsk

In the following period all the German men from sixteen to sixty years old were brought to the collecting point at Muntwims to be deported to Russia. They painted the German swastika (Nazi symbol) on the backs of many of them. Finally, we were all deported to Minsk.[4]

The Poles who accompanied us to the Russian border vented their hatred on us every chance they got. Every morning when we got back on the train after taking care of our personal needs, we were counted and struck time and again. When we arrived at the camp near Minsk, we still numbered about a thousand men.

Here we had to work very hard but were poorly fed, which resulted in the deaths of nearly half of our countrymen. Every day the dead had to be loaded up and carted away. The Russians compelled some German Russians to supervise us. These men treated us worse than the Russians themselves had. Often these were men who had a troubled conscience because of their misuse of Jews under the German occupation. Now they wanted to save themselves by chasing and beating us.[5]

---

4. Minsk is the capital and largest city of what is now Belarus.
5. The time came, years later, that our tormentors' punishments against us were held against them. It was discovered they had committed war crimes from 1941 to 1943.

It was then that I began to meditate on what Mother had taught us from the Bible. I began to pray and to discuss these things with others my age—that all things were possible with God and that His power could preserve us.

One day a Russian officer entered unexpectedly and said, "I have heard from the government that it would like to at least save the young people, since so many people have already died."

Consequently, we were called together several days later and asked, "What trade would you like to learn?" A cabinet shop and a paint shop were available. My friend Heinrich and I chose the paint shop, where the work was considerably easier. Tables and chairs for the workers' kitchen were built in the cabinet shop, whereas in the paint shop we only needed to paint them.

After we had painted all the chairs and tables, the Russian headmaster came and asked, "Have you had enough to eat since you've been living in camp?"

With a clear conscience we answered, "No."

He advised us to take paint and paintbrushes and go to where the new kitchen was being built. There we were to number the bottom sides of the tables and chairs with a small paintbrush. The chef, a good man, would also be present. "Don't work too fast," he recommended. "That way you can be there longer."

We found everything just as he had said. The chef showed us the work we were to do and then left.

At night when he returned, he asked, "Are you hungry?"

"Of course, we're hungry," we replied.

Quickly he wrote a short note on a slip of paper, which we were to present in the workers' kitchen. So when the workday ended, we quickly headed that way. We arrived at the kitchen and showed our paper to the cook, who asked, "Soup or gruel?"

Spontaneously we both said, "Gruel," and held out our dishes, which we always carried with us. He filled them to the brim, and since they held about a quart, it felt afterwards that we actually had something in our stomachs.

From then on, we decided to each carry along two dishes, so we could get soup as well as gruel. This worked for a whole month, allowing us to also share food with our campmates. The chef constantly found new work for us, until one day he received instructions from the authorities that only one of us could stay with him; the other had to work in the factory.

"You stay here," I told Heinrich. "I'll go to the factory. You can eat your fill during the day—that is when the cooking is done—and in the evenings you can bring something along for me." For another month, things went well. God saved us from starvation even though I was not yet converted at that time.

Later on, Heinrich had to join me in the factory. On our way to work, we had to pass the homes of the Russians. Their poverty was so great that men were constantly going out to the garbage cans and picking out potato peelings, bread scraps, and vegetable cuttings—anything that was edible.

One day a man found something wrapped in newspaper that looked like dried bread scraps, but after he had eaten some of it, he decided it was dried yeast. Later, the man began to feel sick and foam came from his mouth. He fell to the ground and began to roll about, and before long he lay completely still. Those who stood near him thought he was already dead and began to help themselves to the man's possessions. One took his belt, and another pulled off his shoes since they were still in better condition than his own were.

But, surprise! A short time later the man revived and got to his feet. His possessions were quickly returned to him. I never saw the man again after that.

We remained in this camp, about fifteen kilometers from Minsk, until the fall of 1945. Then we were moved to the city of Minsk. Since I had learned to paint in camp, I could enjoy certain freedoms here. While others had to march to their places of work under supervision, we painters could go without guards. If our workplace was too far, we could even use the streetcar. This way it was possible for us to beg on our commute, which I did regularly. I was always amazed that the Russians, who had experienced the German occupation, gave us Germans so much bread. They themselves could obtain their bread only with ration cards. I went begging once a week. With this additional bread and our camp food, we got along fairly well.

My friend's name was Heinrich Renpening. He had lived in the Ukraine, in the neighboring village of Liebenau. There I had gone to school with him in grades five and six. Later we had both lived in Warthegau, only three kilometers from each other.

In 1944, Heinrich and I worked together digging military trenches for the Germans. At the end of the same year, we both had to go for military examination under German orders. Since we were both too short, we didn't have to enter the service. Thus, we spent two more years together in Minsk in the Russian prison.[6]

The Difficult Trip Home

In the meantime, my mother, my sister Margareta, and my oldest sister Anna with her two children, Lina and Margarita, were relocated from Poland to the USSR[7] into Krasavino in the district of Vologda.[8] With them were the families of Herr Peters and Herr Thomas, two men who had been imprisoned at Minsk with me.

In late February 1947, when I was twenty years old, we were released and permitted to rejoin our loved ones in Krasavino. At camp we were given money for train tickets, as well as a week's provisions.

Already in Minsk much time was wasted before the tickets were finally issued to us. That evening as we stood in line to board the train, Herr Peters' suitcase and his provisions suddenly vanished without a trace. Herr Thomas could only shake his head, for now the three of us had to make do with his and my provisions. But shaking his head did nothing to change the situation. The suitcase was gone.

When we arrived in Moscow, we had to transfer to another train. At the station we heard that travelers sometimes had to wait up to a week before they could travel farther. This wouldn't have been easy for us since we now had only two bags of food. As we stood perplexed before a kiosk outside the station, a porter

---

6. In 1947, Heinrich and I parted ways, and until 1992, I received no news of whether my friend was alive or not. As I was writing this manuscript, I unexpectedly heard from him. On Monday, April 27, 1992, my wife came home from visiting friends and handed me a letter from Heinrich. He had learned I was living in Ulm, but didn't know my address. So he simply addressed the letter to another person, and in this way it reached me. I learned that Heinrich was still living and that he had moved to Germany in 1990. On May 15, 1992, I traveled to Nagold to visit him and his wife. I was their guest for several days. Our past came alive again. After forty-five years, we were once more together and could talk of how dark the future had looked in 1945.
7. Union of Soviet Socialist Republics.
8. German spellings by Steffen include *Krasawina* or *Krasawino* (on the map). The German *Wikipedia* has *Krassawino*, and the English *Krasavino*. *Vologda* is *Wologda* in German.

suddenly approached us and asked, "What's the matter?"

After we told him all about our plight, he said, "I can help you." We gave him our tickets so that he could get them extended, and we also gave him some money for his help. Herr Peters accompanied the man into the station.

The porter left Herr Peters standing before a door, commanding, "Please wait here a moment. I'll be back soon." In the meantime, Herr Thomas and I waited outside the building. After a while, I set out to investigate what was keeping Herr Peters so long. I found him still waiting at the same door. Unable to restrain myself any longer, I pressed the latch, opened the door, and found myself standing on the platform. The rascally porter had disappeared with our money and our tickets!

What should we do now? How could we get home with no tickets and only a handful of money?

First of all, we set our nearly empty suitcases into the luggage office. The other two wanted to inquire how and when we could acquire tickets and travel on. Meanwhile I went into the city to beg.

I was scarcely on the street when a passing truck lost a package. I picked it up and opened the wrapping. It was full of tobacco, which I sold for fifty rubles at the next street corner. Pocketing the money, I returned to the station where the others were waiting. They had already bought tickets, but only to the next stop, since we did not have enough money to get us to our desired destination. We decided to pretend to be asleep when we reached that stop, so we could travel farther. But it didn't work. When we came in sight of the station, the conductor came and reminded us that we would soon have to get off.

Now it was evening. In the station we ate our last remaining morsels of food. I lay down on one of the benches and fell asleep. While I slept, Herr Thomas sold our suitcases, along with our last belongings. The proceeds from this sale would help get us to Konoscha, but this was still 400 kilometers short of Kotlas, our destination.

In the morning we boarded the train, and the following day we arrived in Konoscha without money, food, or luggage. We had only one cooking utensil left among the three of us. We wanted to sell it, too, but couldn't find a buyer. The train to Kotlas wouldn't leave until the next evening, and Herr Peters and Herr Thomas planned to take the freight train, which was leaving in the morning.

The first days of March were very cold. With my lined jacket and lined pants, such a trip would have been possible, but not with the light shoes I had on. Since I didn't possess the courage to tackle such a long trip on a freight train, I stayed behind by myself.

The first thing I did was go to the market and sell my cooking utensil for twenty rubles. I accepted payment in potatoes and cake. After I had eaten the food, I returned to the train station. Nearby I found a lunchroom where the workers had eaten lunch, but nobody had left anything lying on the tables. So I waited until evening when the train for Kotlas was to come. But how could I board the train without a ticket?

As I sat alone, knowing of no way out, I once again thought of my dear mother and how she spoke with God in all her difficult times. I thought of the words she had so often spoken in the presence of us children, "When the need is the greatest, God's help is the nearest."[9] At the moment I had no understanding of their meaning.

After a long wait, the train finally pulled into the station. Many travelers stood on the platform ready to board. I walked to and fro, noticing how some passengers got off to buy cakes, boiled potatoes, milk, and other things that local women had for sale at the station.

When a woman got off and threw an empty glass jar into the snow, I quickly snatched it up, filled it with snow, and headed for the coach in order to board it. But of course, the conductress asked about my ticket. Now what would I tell her?

Trying to sound natural, I said, "I've only gone to buy milk and want to get back onto the coach." The jar held only snow, which she couldn't see. Whether she believed me, I don't know. Maybe she saw that I had reached the limit of my endurance. In any case, she let me board.

Inside the coach I threw the jar of snow into the first corner I came to, pressed toward the front of the coach, and was prepared to stand until the end of my trip, if only I could stay on the train.

Finally the train departed. Several hours later, after more passengers had gotten off, I clambered onto the baggage rack and was soon asleep.

During the night I heard that tickets were being checked.

---

9. „Wenn die Not am größten ist, ist Gottes Hilfe am nächsten."

The conductor came to me, poked me, and requested my ticket. I pretended to be asleep, but it did no good. Again and again he jabbed me. Now what? I showed him the paper I'd been given at camp.

"I don't need this," he retorted. "I want to see your ticket."

"Read this paper over," I answered. "If you can't read, it's not my fault."

But this, too, didn't work. He only said curtly, "Get off at the next station," and moved on. I waited awhile, but nobody bothered me anymore, and I arrived in Kotlas at two o'clock in the afternoon.

Earlier, Mother had written that I should get a ride from Kotlas to Jadricha. From there I could walk to Krasavino, which was about five kilometers farther. At least, that's how I imagined it.

In the station yard at Kotlas, I inquired how I could travel farther. I was kindly informed when the train would depart for Jadricha. Because I still had some time, I went into the city to beg.

But wherever I went, hunger was evident. No one gave me anything. Finally, a woman gave me several raw potatoes, saying, "Maybe you can boil them somewhere." As soon as I was back on the street, I gulped them down, despite their being raw.

Then I went back to the station. The train, which consisted of a string of old coaches, had already pulled in. Since nobody was standing at the door, I boarded.

Inside was an iron coal-burning stove. I sat down beside it thinking, *It's too bad. If only I hadn't eaten the potatoes raw, I could have baked them here.* More men and women boarded, glanced at me, and moved on. Apparently, I looked rather unkempt.

At last the train drove off. The ticket collection didn't fail to take place. "Your ticket, please," the conductress requested of me.

"Don't you see I'm firing the stove?" I replied. She actually moved on, and I arrived in Jadricha nevertheless. It was already late in the evening, so I wasn't able to be on my way to Krasavino. I spent the night at the station. During the night I became so sick from the raw potatoes that I vomited them all up.

In the morning, with an empty and aching stomach, I was on my way. In about an hour I reached a town, but from the description my mother had given, it couldn't be Krasavino. She had explained that both of my sisters worked in a factory, and there was no factory in sight.

My sister Anna with her two children in Poland, 1944.

Seeing a woman on her way to the well, I asked her, "Could you please tell me the way to Krasavino, and how far it is?"

"It's still twenty-five kilometers," she answered. "You just continue on this road."

I was shocked. I went to the well and took a drink of water. I got up and plodded on again. The road mostly led through forest. At two o'clock in the afternoon, I finally arrived in Krasavino.

At Home

I found number 307 barracks, where my mother was living. The room was filled with people, among them my good mother. She looked very thin and hungry but immediately came to me and greeted me most joyfully. I arrived "home" on March 6, 1947.

Mother led me to a corner of the big room, where she and my

sisters, Margareta and Anna, and Anna's two daughters, lived. "Anna and Margareta will soon be home from work," she informed me.

When my sisters returned from work, our mutual joy was great. Yet, they looked expectantly about, trying to see whether I had brought along any food, while all along I had been hoping to get something to eat from them. Then Anna ventured, "We'll have to buy tomorrow's bread, so you'll get something into your stomach." This they did willingly. Here everyone wanted to, and also had to, help one another. Yet there was nothing to be had.

Four other families lived in the room with Mother and my sisters, among them Frau Thomas and her daughter. We were together again.

Here, just as everywhere else, the Germans were subject to the commandant's office. I, too, had to report the next day. The officer registered me and sent me to work right the next day. I had to unload wood from the railroad cars.

Shortly afterwards I became very sick and had to be hospitalized for a week. By that time Herr Peters and Herr Thomas had also arrived home. The police had taken them off the cold freight train and given them some food to eat. In the end their ride home had been more tolerable and more comfortable than mine.

No sooner was I out of the hospital than I had to unload wood again. For a malnourished young man like myself, this was strenuous work. However, I kept quiet when I heard what the women had to endure in Poland, without any men around. Only old men and boys under the age of sixteen had been left. The children had been separated from their mothers so the mothers could work. Meanwhile, in the children's camps, Polish men and women chose any children they wanted and took them home with them.

Anna's two daughters and a little cousin boy were among those taken. Their mothers had cautioned them always to stay together. Someone came and wanted to take one of the girls, but they had cried together and refused. "We'll go along only if you take all three of us." Nobody wanted to take three children, so they stayed together for a month. By then their mothers were able to claim them again. They had complained to the Russian authorities, who had known nothing of the abduction of the children.

It wasn't long until my sister Anna died of hunger and exertion on May 31, 1947. My sister Margareta and I buried her. The cemetery was outside the village, and the only possible way to transport the body there was by oxcart (with the commandant's permission, naturally).

Mother sent some bags with us so we could gather stinging nettle, which was edible when cooked. It could not be found anywhere else anymore. We didn't have the strength to dig a deep grave but finally succeeded in getting it deep enough so that we could lower the coffin and cover it. Then we picked nettle until our bags were full and drove back to the village.

In the fall we heard that people had gone to glean potatoes on the collective lands. My sister and I decided to do this too. But when we arrived at the field ready to gather spuds, two Russian youths appeared and beat me until I was all bloody. So we had to go home with empty bags. Not until later, when the ration cards for bread and other food were discontinued, could we eat our fill.

This time of hunger was very difficult for my mother; in fact, it was so difficult that she never fully recovered, and she died on December 20, 1948. This time my friend helped me with the burial. We took her to the cemetery on a hand sled. I had dug the grave the day before, but it had stormed and snowed so much that we had to search a long time to locate it. We scooped the snow out of it and buried Mother. It was very late until we got back home.

Goodbye to Freedom

The weeks passed, and one day I heard that the government was checking into my past. Since I knew what lay ahead of me, I had time to prepare for the worst.

One day Commandant Kusminski came and asked me various questions. For one, why hadn't I married? By this time some of my friends had already been married for a long time.

I answered, "I won't need to be concerned about this anymore because you're about to marry me for twenty-five years." By this I meant that they'd put me in prison.

"Get that idea out of your head," he retorted. "Who would be imprisoned for such old matters?"

Things remained quiet for a while until early August 1950 when they arrested Herr Peters and Onkel[10] Kladt. Since I had been

---

10. *Uncle* (English).

in camp in Minsk with these two, I figured my time had come as well.

One of my earlier hearings, at which two men were present, returned to my mind. An older man had directed most of the questions to me, and a younger man had sat by my side. Whenever I had not wanted to answer a question, the younger fellow had given me a good kick with his boot. "Stop kicking!" the older man would say to him.

Then he would ask, "Why don't you answer the questions I ask you? No doubt you were raised on German milk."

I just kept quiet and thought, *You're right,* for my mother was German.

On August 20, the commandant himself came and brought me to his office. On the way, I reminded him that my suspicion had been well-founded after all.

But he held me off with, "Don't say any more about it. It's for a completely different matter that you're being taken to headquarters."

Outside headquarters stood a strange passenger vehicle. When we got inside the building, several men were sitting there. To them the commandant said, "This is the character!"

Immediately they declared, "You're under arrest!" They searched me, and then we left the building. They ordered me into the car, and we drove to my home.

There they searched my whole room. Under the bed they found my packed suitcase. "So! You've already gotten ready to run away," they accused me.

"I didn't prepare to run away," I replied, "but to go to prison."

In the hall stood young boys, anxiously waiting to see what they'd do with me. Quite a few also stood in the yard in front of the house. When I was led to the car and seated inside, they waved to me and went away.

We drove to the city of Veliky Ustyug,[11] which lay near Krasavino. There they put me into prison, and later, into the work camp.

---

11. *Welikij Ustjug* (German).

2. In the Prison and Work Camp

(1950–1959) In this chapter Johann relates his experiences in a Russian prison camp in Siberia. He was not a believer when he came there, but he committed his life to Christ while in the camp. Two years after Stalin died (1953), Johann was released from prison and moved to Kazakhstan where many Mennonites had moved to. Here he met Elfriede at a wedding in Korkino. They married in 1957.

Sentenced

Johann Steffen

In the prison I was again thoroughly searched and led to a small cell. It was already quite late. Glancing about my cell, I discovered a long, narrow crate that looked like a coffin.

Have they put a corpse in here? I immediately thought. But when I moved the crate, it didn't weigh much. Then it dawned on me— this was where I was supposed to sleep! I was so tired that I lay down and was instantly sound asleep.

The next morning the guard rapped on my door and barked, "Get up!" I answered, but went right back to sleep. The guard went along again, checking on all the men he had roused. He knocked on my door the second time, scolding all the while. I answered, "I understood you," but went right back to sleep again.

The third time, the guard opened the cell door and yelled, "If you don't get up right this minute, I'll have you sent to the isolation cell!" These words I did indeed understand and sprang out of bed without a moment's further delay.

I was familiar with the rules of camp, but the prison rules I had not yet learned. I was brought frequently, mostly at night, before the examining magistrate. I was charged under paragraph 54-1(a) USSR. Under that provision, every possible charge had been summarized: my exit to Poland with the German troops, my naturalization there, the work at the military trenches—thereby, I had worked against the USSR. That was the accusation. And because I had belonged to the Hitler Youth Organization, they considered me a serious transgressor, one who was worthy of a severe punishment.

The examining magistrate, Major Lefantjew, was not a bad man. He didn't strike me, but he often pressed his index finger to my forehead. It aggravated me greatly that he called me so often during the night for interrogation.

Among other things, he quizzed me about Herr Peters, but I was unable to provide any answers in his line of questioning. Thereupon he said, "Some people from your town know all about this and you don't?" Now I understood that our neighbor from back home was at the bottom of it all—the one who was bent on getting Herr Peters and some others, as well as me, into prison. He was persistently continuing the work that he had already begun in the 1930s.

Later I was brought by ship and then by train to Vologda. On the train I was confined in a locked compartment. When my eyes had grown accustomed to the dark, I saw I wasn't alone. A German man was in the compartment with me. He was accused of spying because he had succeeded in getting to America during the war; however, he then had returned to Russia.

The man had learned that his family was living in Russia, close to Kotlas, and had been home for only three weeks until he was arrested. When he related how they had tortured him, it became clear that, by comparison, they had treated me quite gently.

Ten days after I reached Vologda, I was sentenced to twenty-five years in the labor camp and was stripped of my citizenship for five years, exactly as they had said all along. After my sentence had been announced, they put me into an individual cell. As I sat there, my past flitted through my mind. The misery I had suffered came sharply into focus although the worst of it took place a long time ago. When the ration cards had been discontinued and we could again eat our fill, my body had also recovered from the effects of the famine.

Other aspects of my past returned to my mind. I could clearly remember May 1, 1948, when I was with several of my comrades, and some girls, drinking schnapps on this state holiday. Mother had often admonished me to begin a new life, but at that time I hadn't yet yielded myself. How many tears I had to shed now because I hadn't listened to my mother earlier! As I sat in my prison cell, I made my decision to make a new beginning. I threw away all the tobacco items I had with me. Then I began to pray to God.

Today I would like to appeal to all children with the words of the Scriptures: *"Children, obey your parents in the Lord: for this is right. Honor thy father and mother; (which is the first commandment with promise;) that it may be well with thee, and thou mayest live long on the earth"* (Ephesians 6:1–3). I should have held firmly to my good vow, but it didn't last long. When I was released from the individual cell ten days later, my good resolutions ended. I forgot all about them and went back to my former life.

In the Work Camp

Shortly afterward we were transported by train to the Komi ASSR[1] in the Russian Soviet Republic. I was part of a group of several hundred men. On the way I met Herr Peters and Onkel Kladt again, for which I greatly rejoiced. It was a long trip. We were traveling over Christmas and New Year's Day, and didn't arrive until the middle of January.

During the trip, Herr Peters told me many happenings from his life and also recounted some of the mistakes he had made.

"The first mistake," he reminisced, "I made in the 1920s, when many Germans were immigrating to Canada. At that time my friends said to me, 'Peter, don't you want to come with us?'

"'No,' was my answer at the time, 'for I have just recently married and have received a considerable inheritance of land, horses, and cows. Now my wife and I want to start up farming—not move away.'

"Suddenly times changed. In the following years everything was taken from us, and everyone was forced onto the collective farms. Then, in 1938 the great famine began.

"The second big mistake I made in early 1945," he related further. "It was then that my brother David came to visit me. At that time he was living near Warsaw, and I in Warthegau. 'Peter, prepare yourself and your family,' he urged. 'Tomorrow we leave for Germany. Take along

---

1. Komi Autonomous Soviet Socialist Republic.

only your ration card and money; leave everything else as I've done. I have seen what the Russian soldiers did where I lived. I just barely escaped with my life.'

"'No,' I again refused, 'I can't do that now. I've brought along all these things from the Ukraine, and now I'm to leave them here? That won't do!'

"'However you wish, but I'm leaving tomorrow,' he said. Today he's in Canada and has all he needs and is enjoying freedom besides. And I, who twice tried to hold on to my bit of earthly goods, have nothing left today. And I'm in prison, separated from my family for the second time already."[2]

When we reached our destination, we were organized for work. My job was to cut wood in the forest, which at first wasn't easy. We couldn't always fill our quota. Whoever couldn't fill his quota got less to eat and had to go to the isolation cell besides. The snow was deep, and it was very cold.

One day toward evening, the brigadier came and told us we were one sled load of wood shy of our quota. Punischo, the group leader, cut a few more trees down, which we worked up while he went to get a wagoner to haul the wood. Two of us, Sinitzkin and I, worked together, he cutting off the branches, and I burning them. Then we sat down awhile by the fire. "Conditions are better now than they were a few years ago," he mused. "Be content with your lot."

All of a sudden, he sprang up and cried, "We've delayed too long!" We raced to the place where the wood was hauled together and where the guards were stationed to take us back to camp.

When we arrived, they had all returned to camp except for one guard. "So! You planned to run off!" he barked at us. "Well, I'll show you!" Sinitzkin wanted to explain everything, but he paid no attention to us—he only stuck a bullet into his gun and commanded us to run.

I was wearing a fur coat and heavy felt boots, so that after we had run a stretch, I was exhausted. But run we must, and fast, for the guard behind us kept hitting me in the back with his gun. "Run faster!" I yelled to Sinitzkin, but he was already running as fast as he could.

---

2. In his old age, Herr Peters did succeed in getting to Germany. In 1988, I visited him, and he knew me immediately. He died in 1991.

There was a sharp crack behind me as the guard fired a shot. But I felt nothing, and neither did Sinitzkin fall to the ground. I breathed a sigh of relief. He had only fired into the air.

A short distance from camp we finally caught up with the other workers. The guards there let us through, with a blow on the back from their rifle butts.

Thus, we reached the camp tower, where we immediately had to step out of the line. They wanted to put us into the isolator, but the brigadier and the group leader spoke up for us and said the fault lay with them and not with us. As a result, they let us go to the barracks.

When we were retiring for the night, Sinitzkin remarked, "The guard wasn't such a bad fellow after all. Anyone else would merely have shot us down." However, I was of a different opinion; my back had to take a great deal from his gun butt.

With the hard work and the scanty, poor food, it didn't go long until I no longer had enough strength to work in the forest. Consequently, the doctor excused me from forest work. Now I and another comrade who could also no longer work in the forest had to tidy up the barracks in which we lived.

During that mad race back to camp when the guard was pummeling my back with his rifle butt, I had to think of my dear mother. During her life, I had often hurt her also with my disobedience and my angry answers. For this reason, I would again like to admonish my young readers: *"Children, obey your parents"* (Ephesians 6:1). *"For whatsoever a man soweth, that shall he also reap"* (Galatians 6:7).

My Life in the Concentration Camp

Hard work, scant food,
    Clothes all in tatters,
Cold stove, frost outside,
    Often not a bite of bread.
When I lay down to sleep,
    I did not remove my clothes,
Slept without covers or pillows.

Bedbugs, lice, filth, and itch
    Surrounded me.

> Hunger, misery, sin, and pain
>   Gnawed at my life.
> Then God, who Himself is love,
>   Looked upon me through Jesus Christ;
> And grace was given to me.

From then on, our work consisted of cleaning the floor, and in the evening, when the workmen came home, we had to put their wet clothes into the drying room, and take the torn clothes and boots to be mended, and return them the next morning.

Every night one of us had to keep watch in the barracks so that nobody could steal anything. At that time several men received packages from home. Those who received packages didn't leave them in the cell, but put them into a room with a lock.

One time a man didn't bring his package to this room but instead locked it up in his own locker. That night this man woke me, asking, "Are you on guard duty?"

"No," I answered sleepily.

He went to my co-worker. "Is it your turn to guard?"

"Yes," the other replied.

"Then why are you sleeping?" he asked. "Where is my locker with all my things in it?"

Someone had carried the whole locker outside, broken the lock, and taken everything that was edible. He found the empty locker the next morning.

After two months I had to go back to work in the forest.

In March of 1953, we heard on the radio that Stalin was very sick. Several days later, he died. Great was our joy, for surely conditions would become easier now. In short order, our earnings increased. We could buy ourselves more food, and we were allowed to rest on Sunday. Life in camp perked up a bit.

My Conversion

Sometime during that year, it was announced that a film would be shown one evening. That was good news, a welcome change for us prisoners. As soon as I returned from work, I washed and changed clothes. Then I went for supper.

When I came back from supper, Onkel Kladt was waiting for me in the room where I slept. He said, "I'd like to read you a letter I got from the young people in Krasavino."

I agreed. How could I tell an old man that it didn't suit, that I wanted to go to see the film?

The letter told how many of the youth whom I knew had been converted. Finally, he also read a "greeting to Johann" (to me) from Psalm 95: *"To day if ye will hear his voice, Harden not your heart . . ."*

Meanwhile, Onkel Kladt had noticed that all the others had gone to the theater, so he went back to his room. But I no longer had a desire to follow my plans to go see the film.

The barracks were completely empty of people—only the guard on duty was left. "Don't you want to go to the theater?" he asked me. "If you aren't going, I'll go." One of us always had to remain in the barracks so nothing would be stolen.

"I'll stay here," I told him, and he went to watch the film.

As soon as I was alone, I threw myself onto the bed and wept and prayed. I called on God for forgiveness of my sins, and God heard me! Later, when I told Onkel Kladt about it, he rejoiced greatly. He also wrote to the believers at home, telling them the good news.

The men who were working with me at the time sensed that something had happened to me, for I no longer smoked. Mockingly they asked, "How in the world did the old man get you persuaded to become a believer?" They knew Onkel Kladt since he often came to see me.

"I have become a believer, and I want to lead a changed life from now on," was my reply. At first they laughed at me, but as time went on, they quieted down.

After I had come to truly know the Lord, I thought back to my mother. Back then she had told us stories about Joseph from the Bible. She had made it clear how God had revealed the future to him through dreams. I thought to myself, *I'll also ask God to show me how many of the twenty-five years I must still serve here in the prison camp.*

Shortly after I made my prayer request, I had a dream. I saw a person selling posters on which the future was written. I bought one of the posters. On it was written in big letters, "Notwithstanding, you will be released in the year 1955, in the month of February, on a Sunday."

Many more things were written on the poster, but in such small letters that I couldn't read them. At that time, I would not have been able to bear all the knowledge of the future. I didn't need to know then how many more imprisonments I still had coming.

The next morning I awoke, overjoyed by the news that I would be free in a little less than two years. I told Onkel Kladt of the dream and wrote to my sister that by such and such a time I'd be home.

Later Onkel Kladt said to me, "I didn't want to discourage you then because you were still new in the faith. I really wanted to tell you not to put too much trust in your dreams. But I kept quiet, and now I can see how all was fulfilled."

When I related my experience to the other workers, they only laughed at me. "You got a twenty-five-year sentence, and you think about going home after only two years? No, only a dreamer could think up such a thing."

In the course of the two years, naturally the others all forgot about it, but I didn't. On December 31, 1954, the other prisoners wrote various words, such as "Freedom" or "Camp" on slips of paper and stuck them under their pillows. On New Year's morning, each drew out a slip. The papers were supposed to tell what the year would bring them.

"Don't you practice this custom?" one of the men asked me.

"No, I don't need that," I replied.

"Have you already forgotten what he told us?" another interrupted. "He wants to go home in 1955. He even said which month—February, isn't it?"

I gave my assent, and a lively conversation on the subject followed. "We shall see," they said, "whether you go home in a month from now."

January passed, and February began. "If it doesn't come true," I thought, "they're going to laugh at me." On the other hand, I had told them I had requested it of God and that He had revealed it to me. I battled with myself. The thought vanished as quickly as it had come, and I held steadfastly to my belief that before the month was out, I'd be a free man.

The first Sunday in February passed, and nothing happened; likewise, the second and the third. On Thursday, February 24, we had just returned from breakfast. I was still making my bed when someone called my last name. I looked at the door. There stood an officer. I came forward, and he said, "Pack your belongings and appear at the checkpoint. You are released and may go home."

Then he left. The other prisoners could only stare at me,

dumbfounded. One of them came over to me, told me his dream, and asked, "What does it mean?"

"I'm no interpreter of dreams," I told him. "I prayed that God would show me when I could go home, and He revealed it to me in a dream."

I packed my belongings, went to the checkpoint, and from there I was taken to the main camp. There they asked where they should send me. "My sister has moved in with our brother in Karpinsk, near Sverdlovsk,"[3] I replied. "I could live there as well."

At that time the Germans were still under the commandant, and they said, "You must have an escort for the trip." So I stayed in the camp for several more days. On Sunday morning I was summoned again. My papers were given to me, and I was told, "You may travel to your sister without an escort." It was just as God had shown me in my dream! What a great God!

From the Komi ASSR, I traveled in the direction of Sverdlovsk. I had to change trains repeatedly and wait at several stations. It was early March 1955 by the time I arrived with my relatives in Karpinsk.

But we didn't live in Karpinsk very long. After two months we moved to the region of Kostanay,[4] where new land was being brought under cultivation. My brother-in-law and I built ourselves houses in this area.

In the summer of 1956, I was able to outwardly confirm my covenant with God through baptism. My sister and her husband were also baptized at the same place.

Elfriede Wall

In November of 1956, a friend of mine was married. The wedding took place in Korkino, and I was an invited guest. At the wedding I met Elfriede Wall, who was also a child of God. As we got to know each other, we saw that we were of one mind in matters concerning the faith. We had a mutual understanding of the love of Jesus Christ.

Earlier, before I had come to the faith, I had once desired to

---

3. *Swerdlowsk* (German), near the Ural Mountains. Today, the city is known as *Yekaterinburg* (romanized *Ekaterinburg*), but the oblast or district is still *Sverdlovsk*.
4. *Kustanai* (German), located in northern Kazakhstan.

marry, but nothing had come of it. Later it became clear to me that if one wants to marry a Christian girl, one has to be a Christian himself so that both belong to the church of God. On March 17, 1957, Elfriede and I were married in Korkino.

Our wedding day was a beautiful winter day; in northern Kazakhstan it is still very cold in March. However, in the following days a severe snowstorm arose, so that the trains were suspended until the tracks could be cleared of snow and made passable again. Therefore, it was several days before we could depart from Korkino, and then only as far as the town of Moskovskiy.[5]

Some days after the wedding, we traveled to Kostanay where I lived. Here my wife Elfriede learned that I was a poor man and had even had to borrow my wedding suit. "It doesn't matter," she said. "The main thing is that we love each other. The rest will take care of itself." When we married, I was almost thirty and Elfriede was twenty-six.

Soon after we got home, I was told that our work gang had been organized for two months' service in the forest. Our assignment was to cut timber.

At first, this was very difficult to accept because I had just brought my new wife home. She was a total stranger here and had to get used to her new home. Now I would have to leave her alone for two months. The parting came much too soon for us, but I dared not stay home. Elfriede had to pack my belongings, and she did her best to provide me with warm clothes, food, and bedding. On April 1st, only two weeks after the wedding, we had to part.

Now my wife and my two nieces had to manage the house and grounds by themselves. The worst part was that in April the spring thaw set in. Because huge amounts of snow had fallen during the winter, spring brought an abundance of water with the snowmelt. Diverting this water was a crucial and difficult job, but if it was not turned aside, it would flow over the sill of the door and flood the whole house. Nevertheless, they managed, and after two months we could joyfully be reunited at my homecoming.

In January 1959, our first daughter was born. That fall, we moved to the warm region of Alma-Ata,[6] to the city of Issyk.[7] I

---

5. The German spelling of this name is *Moskowski*.
6. The current name is *Almaty*, and names either a region in Kazakhstan or its largest city.
7. A city in Kazakhstan, also known as Esik.

couldn't tolerate the cold, especially the snowstorms, and continually suffered from eye inflammations. Our little girl was nine months old then. Margareta, the single daughter of my deceased sister Anna was also living with us. Her sister Lina was already married, so she still lived in Kostanay. We traveled by train to Alma-Ata, and from there took a taxi to our new home in Issyk.

3. Migration and Deportation

(1884–1945) In this chapter, Elfriede tells the story of her child-hood and youth through World War II. Her ancestors had migrated from Prussia to Ukraine and settled along the Volga River, just as Johann's ancestors had.

From 1874 to 1880, when requests for exemption from military service first went unheeded, about a third of the "Russian Mennonites" left the Ukraine and came to America. Many of the rest, like Elfriede's grandparents, went elsewhere, including central Asia. Later military exemption was granted, and some Mennonites, including Johann's family, stayed in the Ukraine.

The 1917 Revolution and World War I disrupted the peaceful exis-tence of those who stayed in the Ukraine. Elfriede's family, living in central Asia at the time, faced far less adversity than Johann's family, who remained in the Ukraine. Eventually, however, the anti-German senti-ment caught up with the Mennonites in central Asia as well.

The Migration

Elfriede Steffen

Heinrich and Anna (Unruh) Schmidt, my great-grandparents on my mother's side, left their beautiful home on the Volga in 1880. They took only one wagon and enough food for a long journey and moved to Asia, a land they had never seen. *What does the future hold for us?* must have been the question that lay heavily on many hearts and caused great concern, especially for the elderly and the women with children, who had left many relatives and friends behind.

During the long journey, they experienced many difficulties and hardships. Their parents, and also some of the children, died and were buried along the way. They were believing Mennonites. Their worship was sacred to them and was not neglected.

The longer the trip dragged out and the deeper into Central Asia they advanced, the harder the conditions became. The strange language, the unfamiliar peoples, the harsh climate with its severe heat, the scarcity of good water, and the absence of shelter for the sick and weary weighed heavily on them.

On the last stretch to Uzbekistan, they joined a caravan and traveled on camels from there. They had to cross the Amu Darja River[1] with a boat. At last they reached the Lausan River, where they heaped up earthen huts as quickly as possible. Lumber and reeds for the roofs were found in abundance nearby.

Yet this was not their final home. After several months they moved again and, with renewed zeal, built other dwellings for their families. They laid out gardens with fruit and potatoes, and everything produced well. Wild animals were the only intruders, but, unfortunately, there were no guns to drive them off.

In the surrounding villages lived Uzbeks and Jamuds. At first their relationship with these people was good. But then the Jamuds began to steal the horses of the new settlers and to cheat and swindle them. This brought the Germans under great peril of life.

The Village of Ak-Mechet

One day Uzbeks from the court of the Khan[2] in Khiva,[3] the "king" of the Uzbeks, came riding to the German settlers and inquired about their living conditions. "We freely want to inform the Khan," they promised.

Shortly afterward, the Khan, whose name was Seit-Muhametscha-Sim Bagadur, summoned the Germans to him. He invited them to take up residence near Khiva. Here he offered them a large park with fruit trees, peach trees, and uruk[4] trees. This orchard was about seven kilometers from Khiva.

The German settlers built a new village for themselves, and in May 1884, they were able to move into it. They named their village *Ak-Mechet*,[5] which means "White Cherry."

In the center of town, a roomy space was left open where the

---

1. The Amu Darja River, also called the *Amu* or *Amo* River and historically known by its Latin name *Oxus*, is a major river in Central Asia.
2. *Chan* (German).
3. *Chiwa* (German.)
4. Definition of *uruk* unknown.
5. *Ak-Meschet* (German) means *White Mosque* according to *Wikipedia*.

church, the school, and the parsonage were built. The houses were constructed in such a way that the front doors faced the center of the village. Behind each house were a garden and a stable for the animals. Large-scale farming wasn't possible in this region. Also, they had to promise the Khan they wouldn't raise pigs since this was contrary to the beliefs of the Moslems.

Because the settlers bore no weapons and were a peaceful people, they were received as guests. The Germans and the natives soon established a mutual trust. They were allowed to carry on their Christian church life in complete freedom.

Most of the men worked in the palaces of the Khan as carpenters or furniture makers. The women, too, were given work. As seamstresses, they made dresses and coats for the people in the palace. The Germans were good craftsmen and diligent workers.

Because they were short in ministers, my maternal grandfather, Heinrich Schmidt (March 24, 1874, to September 20, 1944) received the solemn duties of a church leader in his younger days. His wife, the former Anna Toews, lived from March 12, 1878, to August 13, 1940. His brother-in-law, Otto Toews, was chosen as chairman of the town council.

My Mother

My mother, Emilie Schmidt, was born July 10, 1903. She enjoyed a pleasant childhood and youth in Ak-Mechet. Many times she spoke fondly of her school days and of her beloved teacher, Wilhelm Penner. She also frequently reminisced about the warm Christian fellowship they had when they gathered at the church. There she learned to know Jesus Christ as her Savior and found peace for her soul.

She had a younger sister, Helene, and four brothers, and they all grew up together in a happy family setting. At a young age she had to help her mother with the housework, so she learned to lead a good Christian life. When she was twenty-three, she traveled to the village of Orlovka in Kirgizia[6] with her father to visit his sister. She stayed there for quite some time, learning the vocation of a seamstress. She attended church regularly with her aunt.

---

6. Orlovka is located in north-central Kyrgyzstan, formerly known as *Kyrgizia*. Johann used the older German form of *Kirgisien*.

My Father

My father, Hermann Wall, was born July 11, 1903, in Kirgizia on a farmstead his father had built. It was set in a valley filled with beautiful fields and meadows and stately farmsteads. The giant mountains of the Tian Schan[7] range, whose peaks were snow-covered year-round, rose majestically in the distance. The region was absolutely beautiful and the climate milder than in Ak-Mechet. Later, some Germans from the settlement at Samara on the Volga also migrated there.

My father had a pleasant childhood and grew up under Christian parents with his two brothers, Cornelius and David. They lived out their childhood, school days, and youth on the farm. The church was nearby, and my grandfather was a minister there.

As a child, Grandfather Hermann Wall with his future wife, Helene Janzen, had migrated from the Volga tract to the village of Keppenthal in Kirgizia. They died in the village of Thalmann in Tajikistan[8] after being deported.

Many of the believers drove to church services in wagons. From childhood, my father attended the services and enjoyed being in the fellowship of the believers. During this time, he came to the faith and found peace for his soul.

Aunt Mariechen

I loved my Tante[9] Mariechen as I loved my mother, for she was as dear to us as only a mother can be. I often think back to her, and I can't recall that she was ever unkind to us. She was a model of love, patience, and true humility of heart.

Tante Mariechen was of a delicate build and had a pleasant voice and friendly eyes. Her face was full of wrinkles, and each wrinkle radiated friendliness. From morning until night, she fulfilled her duties cheerfully and faithfully and was a blessing to others. She told us numerous stories of her childhood in such a way that her experiences seemed to come alive.

She and her siblings had a happy childhood with their parents,

---

7. Also spelled *Tien Schan.*
8. Also *Tadzhikistan* (English); *Tadschikistan* (German).
9. *Aunt* (English).

Elfriede's Mother   **Aunt Mariechen**

but then Tante Mariechen's life changed. Soon after the birth of her youngest sister, her mother died. Only a few months after her mother's death, her father died too. This was the beginning of a hard life, for she was put out to various families from time to time. Tante Mariechen had to work as a child nurse in her youthful years. She was not physically strong, and the work was strenuous for her.

My aunt had learned to know the Lord Jesus early in life and had found peace for her soul. Then she experienced the great joys of love. She married Cornelius Wall, my father's older brother. Tante Mariechen had been happy and thankful for her new and permanent home with her husband. She was happy for her newfound parents, to whom she could once again say "Mama" and "Papa." She was affectionately received by her in-laws.

A year later their first daughter, Helene, was born, and three years after that, they welcomed another daughter, Maria. Joy and happiness abounded, but unfortunately, it didn't last very long.

When little Maria was nine months old, the family received the shocking news—their beloved husband and father was seriously ill. Only a short time later, he was called out of his illness and home to his heavenly Father and eternal rest. Tante Mariechen grieved for her husband, but she also trusted that God would care for her as she had learned earlier. Her two daughters and her in-laws were a great comfort and help in this sorrowful time.

Tante Mariechen did receive another proposal of marriage but refused it, considering it much better to stay with her daughters and her in-laws. She proved herself to be a faithful daughter-in-law, looking after her parents-in-law to the ends of their lives. They are all buried in the same cemetery—the in-laws, Tante Mariechen, and her daughters.

My Parents

My father learned to know his future wife while she was under instruction in the church parish in Kirgizia. After my mother had finished her time of instruction, she returned to her parents in Ak-Mechet.

During this time, my parents wrote many letters to each other. On June 8, 1927, they solemnized their wedding in Ak-Mechet. Soon afterward, as happy newlyweds, they traveled to Keppenthal in Kirgizia to my father's parents. There they were given a room in which to live. Both were born-again Christians and gladly lived in the community of believers as if nothing could cloud their happiness.

Yet, with socialism and communism spreading rapidly over the country, they looked with concern at the future. They had already heard from other districts about farms being destroyed and farmers' properties being seized.

My father had inherited his portion of land and cattle from his father. Erecting a house of his own and building up his own business would not have been profitable, so he worked with his father. The land and cattle-raising were jointly managed because my father's brother David also lived there. At seeding and harvest time, the Kirgizians came and offered their help in order to earn a little money.

My parents did build a small house in Grandfather's garden when they were expecting a child. In May 1929, Helmut was born, a source of great joy for the Wall family.

God blessed the fields of my parents, and in the fall we celebrated the harvest thanksgiving service in the church. The whole congregation thanked God for the abundant harvest.

In 1929 and 1930, what had long been feared came to pass.

The Russian dictators took control of the local government. The Kirgizians rebelled and fought the Russians. Nearly all the property of the Germans was seized and put into a collective. My father and my uncle David were drafted into the military in 1931 and sent to Fergana,[10] which is in the mountains. Because they didn't bear arms on religious grounds, they had to perform another kind of work.

In Uzbekistan, the Russian government already had everything under its control. Since the village of Ak-Mechet wanted to retain its religious freedom, Grandfather Schmidt and several other men journeyed to the central government in Moscow with a written request for religious freedom. They received a positive answer, yet no one knew how long it would remain in effect.

Mother's Homecoming to Ak-Mechet

In the summer of 1931, Mother's brother Otto came to Kirgizia and brought Mother and Helmut back to Ak-Mechet. At that time Father was working in alternative service, doing forestry work in Fergana. Grandfather Wall's possessions had already all been confiscated. Later, my grandparents, together with Tante Mariechen and their children, followed them to Ak-Mechet.

Twins—my brother Siegfried and I—were born to my mother on August 8, 1931. At that time, she was living with her parents, who were a great help and comfort to her.

There was great unrest in the country, and the family lived in suspense and uncertainty as to whether Papa and Onkel David would ever return home alive. However, God answered their prayers, and both returned in good health. Their homecoming was an occasion of great joy.

In Ak-Mechet, Onkel David married Margareta Toews, a cousin of my mother's. Soon afterward, they moved to Urgench,[11] where Onkel David found a home and work.

My parents, however, continued to live in a room with my mother's parents. Building their own house or setting up their own business was impossible for them at that point. They also faced great uncertainties. Everyone was waiting anxiously to see what

---

10. Fergana is in eastern Uzbekistan, about 260 miles east of Tashkent.
11. Urgench (*Urgentsch* in German) is a city in western Uzbekistan.

time would bring. The believers stood together in faithful fellowship and persevered in prayer, trusting God.

In May 1934, the fiftieth anniversary of the Ak-Mechet settlement was celebrated.[12] *"Hitherto hath the Lord helped"* (1 Samuel 7:12) was the saying on that day. It was a day of thanksgiving and praise for God's leading.

In these fifty years, the church had received much good from God, even though it had had to undergo severe testing. The robbers of the Jamuds, who dwelt in the Karakum Desert, had attacked the village. Though they hadn't killed anyone, they had stolen food and searched for money. Various diseases had been brought on by the hot, desert-like climate in summer. Infants, especially, had suffered, and once, as a child, I also had been deathly sick.

Deportation of 1935

At the beginning of 1935, severe testing and great grief engulfed the village of Ak-Mechet. To begin with, seven men, all of them either church leaders or members of the town council, were arrested. Among them were my maternal grandfather Heinrich Schmidt, who was the leading elder in the church, and his son-in-law Otto Toews, the head of the town council. The other five were members of the town council: Otto Schmidt (Heinrich's son), Hans Toews (Otto's son), Hermann Riesen, Aron Lepp, and Gerhard Hamm.

Urgench

Russian soldiers now besieged peaceable Ak-Mechet. The rest of the men were arrested and taken to a camp in Urgench. Everything found in the village, and in each house, was carefully registered. Many things were confiscated and only the most needful things left to the families. Great hardship came upon the tiny village, for none of the inhabitants had been large-scale farmers. Nearly all of them had worked as craftsmen, most of them as carpenters.

My father had learned that the Russian government also planned to take away the children and place them in children's homes, where they would be raised under communism. This news

---

12. Mennonites involved in the *Great Trek* to central Asia founded Ak-Mechet in 1884.

was shattering, but Father dared not speak to anyone about it. Desperately he sought for a way out. He sent a man into the village with an "Arba-wagon" to which a donkey was hitched. This was perfectly inconspicuous, since this small, two-wheeled cart was widely used in Asiatic countries.

Mother and we three children were stowed away in the body of the "Arba-wagon" where we had to sit perfectly still. Grandmother Schmidt brought out a bag of toys so that we would have something to play with at the secret place to which we were being taken. Thus, I left my home village and never saw it again.

In another village we were secretly taken in as guests and hospitably entertained by the family. My mother dared not let herself be seen. My father was then working as a surveyor and made frequent inquiries as to how the residents of Ak-Mechet were faring.

All the women and children who had remained in Ak-Mechet were loaded onto trucks and taken to a camp in Urgench, where the men had been sent earlier. Not a soul was left in the village of Ak-Mechet. They were allowed to take along only the most necessary things. Everything else remained in the houses, stables, and gardens. But now the families were reunited. Their children hadn't yet been taken from them, since no suitable building for a children's home was yet available. God had not permitted it.

Only the seven men who had been arrested early in 1935 were missing. Of those seven, only two remained alive, Otto Schmidt and Gerhard Hamm, and they weren't allowed to return to their families until 1946, after an imprisonment of nearly twelve years. God protected them, and they remained steadfast in the faith. During this lengthy interim, in January of 1943, their wives were brought to a work camp. They were able to see each other again in Korkino, in the district of Chelyabinsk.[13]

By and by my father brought us out of hiding. He decided to go to Urgench, where many of the former Ak-Mechet residents were living. Father's parents and his sister-in-law Mariechen, with her older daughter Helene, lived there. Mariechen's second daughter Maria was then living with Onkel David in Urgench. My maternal grandmother and four of her siblings with their families were also in the camp. My parents preferred to travel the hard road of

13. *Tscheljabinsk* (German); located just east of the Ural Mountains.

the future in a group, rather than stay back alone. Nobody knew where the road would lead us.

Deported to Tajikistan

Soon afterward we were all loaded onto a steamship and sailed southeastward on the Amu Darja River to Türkmenabat.[14] From there we traveled by train to Dushanbe[15] and finally by truck through the Pamir Mountain range. An old man named David Pautz died along the way.

In Tajikistan,[16] near the Afghanistan border, we were unloaded onto an open plain. Tents were set up and barracks of reeds were built. There were no private rooms—one family with its few possessions camped beside the other—and there was a common kitchen where all got their meals. My grandmother, Helene Wall, died after we arrived at the new camp.

The beginning was very hard. The newly resettled people were divided into groups and had to work either in the fields or in the kitchen. Work in the fields was very strenuous, especially for the women.

Bricks had to be made out of clay. The daily quota was extremely high: 400 bricks per person. Whoever couldn't fill his quota during the day had to finish by moonlight or lantern light until he had produced his 400 bricks.

Others were assigned the work of building houses out of these bricks. The roofs of these houses were covered with reeds that were daubed with clay on the topside. These "two-family houses" were built exactly alike. Each family had a bedroom and a kitchen. No furniture was available, and the beds, tables, and benches had to be nailed together from boards.

Thus, the collective farm of Thalmann came into being. The chief work on this collective was cotton growing. All jobs connected with cotton growing were done here. And this is where I grew up. Already in nursery school the teacher took us out to gather cotton.[17]

---

14. *Tschardschou* (German); *Chardzhou* (Russian). The second largest city of Turkmenistan.

15. *Duschanbe* (German), the capital and largest city of Tajikistan.

16. *Tadschikistan* (German); now a small mountainous country of Central Asia.

17. Years later, in 1972, my brother, Helmut, and Herr Ewert, an older man from our village, decided to make a trip back to the village of Ak-Mechet,

Papa's Time of Suffering

During a train trip from Türkmenabat to Dushanbe, when the train braked suddenly, my father fell from the upper berth and seriously hurt himself. His ribs, his back, and even his lungs were injured.

In November 1935, he had to take on the duties of night watchman. While on duty, he caught a bad cold and ended up contracting pneumonia. In addition, he became partially paralyzed and from then on was confined to a wheelchair.

The house we'd moved into was wet and cold. When it rained, water dripped down through the leaky reed-thatched roof so that there was scarcely a dry spot in the house. Then there was also the scant supply of food. Under such conditions, how could a seriously ill person hope to ever get well? All the adults had to work; only the children, elderly, and sick were allowed to stay at home.

At the age of seventy, Grandfather Wall had to tend the pigs in the pigsty of the collective. Tante Mariechen worked as a milkmaid in the cow stable. We children passed our time in nursery school or at home. I liked best to be with Father in his room so I could help him.

In the evenings, Mother would come home exhausted from the hard work and the intense heat, which ranged from 40 to 43 degrees Celsius (104–109°F). Then she still had her housework to do.

My parents put their complete trust in God. They prayed often and fervently. They encouraged and comforted each other and had a blessed married life. They discussed all their sorrows and joys with each other. We three often sat beside Father's bed while he related something from the Bible to us.

In March 1937 and the following months, Father's condition

---

their former home. First they visited the city of Khiva and also the palace of the Khan. The Khan's palace is now open as a museum, where tourists admire the magnificent old buildings. Herr Ewert had spent his childhood and youth in Ak-Mechet and had vivid memories of how things had been. He also had good command of the Uzbek language, so they soon struck up a lively conversation with the older Uzbek men. From Khiva they drove on to Ak-Mechet. The old townspeople still remembered the Germans who had once lived there and were overjoyed to have them as guests. Herr Ewert and Helmut were warmly received and entertained according to the Asiatic custom. The Uzbeks have a high regard for the German Mennonites and pass on their experiences with them to their descendants.

steadily worsened, and his lungs began to fester. A bed was made for him on a wagon, and he was transported to the hospital. Sorrowfully we children followed on foot. The parting was hard. After a while we stood still and waved after him. There were tears in Father's eyes. Would he ever see his dearly beloved children again?

He left behind a fatherly blessing for us—a true faith in God, a devout heart, his faithful conduct during his life, and the many prayers he had directed to God on our behalf. God be praised and thanked—all of us children put our faith in Jesus Christ.

Onkel Willi Pauls accompanied Papa to the hospital in Leninabad[18] and then returned home. They operated on my father, making a small opening in his lungs, and inserting a tube so that pus could drain out. The doctors went to great pains to help him recover, and it looked as if the procedure would be successful

On July 10 and 11, his birthday, his brother David visited him in the hospital. They were able to discuss many things together and to encourage and console each other.

Then they parted with the question, "Will we see each other again?"

"If not here, then surely with God in eternity." It was a good thing the future was hidden from them. David was arrested on August 20, and on October 5, he was shot in prison.

Tante Mariechen, Helene, and Grandfather Wall had obtained a home close to ours. This was a good thing because Grandfather Wall could keep watch over us children. Tante Mariechen's second daughter, Maria, had stayed with Onkel David in Urgench to work there.

Then one day came the sad news from the doctors that, in addition to his other problems, Father was very ill with a nerve paralysis. Consequently, Mother left for Leninabad to see him in the hospital.

She arrived safely and thanked God that she was able to see him still alive. The reunion was joyful, but the reality that they had to meet each other in the hospital, like this, was also very painful for both of them. Hope of recovery had disappeared. Yet my parents thanked God that they were able to see and to talk to each other once again.

---

18. Now *Khujand*. The *Leninabad* name was used from 1936 to 1991; earlier it was called *Chodschent*. The second-largest city of Tajikistan.

The head doctor at the hospital was a kind man. Mother received employment as a cleaning lady there. She found night lodging with a German family, who had a small room where she could sleep. She was thankful for the warm reception she received at Julia's house and for the work she had found.

Every day, before and after work, she was allowed to visit Father and look after his needs as well as she could. Only at night did she go back to her boarding place. During these days, Father's favorite song often resounded through the sickroom:

> Let me go, let me go,
> That I may see Jesus.
>   My soul is full of longing
>   To embrace Him forever
> And to stand before His throne.

Papa's strength deteriorated further, and talking became harder for him. One day when Mother came to see him, he said, "Soon, soon!" and pointed toward heaven. His joy in the Lord was his sustaining strength. As long as he was able to move his hand, he held the picture of us three children and gazed at it. He commended us to God in love, for before long he would have to die.

On the evening of November 10, 1937, the doctor told my mother to stay with her husband that night because he was very weak. The nurse cautioned her, "Tante Emilie, your husband will die tonight, but you must not weep. You must remain quiet, for there are other sick people in this room too."

All was quiet throughout the hospital. In Father's room everyone was also asleep, except my mother who sat awake at the bed of her dear husband. She prayed and entreated God for comfort and strength.

The nurse came back and felt his pulse. "Yes, he is very weak," she said and repeated her earlier words, "Tante Emilie, your husband will die today."

Mother stood at the foot of his bed and prayed once more to God, "Oh, let me see his opened eyes once again." God heard and answered her prayer. Father opened his eyes and looked at her. For one last time, love radiated from his face, and then he fell asleep. His soul had now entered the heavenly home in peace, where there will be no more pain or suffering.

Mother left the hospital. It was midnight, and all was dark outside. Only the stars sparkled in the sky as if they wanted to tell of the glories of heaven, to which the soul of her beloved husband had been called. Father had ended his earthly pilgrimage and had now entered into glory.

Now my mother was alone in this strange city, far from home and without relatives or acquaintances. She felt utterly forsaken. Where could she possibly obtain a coffin? How would her husband be transported to the cemetery? Who would dig the grave, and where? Who would help bury him? All these cares and questions weighed heavily upon her. Yet God heard the widow's prayer.

The next day Mother went to the hospital, intending to ask for help with the burial. There she was informed, "Don't worry about it. Everything is being taken care of."

They helped her lay Father into the coffin. Mother had brought a suit from home, as well as a white sheet and a white pillowcase. As well as she could, she put everything in order.

The hospital ordered the wagon, on which the coffin was placed. Mother walked along behind, and the driver led the horse. The couple with whom she was living accompanied her. On the way to the cemetery, more people showed up and walked with the widow.

When they reached the cemetery, more people had come for the burial and were waiting there. Several German women spoke words of comfort to my mother. A man conducted a Christian service for the burial, and Christian funeral hymns were sung, all exactly as Mother had been accustomed to.

When they left the cemetery, a woman came to Mother, embraced her, and asked, "Do you know who buried your husband?"

"No," my mother replied, for she truly didn't know.

The woman nodded kindly and said, "He is an Evangelical preacher."

Mother thanked the people for all the sympathy they had shown her.

All this was unexpected for Mother, because already in 1937, many believers had been arrested. Now here were more than she had expected. *Where did these people find out that my husband died?* she asked herself.

Many of them had learned to know him as a believing Christian in the hospital and had frequently visited him. When they heard of his death, they told one another about it, and they all came to the burial. *"Blessed be God, which hath not turned away my prayer, nor his mercy from me"* (Psalm 66:20).

> How great is the grace of the Almighty . . .
> O, to comprehend His love
> Shall ever be my greatest duty.
> The Lord has never yet forgotten me;
> Likewise, my soul, forget not Him!

After Father's death, the head doctor said to Mother, "Don't sorrow any more for your husband. Some men from the secret police (NKVD council) came here to take him to prison. I told them, 'Hermann Wall can't go with you; he's crippled and has just had a lung operation.' Whereupon the police responded with, 'We'll come for him when he's well again.'" Now my mother understood that God had preferred to take Father home to Him rather than to let him fall into the hands of the ungodly.

Mother prepared to leave for home. She went to the grave one more time to bid farewell. That was her last visit to this cemetery. She picked up a small stone from the mound over the grave and took it along for a remembrance. She devotedly held on to this stone. She'd often hold it in her hands and gaze at it, with several tears trickling down her cheeks. She loved her husband until her death.

It wasn't easy at that time for Mother to set out on the trip home. True, she could speak the German and Uzbek languages, but she knew only a few words of Russian. Yet God protected her on her homeward journey on the train until she safely reached home.

While Father lay in the hospital, many letters arrived from relatives, even from Grandfather Heinrich Schmidt in prison. These were often letters of comfort with encouragement from God's Word, but there were also some that told of difficult experiences. Several letters had also come from my sick father. Mother saved all these letters as a precious treasure. Today they're still a valuable inheritance to me, for I can draw much comfort from them. The poem following is one that Father wrote.

On the field of Tajikistan
    We sit and weep:
The plaintive sound of our sighing
    Must for this reason unite.

On the field of Tajikistan
    We labor and moan
Over these hard conditions:
    We give up all of life's happiness.

On the field of Tajikistan
    We crouch on the ground, sighing
Over the fate of our days,
    As once did the prodigal son.

On the field of Tajikistan
    We lie cowering on the ground,
The wages we get for our work
    Are disgracefully small.

On the field of Tajikistan
    We look beseechingly toward heaven,
For the mockery and scorn
    Would cut our courage to the ground.

On the field of Tajikistan
    We must take care of the cotton—
Oh, so much rather would one
    Take care of one's own dear children.

For from the early light of dawn
    Until the evening twilight
One may not look after his children,
    Who are still so tender and young.

Still asleep, they are left behind,
    Sleeping, one finds them again at night.
These glimpses of beloved children
    So soon are lost to us.

Oh, my heart trembles for sorrow
    When I think of the future,
Oh, what a high wall
    Has set itself between my child and me.

If they, without their parents' love,
Are thrust out into the world . . .
If they, in this world's confusion,
Are completely corrupted, completely lost . . .

If no father can advise them . . .
If they get to see no mother . . .
If, then, in bad boys' evil deeds
They so often become entangled.

My God, my God, how long
Hast Thou still forgotten us?
Oh, we asked so long already;
Hearest Thou not, and art yet angry?

Yet, Thou dost consider our suffering,
Suffering, of which we are not worthy.
We will thank Thee with joyfulness
For the way in which Thou leadest.

Lord, Thou givest patience for suffering.
Give us strength and courage as well!
Make us ready for that parting
From the earth to the better rest.

Thanks be to Thee for this faith,
Thou dost not forsake Thine own!
All those who build upon Thee here,
Will be with Thee in heaven's light.

—*Hermann Wall (1936)*

My Schmidt Grandparents

During the time Mother was staying in Leninabad, I often visited Grandmother Schmidt. She, too, had heavy sorrows to bear. Her husband and two of her sons were in captivity for their faith. Her son-in-law had been sick for years and had now passed away. She herself had had a bad fall and was confined to her bed for a long time. Her knees had become stiff, and she could only sit or lie in bed. She was often alone, for the other adults had to work during the day.

At the age of six, I was allowed to be her little nurse. I brought everything that she needed to her bed, but she was responsible for the cooking. She had a little oil stove standing in front of her bed. When I had spare time, she helped me with small craft projects. My little hands sometimes had great difficulty working on these projects. When Grandmother took a nap, I was allowed to play with a doll.

If one of us children was hurt or became sick, we went to Grandmother. She would clean the wounds and bandage them.

To this day, I have a clear picture of her in my memory: her thin, gaunt, pale face with its brown eyes and gray hair. Grandmother was always eagerly awaiting letters from her dear ones who were confined to prisons. On August 13, 1940, she died in her sixty-third year of life. This was a great blow to me.

Grandfather Schmidt died September 20, 1944, in a hospital in Tashkent[19] soon after his release to freedom. When he was released, there was no one there to meet him or give him a home. It was in the war years, when most people were in the work camps or in prison, and we grandchildren lived in desperate poverty. Only after his death did we learn that he had been released and had died in the hospital in Tashkent. He had been buried there as well.

Grandfather's years of imprisonment were especially hard on him because of his age. The conditions in such camps were unbearable. Sickness, lice, and bugs gnawed at his weakened body. The hot Asiatic climate and meager camp rations contributed to the severe living conditions.

Onkel David and Tante Margareta Wall

From time to time Onkel David would send us packages containing clothes and food. These provisions made the first years in our new home somewhat easier.

In July 1937, as mentioned before, he paid Father a two-day visit in the hospital. That was the last time he was able to visit Father, because on August 20 he was arrested and imprisoned in Urgench without any charge ever being made.

One hardship followed another. Onkel David and Tante Margareta's little son died. Then Tante Margareta herself was also taken into custody and sent to Siberia. There she had to work in the forest. She became sick with scurvy and had to endure terrible hardships.

---

19. The largest city and capital of Uzbekistan.

When the war[20] ended, she was released and permitted to go to her relatives. She worked as a bookkeeper in an office. After a long, hard illness, she died in peace on November 20, 1963.

As long as she lived, she never gave up hope that her husband David was still alive. She submitted letters of request to try to obtain information about him. The response from Moscow was that he had died of a lung disease. However, years later, during President Gorbachev's term of office, my brother again wrote to the Kremlin in Moscow to obtain more definite particulars about his uncle David Wall. The reply was that he had been shot on October 5, 1937.

Grandfather Wall

My dear Grandfather Wall had to go through many difficulties in life. Two of his sons died, and the third one was imprisoned with little hope of another reunion. Grandfather didn't find out that his son David, though innocent, had lost his young life already two months before my own father died. Grandfather, a loving, true Christian, bore all these hardships patiently.

He related many things to us from the Bible and was a praying, sympathetic grandfather who had great concern for our well-being. He helped us with our schoolwork, teaching us to read and write. I can still clearly remember his pleasant face, his gray hair, and especially his patience with us children. In the evenings, when he told us stories, a neighbor boy also came to listen.

My mother and Tante Mariechen cared for him as well as they could to the end of his days. He died in peace in the summer of 1939 and followed those who had gone before him into eternal rest. This was indeed painful for all of us.

Tante Mariechen's daughter Maria, who had been arrested in Urgench, was released after several months and came back here to her mother. Now we were all together, Tante Mariechen with her two daughters and Mother with us three children.

By then religious services were no longer permitted on our collective farm. More and more of the Christian men were arrested, and nobody knew who would be next. People were afraid, and the hard work in the cotton fields exhausted them.

---

20. World War II.

Little children died of scurvy, and other diseases, such as malaria and dysentery, occurred frequently. From August to October 1937 alone, eighteen children died.

The Years Before the War

With fieldwork, the workers' concern was to always fill the quota. To promote the quota system, an award was given to the worker who picked the most cotton in a given period. The reward was either a sewing machine, a young pig, a sum of money, or material for clothes. The Stachanows were among those awarded, and their names were written on an honor roll.

In the fall, the harvest thanksgiving service was celebrated. At that time all the good workers were honored and favored with words of praise. An open meal was prepared, to which everyone, great and small, was invited. Nobody was allowed to work on this holiday. I can still clearly remember those days.

My mother and Tante Mariechen didn't attend the festivities, but we children delightedly hurried there, curious to see what all would happen and eagerly anticipating the good meal.

"HER CHILDREN . . . CALL HER BLESSED"

When I was eight or nine, I watched the festivities for a short time, but they soon lost their attraction because Mother wasn't there. Without her, these amusements no longer held joy for me. I ran home to Mother. There I found her dressed in her Sunday best, sitting at the table reading the Bible. The house was in good order, and all looked so peaceful. From then on, I had no desire to go to the festival, for here in our poor cottage all was so peaceful and pleasant.

As a child I was often unable to go to sleep in the evenings until my mother also went to sleep. She wept much and grieved for all those who had died. Mother had a great concern for us children. She provided a consistent godly influence on our lives, guided us to what was edifying, and kept a constant vigil over our conduct. She carefully weighed matters and admonished us to live in uprightness, to love our neighbors, and to read the Bible. She herself often prayed with us. When we siblings got into arguments in our play, she'd quote the following Scripture: *"How good and how pleasant it is for brethren to dwell together in unity!"*

(Psalm 133:1). We would repeat it after her, make up again, and embrace each other.

Since we had learned very little German in first grade in school, Mother gave us lessons from the German reader during the summer holidays, so we could learn to read and write. When she came home from work in the evenings, she reviewed what we had learned. We also memorized stanzas of songs and Bible verses.

During the winter, when she had more time in the evenings, Mother read stories to us from the Bible. At such times, we draped the windows so no one could look in. We would all sit at the table, on which an oil lamp stood, and listen attentively to our mother's voice. One evening when we were reading, we suddenly heard footsteps outside. Someone was approaching our window!

UNDER ARREST

Instantly my mother was silent and frantically hid the Bible. We listened fearfully. Soon we heard several men enter the yard, come up to the door, and knock heavily. Rough men's voices called out, "Open up!" Naturally, the door was barred.

Fear gripped us. Would they take Mother from us? Mother was pale and hardly in a condition to go to the door.

When she opened the door, two policemen entered and barked a question. But my mother understood very little Russian. Then another man, from our own village, entered. He asked her name, and she gave it. At that, the men left because they had not been looking for us. "We came to the wrong door," they explained.

Mother again barred the door, put out the lamp, and then prayed with us. Finally, we lay down to sleep, but sleep was out of the question. It took us a long time to quiet down.

Since we lived in a double house, we could hear knocking at our neighbors' door. A commotion followed—hasty steps, noises. Then it became clear to us; they were after our beloved Onkel Quiering.

The next day we learned he had been arrested. The only charge: "He keeps Sunday holy and doesn't work on that day."

Through this nighttime incident, we children learned already in our early years what it was like when relatives and neighbors were taken into custody. The darker the future looked to us, the more we prayed. *"They that wait upon the LORD shall renew their strength"* (Isaiah 40:31).

Memories of Neighbor Onkel Quiering

Mother and Tante Mariechen had gone to work, and my twin brother and I were playing in front of the house. Nearby was a pond where we got our water for use in the house. My brother and I had long sticks, which we plunged into the water to see who could reach the greatest depth.

Then the mishap occurred! Bending forward too far, Siegfried lost his balance and fell into the pond with a resounding *plop*. I screamed frantically, frightened at the thought that he could drown.

Onkel Quiering, who was working outside at the carpenter's bench just then, heard my frightened screams and immediately came running. He snatched my brother out of the water at the last second. As a result, Onkel Quiering saved my brother's life.

At Home

In those days, heavy sorrow lay over many families for loved ones placed under arrest. Only God could comfort and strengthen. Added to this sorrow were the great poverty and the strenuous work in the cotton fields. Most of you readers probably can't quite imagine what it was like to work on a cotton plantation in 43-degree Celsius (109° F) temperatures.

My mother had saved up some money and bought two goats. We children were delighted with this small treasure. Now there was milk and cream. During the winter the goats gave birth to little kids. The stable was too cold for them, so the kids lived with us in the house during the first few days of their lives. That was a happy time. We adored the baby goats and laughed at their funny capers. We fondly gave each of them a name.

Whenever it rained or snowed, water continually dripped down into the room through the leaky, reed-thatched roof. Buckets, basins, and dishes were set about to catch the water. Fortunately, the winter did not last very long. Always, there would be warmer days when everything could dry out again.

In March the cotton was planted. Then it was cultivated, and from September until New Year's, it was harvested. During that time there was very little school for us.

During 1939 and 1940, our situation improved slightly. Not quite as many believers were arrested, and one could earn a better living. Now we could buy clothes and other necessities. During that time, Tante Mariechen's daughter Maria was also released from prison and returned to her mother. This was a cause for great joy for all of us.

Meanwhile, the people had organized themselves for daily life and grown accustomed to the affairs of the collective farm. There were no church services there, and we were not permitted to build churches. My mother and many other steadfast Christian women were good examples for their children and brought them up according to the Word of God.

Mother often said to us, "I have a great concern when I think of your future. Here you're growing up, not learning to know any Christian church. What will become of you?"

At Christmas time, December 24, some friends came to our home to visit us. There was Bible reading, and we children recited our poems. We also sang several Christmas carols for the glory of God.

Then, on June 22, 1941, came the shocking news that war had broken out.[21] Again, fear and terror seized the people. What would the future bring? Every family thought of the men who were still living and of their grown sons. Wives who had entertained hopes of seeing their imprisoned husbands again, now lost all hope. My mother loved to sing, but now she could sing many of the hymns only in tears. Here is one hymn she often sang, which I'll give in memory of her:

> Be afraid no longer,
> Behold, I am with you!
> This is my guiding light upon the way,
> > The light of promise shining through the clouds:
> > "Behold, I am with you and will not forsake you."

Chorus:
> No, never alone, no, never alone,
> > Thus, the Lord has promised me:
> He never will leave me alone.

Women whose husbands were in custody said to Mama, "For you it is more bearable: you were able to care for and comfort your

---

21. Nazi Germany invaded the Soviet Union on this date.

husband in his illness and also to bury him. On the other hand, we know nothing of where our husbands have been. We receive no news of them and can't write letters to them. In fact, we don't even know whether they're still alive or not." During the captivity of 1937–1938,[22] these men had been taken away and had vanished without a trace.

The War Years

In the neighboring Russian villages, the men were now being called to the battlefront. Men and boys of German descent from sixteen years upward were drawn into public service and sent to various places in the cold North. Many of them, including Mother's two brothers and a nephew, were in the region of Chelyabinsk and had to work in the coal mines. Everyone put forth great effort to prepare warm clothes and food for those who were leaving.

Those who were called to go were loaded onto wagons and hauled away. Once again there were painful separations, and no one knew whether they'd ever see each other again.

Soon afterward, letters and news reached us that told of the pitiful condition of these men. The war front kept pressing ever deeper into our Russian homeland, and there was no longer any hope for a quick end to the war.

In 1943, all the women from the ages of eighteen to fifty were required to take a medical examination. If they were considered able, they were called into alternative service. Only the sick, the old women, and the mothers with children under age three were allowed to stay at home. All had to be prepared for departure by January 20. They were permitted to take along only a few items such as clothes, bedding, and food for the long time ahead.

The evening they left was a night I shall never forget. For our region, it was very cold, and deep snow had fallen during the previous night. Everyone had to gather in a large meeting place. Then came the parting, which was fraught with many tears.

The two-horse wagons were loaded with hay. Four or five women, with the few possessions they were allowed to take, climbed onto each wagon. Time and again, the roll was called to

---

22. This period of intense political repression and persecution, that lasted from 1936 to 1938 in the Soviet Union, was known as the Great Purge or the Great Terror.

make sure not one was missing. The evening twilight had already fallen when at last the command came to start off.

The wagons started out, one after the other, in a seemingly endless snaky line. On the wagons sat praying mothers and daughters. Only the snow could be heard crunching beneath the wagon wheels.

The ones who remained behind stood gazing after the wagons. Many walked along after them for a distance. Tante Mariechen and we three siblings also followed until the wagons could no longer be seen. Only the twinkling stars looked down on those sorrowful circumstances that evening, as if to say, "Do not be afraid. I am still the same God who sees all. I am with you until the end of the world."

Tante Mariechen's daughters were with my mother on the wagon. When the wagons were out of sight, we went to Tante Mariechen to console her. We were all chilled to the bone, tear-stained, and discouraged.

That night we stayed with our aunt. The next morning, we brought the few remaining things from our house over to Tante Mariechen's: a table, the beds, and a few other things.

Mother's sister Helene and three sisters-in-law were among those taken to the work camp. As it was in many families, their children were left at home. The women who stayed behind took these "orphaned" children into their homes. Many houses stood empty.

SUFFERINGS AND DEPRIVATIONS

In a year's time, a large portion of the village became overgrown with weeds, and the empty houses were in ruins. Mice, rats, and other vermin had moved in.

Everyone who was able to work—we children, the few remaining women, and a few old men—had to toil on the cotton plantation. The many weeds grew faster than the cotton plants, and we worked from morning until night in the fields. Working with farm machinery was practically brought to a halt, for all the trusty old horses had been taken to the battlefront.

How could we till the land now? Our strength was meager, the cotton harvest was poor, and our earnings remained slim. Food was very scarce, and our diet was unbalanced. Many people suffered hunger. Each family had a small plot of land outside the village where they were allowed to plant and harvest as they saw fit. But when were we to find time to till this land? Besides, no one had the strength left to do it.

The vegetables had to be watered often. If neglected, they dried up in a few days' time in the great heat. But often there wasn't enough water available, as the canals were choked with silt. They should have been cleaned out regularly, but there wasn't extra manpower to keep them in shape.

One difficulty led to another. Rats and mice multiplied unchecked, eating up our potatoes and turnips. Flocks of birds got their food in the fields, causing great damage to the crops. In the cotton fields, we often ran into snakes and lizards, of which we had to beware.

Our clothes were scanty and shabby. Now they became even more inadequate, because in Asia more clothes are needed even during the summer. The material doesn't wear long on account of the intense heat. Bags, bedsheets, and many other things were used to make needed clothes.

Shoes were nowhere available and would have been much too expensive anyway. During the summer we ran barefoot, which made the soles of our feet hard and thick. Over the hottest part of the day, it was almost impossible to walk in the sand or on the roads. Then we would run at top speed to quickly reach a place where we could cool our feet. In winter we wore wooden slippers. The soles were made of wood, and in front were straps fastened to the soles with nails. We counted ourselves very fortunate if we received such slippers.

The majority of the people suffered from lack of food—and hunger is painful! People searched desperately for food of any kind. Horses that were too old for work were butchered, and the meat prepared for food. Several of our villagers went into the mountains to hunt for turtles, whose meat was also eaten. In May there were finally fresh fruits: mulberries and apricots. In summer, peaches and blackberries were gathered and dried for winter provisions. We children received from 200 to 300 grams of bread a day. The most prevalent sicknesses were malaria, scurvy, and dysentery. I myself suffered much from these diseases.

During this time, we also received the first news from our fathers. They informed us of the heavy work they were required to do, and that some of them had died of starvation.

One day my cousin Anni visited me. Weeping, she told me, "My father died! I have no father anymore." Her mother had also been taken to the work camp.

We clung to each other and wept. I felt so sorry for little Anni, who had to go through tremendous hardships in those years. She lived with an elderly aunt, and in winter she had a hard time finding enough fuel for the stove. So we went with Anni and hunted along the roads and in the fields for shrubs. These we chopped off, tied into bundles, and carried home on our backs. Since the shrubs had sharp thorns on them, they pierced through our clothes and into our backs. By the time we reached home, the wounds really smarted.

In many homes, the poverty was even greater than in ours. We always had the means to buy a little extra food, such as barley or corn. We ground the kernels with a hand-cranked mill. In our garden we grew pumpkins, beans, and sugar beets. These foods, plus the bread we received, made up our meager meals. Tante Mariechen never had to cook a turtle. She also packed many a parcel for her daughters and for our mother to help support them.

Most of the children no longer attended school at all. Tante Mariechen would by no means allow this for us. Even though we didn't learn very much, we still had to go to school. In doing so, we covered a distance of three kilometers every day.

4. End of the War and the Post-War Years

(1945–1963) At the beginning of this chapter, Elfriede's father had died and her mother was in a work camp near Chelyabinsk. These camps provided support for the Russian war effort and were a means the Russian Communists used to control the German-speaking believers. Elfriede's mother spent nearly five years in a labor camp. Elfriede was eleven when she left and a young lady of sixteen when she returned.

In January 1955, at the age of twenty-three, Elfriede moved north to the area where her mother had been in camp and lived in Korkino with relatives. Here she met Johann. After Johann and Elfriede married, they moved back south to Issyk, close to where Elfriede spent her youth. Here Johann was arrested four more times throughout his life.

The War Ends

Elfriede Steffen

On May 9, 1945, we children came back to the classroom after recess as usual. There we waited in vain for our teacher, Emilija Osipowna, who was always so punctual. What had happened? Why didn't she come?

Suddenly the schoolbell rang mightily. We rushed into the hall corridor, and the teachers came running. The headmistress shouted, "The war is ended! Our side won!" Joyous shouts rang out everywhere. Most of our classmates were Russians, whose fathers and brothers fought at the battlefront. Many of them had been killed in the war.

On the way home, plans were suggested, and we discussed at length how our relatives who were still alive would soon be at home.

"They shall obtain joy and gladness, and sorrow and sighing shall flee away" (Isaiah 35:10).

However, things didn't turn out as we had imagined they

would. The men had to keep on digging coal. The years 1945 and 1946 went by, 1947 began, and the wait became harder all the time. Only the sick were released from the work camps and allowed to come home to their families. A few children were granted a trip to the Chelyabinsk region to see their mothers, among whom was my cousin Anni.

RELEASED!

Finally, my brother Helmut sent a written appeal for our mother directly to Stalin at the Kremlin in Moscow. God heard this plea. In September Mother was unexpectedly called before the authorities. There she was handed the documents from the Kremlin. She was free and could go home!

This was an unexpected, yet tremendous, joy for Mother. Finally, after four years and eight months, she was allowed to see her children again. The officer said, "Your son directed a plea to Stalin, and the plea has been heard." This was miraculous, for in the years right after the war, Stalinism prevailed, even stronger than before.

Mother prepared for the trip home. At the same time, Herr Franz Pauls, a man from our village was also released. As a result Mother didn't have to make the difficult trip all alone.

Such a trip wasn't easy since the stations and passenger coaches were overcrowded. Herr Pauls and Mama had carefully made provisions for everything and had bought the tickets for the trip home. Yet, when they went to board the coach, the conductress wouldn't let them on. No amount of coaxing helped, neither did the purchased tickets do any good. The conductress stood firmly on her ill-natured resolve.

If they had been able to leave even on the next train, the tickets would have become partly invalid. So nothing else remained except to jump onto the steps of a coach as it pulled away and ride along standing up!

During the trip they clung fast to the railing. It appeared impossible to hang on like that for an extended period of time, but love for their children and the hope of a speedy reunion gave them the needed strength.

They rode along in this way until the next station. Then they clambered onto the roof of a coach and settled themselves there. The train traveled at top speed! The cold wind blew about their ears, yet it was much more comfortable here than it had been standing on the footboard. Slowly they were making their way in a southerly direction.

After four days and four nights the train pulled into Tashkent. There they had to change trains once more. Then they could reach home without further interruption.

From there on, they were allowed to ride in the coach until Dushanbe. There they had to change to the narrow-gauge railway and ride 200 kilometers farther through the mountains, since we lived close to the Afghan border.

On the evening of September 20, 1947, Tante Mariechen worked in the dairy as she did other evenings. We three siblings and our neighbor boy Willi Lepp sat in the farmhouse by the light of flickering oil lamps. Our supper consisted of stewed pumpkins. We knew nothing of our mother's release. No one from the government had informed us of it.

Suddenly one of our group shouted, "There's someone coming toward us!"

Jokingly Willi said, "It's your mother."

"What!" my brothers retorted. "It's just another one of the many beggars that come to town." Meanwhile I had hurried toward the visitor to see who it was.

All at once Mother called my name. "My dear children!" she said in a flood of tears. What a joyful moment!—one that would never be forgotten.

One of us immediately raced to the dairy to inform Tante Mariechen of the joyous reunion. We were all overjoyed that we could be together again and rejoice together. Tante Mariechen could give us three children back to our mother. After a long separation, we had actually survived the hard times.

"Hitherto hath the LORD helped us" (1 Samuel 7:12).

We continued to live with Tante Mariechen all that winter. Then in February 1948, I became seriously ill with pneumonia. There was little hope of recovery. I was only sixteen years old, yet I was prepared to go meet my Lord and Saviour.

But God had other plans for me; my pilgrimage was not yet completed. Mother and Tante Mariechen devotedly cared for me and prayed to God unceasingly for my recovery. And I did recover. *"Ask, and ye shall receive, that your joy may be full"* (John 16:24).

A year later, I came down with pneumonia again, and a second time God granted grace for my recovery.

In 1948, Tante Mariechen's older daughter was allowed to return home from the work camp. Her second daughter seriously injured her spine in a fall while she was doing stuccowork. Tante Mariechen had to care for her, which she did with devoted love and patience.

In the following years, it was again possible to buy more food. Now we no longer needed to go hungry. Clothing was also more readily obtainable by that time, and the workers were using new farm machinery on the collective farm. More and more people moved back into the village, and before long all the houses were occupied again.

We still had to work from morning until night, but in summer when it was extra hot, we were allowed a three- to four-hour break over noon. Days of rest came very seldom, and only on state holidays. The work was especially hard during the cotton-picking time when everyone had a struggle to try to fill his daily quota.

In the winter we had to clean out the canals. This job also carried a quota. A certain number of cubic meters of mud had to be shoveled out of the canal bed every day.

During the winter there was more free time in the evenings. Then we would catch up on the smaller jobs that had piled up or work on small handicraft items. This was the time when we could learn Christian hymns. We were still not permitted to meet as a church, yet several house groups existed where Christians met to study the Bible and sing together. These evenings were always a blessing.

A BIBLE OF MY OWN!

In 1950, we were able to buy Russian Bibles in a church in Dushanbe. A friend and I went together and bought a Bible for the two of us. The Bible stayed at her house for a while, and then at our house for a while. This way we could at least take turns to read the Word of God.

At that same time, Mother bought me some silk dress material, which in those post-war years could seldom be bought. Soon afterward, my girlfriend became engaged. "Please, would you give me your material so I can sew myself an engagement dress?" she pleaded. "In return, I'll give you the Bible, for my fiancé is also a Christian and already owns a Bible." I immediately agreed to this proposal. It was a joy to finally own a Bible that belonged to me alone.

In our village there lived a very poor family who had moved in after the war. The man was seriously ill, and they had a number of small children. My girlfriend and I agreed between us to make a Christmas gift for this family. We prepared clothing, shoes, and socks. Many food items were also added to the pile.

On Christmas Eve, we, who had grown into a bigger group by then, visited the poor family. Our visit was totally unexpected. The family was overwhelmed with the gifts we gave to them. We sang Christmas carols and read Luke 2. That Christmas Eve was a happy time for all of us.

Even though we were still not allowed to meet as a church in the village, the desire for God's Word continually increased. Among ourselves, we were all bound together in the spirit and love of Christ. More and more, I had a longing to live my life wholly according to the Bible.

Our Life After Stalin's Death

In March 1953, unexpected news reached our ears: "Stalin is very ill." Several days later, we heard he had died. In the following days the authorities expressed great mourning. The great and alarming question that faced us was, "What will happen with us now?"

In the summer of 1953, it was announced in a meeting in the field of the collective that Sunday was to be a general day of rest. It was also announced that we would see other concessions to make our living conditions easier. And it actually happened! We were overjoyed at these changes.

In September 1953, a night school was opened in our village, and I was able to go to school again. Naturally, it wasn't easy, working hard to pick my quota of cotton during the day and then studying in school at night. But I stuck to it for a whole year.

In August 1954, we were released from the jurisdiction of the commandant. Our identity cards were returned to us, and we could travel about freely.

My two brothers had already completed their vocational training in Dushanbe. At that time my older brother had finished his training as a hydraulic engineer. My second brother had studied to be a mechanical technician. I was able to pursue a five-month course on accounting.

During this time, I lived with a family of believers who attended a Christian church in Dushanbe. There I sought out the fellowship of believers, recognized myself to be a sinner before God, and received peace for my soul (Psalm 66:16–17). I wrote to my mother of my newfound joy, and she came to visit me and rejoiced with me.

KORKINO

My training ended in January 1955. Since I didn't want to return to the collective farm, I traveled to my relatives in Korkino, close to Chelyabinsk in February. I lived there for some time.

The trip to Korkino was an unusual event for me. I had grown up in a village and had never taken such a long trip. Added to that, it was winter. Fortunately for me, a married couple whom I knew was traveling with me. We traveled together to Aktyubinsk,[1] at which point, alas, they got off, and I was left alone among strangers.

In Orenburg, I had to change trains and have the tickets updated for the next train to Chelyabinsk. Here the station was overflowing; before me stood a horde of people. First, I looked when the train would depart for Chelyabinsk and what time the ticket office would open so I could have the tickets updated. But nowhere could I obtain reliable information.

I pondered how I could reach my destination. The situation looked hopeless, but then I had an idea. Taking a paper and pen from my pocket, I shouted into the crowd, "Who is going to Chelyabinsk? I'll record all of you here."

Four men gave me their names, and I wrote them down, also adding my own name to the list. I looked the men over carefully, so I'd be able to keep close to them in the ever-lengthening line of waiting people. The men also said, "You can register with that girl there." Hours passed, but at least I was confident that I was where I needed to be. When the ticket office opened, the crowd pressed forward, and I had to be brave and use all my strength to keep from being pushed to the side.

Then someone shouted, "Where is the girl with the list?" So I was able to advance farther toward the front. I handed the list over

---

1. City in western Kazakhstan where Johann was later imprisoned, page 128.

to a man, and with great effort I finally got to where I could have my ticket updated.

Then we had to wait until the train arrived. It was already late at night, and it was an exceptionally cold, frosty evening. Finally, I was able to board, and my journey continued.

The next night I arrived in Chelyabinsk, where my cousin Andreas Schmidt was expecting me because I had sent him a telegram announcing my coming. How I rejoiced over the warm greetings from my relatives! It was so good that I was able to stay with them!

In Korkino there had long been a Christian church with a choir. The conductor, my uncle Otto, had been imprisoned for more than eleven years for his leadership of the choir. He now lived in Korkino with his family.

A SPECIAL CHRISTMAS CELEBRATION

In the meantime, I worked in a sewing factory and learned cutting and sewing.

The church also had a Christian youth group with which I participated regularly and soon formed many friendships. Another year had passed and Christmas was fast approaching. How would we prepare for this year's Christmas festivities? Each of us was allowed to make suggestions. I related how, in my home village, we had once made a poor family so happy at Christmas time.

"Yes," several others chimed in, "That's a good idea!" So we began making our plans. "But whom should we call on?" someone asked.

One girl in the youth group said that, as a mail-carrier, she had come to know a poor family whose children didn't have sufficient clothing and shoes to wear into the winter streets. They had also adopted a thirteen-year-old orphan girl even needier than themselves.

So we pondered how we could help them. First we needed to collect money to buy things for them. The lady mail-carrier and I visited the family and observed the children closely, noting their approximate sizes.

Then we bought cloth. I did the cutting, and we soon got the sewing underway. Our entire congregation had learned of the youth group's mission. Many people donated money and food items, as well as clothes for the parents and children.

Finally, it was Christmas Eve. The gifts were checked one last time, and then wrapped and packed into a basket with the food items. So many gifts had been donated that we had to use a hand sled to transport them to the family.

It was a great surprise for the family. In their small cottage we prayed together and read from the Bible. The children recited poems and opened gifts. Meanwhile, the table was spread for a meal. Finally, we left the happy family. Later, they began to attend the meetings of the believers.

Baptism

In 1956, a baptism took place at the Korkino church. It was my heart's desire to also be baptized. It was a blessed day when we were baptized in a stream close to the city.

My girlfriend was engaged to Emil R., who lived in the district of Kostanay. Their wedding was held in Korkino on November 7. Diligent hands had prepared everything lovingly and beautifully. Eagerly we awaited the bridegroom and the other invited guests, among whom was Emil's friend Johann Steffen. As Irene's best friend, I was allowed to deck out the bride with white flowers and green myrtle.

The ceremony was performed, and we celebrated a Christian marriage. Johann Steffen contributed a speech as part of the service.

JOHANN STEFFEN

At this wedding Johann and I met for the first time, became acquainted, and found out we were of like mind concerning the faith. From the beginning we had a mutual understanding of the love of Jesus Christ.

A short time later, Johann asked me, "Would you like to become my wife?"

"Please give me some time to think it over," I requested, because I first wanted to inquire after God's will. I received the joy and assurance that in this serious decision about my future, it was right to give Johann my consent.

He lived in the district of Kostanay, so for the time being we could become better acquainted only through letter writing. In December 1956, Johann visited us, and we celebrated our engagement.

At the train station.

In February 1957, my mother and oldest brother moved to Korkino. Mother made one last trip to Tante Mariechen to visit her and say good-by to her. When she came back, we had already bought a small house.

Our Wedding Day

On March 17, Johann and I were married by Preacher Jakob Janzen in a very beautiful Christian wedding. Several days later, we took our leave. Mother and my two brothers and sisters-in-law accompanied us to the train station. Parting from our beloved relatives was hard, especially for my mother since she had already endured so many hardships in life. She wished us God's blessing and commended us in prayer to trust in God, that He might lead us and that we might meet again. We were both very happy and hopeful of a prosperous future. I knew I had a Christian husband, to whom I could entrust myself, and with whom I could bear joys and sorrows.

The train moved ever farther away from the home of my parents, heading toward Kostanay, which was to become my new home. New duties in life would present themselves to me there. We would not be living alone since Johann had taken in two of his orphaned nieces. The older one was eighteen, and the younger sixteen.

The next morning we reached the village of Moskovskiy. The weather there was bitterly cold, and a great deal of snow had fallen in the last few days. Lina and Margarita, the two nieces, had the house warm and the table spread, and they greeted us warmly at the door. Johann's sister and her family were neighbors to us. They all attended a Christian church that had a meeting place in the village. Johann already had a house of his own and a small farming operation. Life went smoothly for us here, and I was soon accustomed to my new surroundings. The only thing that bothered me was the severe weather with its many storms.

Our first daughter entered the world in January 1959. We named her Maria, but often affectionately called her Mariechen after Tante Mariechen. By that time our oldest niece Lina was already married and living in the same village.

Issyk

In September 1959, we sold the house and the small farm and moved to Issyk, in the region of Alma-Ata. This was a necessary move because Johann's eyes had become badly inflamed on account of the cold winds and the severe snowstorms of northern Kazakhstan. In Issyk, Johann bought a small house with a kitchen, rooms, and a vestibule. It was surrounded by a garden. The area was very attractive, and the climate was moderate.

The little town of Issyk lies at the foot of the lofty Tian Schan Mountains. We attended a small Christian congregation which held services there. The only thing painful was that we were even farther away from my mother and our relatives on both sides.

Called to the Ministry

In January 1960, a son Willi was born to us. Also, at that time the office of church leader was committed to my husband Johann. When Johann told me of this, he asked, "Are you agreed?"

"Yes, if God so desires it," I answered, for we both wanted to commit our lives to God and not resist His will. We knew that it meant accepting a great responsibility before God and the church.

As time went on, more and more Germans returned from the

The town of Issyk lies at the foot of the lofty Tian Schan Mountains.

North, where they had been sent during and after the war. Now, when they had been released from the commandant's oversight, they chose to settle in the South. It wasn't easy for these newcomers to build new houses and establish everything that was needed. People helped each other with this challenge.

The congregation grew, but there was no church building. Therefore, meetings were held in three different homes. Yet, all were of one mind, and that gave the church strength. Also, the youth group met frequently.

In February 1961, our second son was born. We named him Peter and were thankful to God for our three children. My mother, who had been visiting us during this time, returned to Korkino in May.

Here in Issyk, there was increasing atheistic interference with our worship services. They watched where and when the believers gathered, and then listed the names of those present. Bringing children along to the services was no longer permitted. Conditions became continually harder for the leaders of the church.

In January 1962, Johann Braun married my husband's youngest niece. They had a wonderful Christian wedding.

Beginning in 1963, it again became very difficult to buy food. In order to buy bread, one had to get in line early in the morning. Every day we were thankful anew if we only had bread for the day.

In July 1963, there was a terrible flood, caused by the mountain lake Issyk. A raging torrent of water poured out of the mountains and rushed irresistibly through our village. Since we lived along a tributary of the river, we had to immediately flee to the foothills. When we returned after some time, we found devastating damage done by the flood. Gardens, lawns, and cellars were laid waste.

ARREST

Pressure from state authorities continued to increase. This included threats that believers would be arrested in the near future. For this reason, worship services were held in various homes, and services were begun at different times of the day. Conditions became almost unbearable for Johann and the other ministers. During the day they had to work hard, and afterward they ministered in the meetings of believers.

One evening when Johann was still not at home, I heard someone enter our yard and walk up to the front window of the house. I went out to see what was happening. Several men came to the door and wanted to come in. I tried to prevent their doing so because I could not let them frighten the children, who already had been sleeping for some time.

But they wouldn't be dissuaded. They entered and looked about to see if they couldn't discover a church service in progress. Having satisfied their curiosity, they left again. I thought back to the events of my childhood, thirty years ago, when the circumstances had been similar to this.

Soon after this occurrence, there was more and more unrest. Several of the brethren were questioned. "It won't be long until they arrest me," Johann told me. "Prepare yourself and don't be too sorrowful, but take good care of the children. A difficult future lies before us."

He also said his goodbyes to the children and admonished them to be obedient and to love each other, for, "Your daddy will have to go away." He felt it would be extremely hard for me because I had no relatives in our community. But he urged me to take courage, trust in God, and not weep for him, but to be more concerned in my care for the children.

In September 1963, Johann was ordained as bishop of the church. One day in October of that same year, a car drove into the village. It stopped at our gate, and a uniformed man with several government agents came striding toward us.

"Now they've come to take your daddy away," I told the children. I snatched the Bible from the bookshelf and hid it under my apron.

"You! What are you hiding there?" demanded one of the men, pointing to my apron. Therefore, I had to give up the Bible.

"Are you taking my father away?" little Maria asked the men.

"No, no," one of them said. But Johann was immediately brought home from work. A thorough search of the house was made, for the purpose of confiscating any Christian literature we might have there. But we owned only the Bible and one hand-written hymnbook. We weren't allowed to converse anymore, and Johann was immediately taken to Alma-Ata and put into prison.

5. Arrested for the Second Time

(1959–1968?) Johann picks up his story after their marriage and his ordination as a minister. In 1963, he was ordained bishop of the local congregation. His arrests and imprisonments were under the post-Stalin Communist regime.

In Issyk

Johann Steffen

Upon our arrival in Issyk, we rested for a bit. Then we bought some fruit at the market and ate our fill.

While my wife and niece guarded the baggage, I went to look for a temporary residence until we could buy a house for ourselves. As I walked the streets, I met an elderly Christian woman whom I knew from having seen her at church services. I told her why we had come to Issyk. She kindly offered us her home to live in. In October I found a job, but the pay was initially very poor. Later on, when things were going better financially, we were able to buy a small house.

Sometime during the summer of 1960, church services began to be disturbed by the government. The names of Christians were recorded, and we were forbidden to assemble.

In spite of all the difficulties, we brethren were agreed to continue holding services in accordance with God's Word. We alternated the time and the homes where services were held. God wonderfully blessed us these many years.

Imprisonment in Alma-Ata; Sentencing in Issyk

Three years later, on October 24, 1963, a brother in the church and I were arrested. His house and mine were thoroughly searched. We were both taken to Alma-Ata and incarcerated in single cells in the prison for political prisoners.

Ten o'clock was bedtime, as was the custom in prisons and labor camps. I knelt down and prayed. The guards always looked through the peepholes in the cell doors to see whether the prisoners had retired. When they saw me praying, they repeatedly said, "Lie down and sleep!" But after seeing me doing this every evening for a while, they became accustomed to it and accepted it without comment.

LOVE YOUR ENEMIES

In the course of time, the examining magistrate began calling me to his office day after day. Finally, he informed me that he was finished examining me. He asked me to read the summary he had written up about me. First, however, the public prosecutor asked me some questions, which I was to answer in detail. "Very well," I answered.

The first question he asked me went like this: "How can one love his enemy? I can't understand the saying in your Bible: *'Love your enemies.'"*

"Yes," I answered, "that's how it's written."

Whereupon he rejoined, "How can a man love his enemies? Please clarify this for me."

Then he pursued the matter further, "Do you have a daughter?"

"Yes," I answered.

"Now then," he continued, "if an evil man raped your daughter, and the police apprehended him, and you had the opportunity to see the man who had ruined your daughter's whole life, how could you possibly love that man?"

While he was laying all this before me, I thought of the words of the Lord Jesus in Luke 12:11–12: *"And when they bring you unto the synagogues, and unto magistrates, and powers, take ye no thought how or what thing ye shall answer, or what ye shall say: For the Holy Ghost shall teach you in the same hour what ye ought to say."* And I thought, *That's exactly how it is.*

I answered, "You've made not only my daughter miserable, but all my children and my wife, and me too, because you've thrown me into prison and want to judge me. And that solely because I'm a Christian, yet I hold nothing whatsoever against you."

When I said this, the examining magistrate held the papers before his face because he couldn't refrain from laughing. Then he asked the public prosecutor, "Do you have any further questions?"

"No!" snapped the prosecutor.

Thus, God gave me the proper answer in a wonderful way. After I had read through all the papers, they brought me back to my cell. After the interrogation was ended, they put another young man in my cell with me, a Russian who, with a companion, had tried to cross the border into China to escape military service. He had been caught before he could accomplish his escape and had been in this prison for some time already.

After lunch on January 1, 1964, we lay down to take a nap, and as I was adjusting my pillow, I noticed something was hidden inside. I carefully opened the seam of the outer pillow cover. Inside was a second cover, which I likewise opened and then pulled out its contents. It was money—forty-five rubles—neatly folded. I sewed up all the seams again, and then awakened my cellmate, the soldier. "Get up," I said, "and see what I've found!"

When I showed it to him, he rejoiced, "Now I can buy myself something to smoke."

"But it's all old money that has been replaced since the war," I countered.

But he, not listening to reason, went to the door and snapped on the corridor light. Therefore, the guard could see that someone in the cell wanted something.

When the guard appeared, he gave him half the money with the request, "Go buy me something to smoke."

"Where did you get this money?" the guard inquired because we weren't permitted to have money in prison. Also, it was impossible to smuggle money into this prison for political prisoners because the security was very strict. Thereupon the guard locked the cell door again.

At night when the guards had been changed, my cellmate gave the other half of the money to the new guard and said, "Bring me something to smoke."

This guard also merely asked, "How did you get money in here?"

Whereupon my cellmate answered, "Someone slipped it to me a week ago when I showed him how he could secretly slip across the border into China."

"That may well be," came the reply, "but how did you smuggle it in here? Who searched you?"

He answered, "The one who is always nasty to everyone."

The guard disappeared with the money. After a while he came back laughing. "This is old money."

After breakfast the next morning, our door was opened and the young man was called for questioning. When they brought him back, they got me and took me to the captain of the prison. After he had shown me to a seat, he brought out the money and asked, "Where does this come from?"

"Out of my pillow," I answered simply.

"Now, I'll believe you," he replied.

Back in my cell I asked the young man, "When he asked you, where did you tell him you got the money?"

"I told them," he returned, "The Baptist gave it to me. Ask him where he got it." And this is how the new year began.

Later they came and searched the whole cell, including the pillow. They saw where I had ripped it open and sewed it shut again with black thread. Then at last the matter was settled.

THE HEARING

My hearing took place in Issyk from January 14 to 16, 1964. The television station from Alma-Ata was present and filmed the whole process. I was sentenced to five years in a strict prison camp. The other brother who was arrested with me was given four years in the common labor camp. Afterward we were allowed to meet with our wives for several minutes in the presence of the police, as was the common practice. They also gave us something to eat.

Finally, we were taken back to Alma-Ata, where we believers were separated. When I entered the cell, my fellow prisoners asked, "Why were you sentenced?"

I answered, "You wouldn't understand the sentencing."

Generally, the prisoners know every article of the penal code, so they pressed me for a more definite answer.

"Because of my faith," I told them.

"Are you a Baptist?" they promptly asked.

"Yes," I answered, because the people were most familiar with the Baptist faith. Then the questions came flying from all sides.

Abruptly someone shouted from a corner, "If you wanted to be instructed in the faith, you could have done it when you still had your freedom." Everything grew quiet. I gathered that this comment had come from the chief because every cell had a "chief," who was the leader of the so-called thieves.

I was given a sleeping place in the lower berth of a double-bunk bed at the end of the table. There I could lay my mattress and my other personal effects. Whenever someone new was brought into the cell, the others took special note of what he brought with him. I had brought along a nice bag of food.

Before long, supper was served—a bit of gruel. I sat at the end of the table. Preparing to eat, I took some food from the bag my wife had prepared for me and proceeded to eat. Only the chief and his friends ate at the table. All of the others ate sitting on their beds. The men watched as I ate the sausage and bread, expecting me to give them some too. When they were finished eating their gruel, I asked, "Would anyone like something more to eat?"

"Yes, gladly, if there is anything more," one of them answered.

I took a loaf of bread, a nice piece of sausage, and a package of lump sugar and gave it to them. "Share it!" one of them commanded. Now I knew who the boss of this cell was, but he shared the food only with those who sat at the table.

After supper one of them stayed sitting at the table and conversed with me. He informed me that his parents were planning to go to the Baptist meetinghouse in Alma-Ata. Then the others came to the table, one after the other, and we conversed about God's Word. No one reviled me anymore.

In no time, it was ten o'clock, and we had to go to bed. I prepared my bed for sleeping and then knelt to pray. From others, I had heard that when a Christian begins to pray, the boots start to drop. And this had sometimes happened to me, but not always. I knelt on my bed and prayed silently. Usually it's very noisy right at this time when everyone is preparing for bed. Suddenly one man cautioned another, "Quiet! He's praying." It became very quiet until I had ended my prayer, and that night I could sleep undisturbed.

Newly admitted prisoners are usually brought into the cell in the evening. One evening a newcomer came in, a Kazakh, who had brought along two big bags. These were filled with food—how could it be otherwise? On top of the lounge sat two of his fellow countrymen. They greeted each other, and the newcomer handed his things up to them.

He seated himself beside them, and they proceeded to eat while carrying on a lively discussion. The thieves sat on the sidelines watching, expecting him to share with them also.

After the three had their fill, the new fellow took some candy and went around the cell, giving two pieces to each man. I seriously doubted that the thieves could be bought with two sweets. As ten o'clock approached, we retired for the night.

During the night, someone suddenly crawled over me, dragging a heavy object behind him. When I looked up, I saw someone was dragging the Kazakh's heavy bag. Then all those who slept in the lower bunks had a feast. They wanted to give me some too, but I refused it.

The Kazakhs slept soundly, but in the morning when they awoke and discovered the thievery, they were quite upset. But what could they do? They hadn't seen who had stolen the bag. When breakfast came—gruel again—each man dipped out a portion for himself. By the time I had dug my spoon out of my bag and seated myself at my usual place, they had already set my gruel there for me. As I stirred the contents of my bowl, I discovered a nice piece of butter at the bottom. The thieves hadn't been able to eat everything in the night, and now they had put some of it into each man's dish of gruel. I shoved the dish to a side. When they saw I wouldn't eat it, they pushed another bowl of gruel toward me in which there was no butter. This was the criminals' way of testing me to see whether I, a Christian, would eat stolen food. Even in prison and in the camp, it wasn't enough to merely profess to be a Christian. My fellow prisoners wanted to see my faith put into action in my life.

In the Work Camp Again

One February night in 1964, they took me and sixteen others to the camp. I was sentenced to Alma-Ata. We were summoned individually. When I arrived, I gave my last name as usual. The camp leader looked at me and shouted, "You should have been shot without a trial!"

Instantly the other officers all looked up, expecting to have a hardened criminal on their hands. "On what grounds were you condemned?" one of them asked.

"He's a Baptist—one of those people who believes in God!" the camp leader snapped.

After several minutes they had calmed down, but another of the officers threatened, "If you tell others here of your faith in God, we'll find another place for you in a hurry. You may pray by yourself, but don't teach others to pray."

Thereupon the leader barked at him, "That's what they condemned him for, and you allow him to pray here? Nothing doing!"

"What is your occupation?" another inquired.

"I'm a stucco worker," I replied.

"We don't want to know his occupation," the leader stormed. Then turning to me he said, "The tenth palatka—the tenth brigade—that's the place you're going, to work in the stone quarry. Understand?"

"Yes," I said, and he dismissed me.

The camp wasn't far from the Ottar station. The next day I had to go to work in the quarry. The food was scarce and the work hard. There were no leftovers to be found in the canteen. When we went to the canteen to eat, I prayed as usual, standing before the food. One day I heard one man whisper to another, "If Pugatschow were here now, he'd deal with this Baptist." Still, no one harassed me or disrespected me.

One evening I was fortunate enough to get to go to the kitchen to peel potatoes. There I also received gruel to eat.

In the summertime I fared better. Then I was transferred from the quarry to construction, where the work was lighter and the pay better. Now for five rubles a month, I could buy bread or some sugar. This was already a great relief.

After we two ministers were sentenced, many others from our church had also been arrested. These brethren had all been released again. One evening when I was at the barber getting a haircut, he asked me, "How's it going?"

"I'll soon be going home," I answered, "I've received letters from home, telling how Christians have been released."

He laughed because he knew I had served only a small part of my five-year sentence. "You'll sit out your five years, and they'll add some more to it," he predicted.

Released

When the barber's work was finished, I went out and headed for my barracks. On the way, I met one of my fellow workers who said, "The officer was looking for you." He described the officer to me.

Immediately it clicked—I'd be released to go home! His wife worked in the office where the papers for all the prisoners were processed. I went straight to the office, where the camp leader and this officer were sitting. "You were looking for me?" I inquired.

"Yes," came his terse answer. Then he asked, "What did you dream about?"

"That I'd soon be going home."

"That's right!" he said. "Tomorrow you won't have to go to work anymore. You may collect your papers and go home."

"Well, why do you stand there so stiff?" the camp leader asked. "Why don't you dance for joy?"

"I can't," I replied. I thanked the men and left the room. Only a year earlier when I had arrived in February, the leader had screamed at me, "You should have been shot without a trial!" Now he was saying, "Dance and be happy."

I took a bath and prepared my belongings. Then I made another trip to the barber to tell him what the officer had told me. He could only gape in surprise. I shared the news with my fellow prisoners in the barracks. There was little sleep for me that night.

Next day when my papers were ready, I could go to the station without an escort. It was already nearly evening. A few hours later, I was sitting in the train. In this way I arrived in Alma-Ata. The next morning I took the first bus to Issyk.

When I arrived at home, my wife and children still sat at the breakfast table. They saw me coming and came running to meet me. Their joy was boundless. This joyful homecoming occurred March 6, 1965.

The reason I was released early, and not required to serve the entire five years, was that people in many foreign countries became informed of the things that were happening in the Soviet Union and openly voiced their protests. Therefore, most of the Christians were released.

Home in Issyk

To Register or Not to Register

At the time when we were released and sent home, things were pretty quiet as far as the government was concerned. During the time when so many brethren were away from home under arrest, the council had offered the church leader the chance to register these brethren. He was agreed to this proposal.

Several years before, we had wanted to register, but at the time the government hadn't permitted it. But now when the matter was brought before the church, not all were in favor. Why so?

In the meantime, a new brotherhood[1] had been formed, which withdrew from the Moscow Union. This group advised the churches not to register with the government and to leave any group that was associated with the Moscow Union. This brotherhood had also given their reason: "Whoever registers, particularly under the Moscow Union, will be controlled by the government."

When we came home, the church was called together and this concern was discussed. A third of the church was in favor of registration and associating with the Moscow Union. This minority group began to meet separately. After they were registered, they were even allowed to build a house of worship, which was a cause of great rejoicing to them.

However, we continued to meet in several of our homes. Then a Sunday school for children was established, and God blessed this work.

---

1. This new brotherhood was formed in 1961 and was often referred to as Non-Registered Baptists.

6. Alone With the Children

*(1963–1975) In this chapter Elfriede writes of Johann's first impris-
onment in a prison camp in Ottar (1963–1965), and his second incarcera-
tion at Dzhambul[1] (1969–1972). As a youth Johann had been in a labor
camp, but these now were prison camps. During this time Johann and
Elfriede and their growing family lived in Issyk. They enjoyed a brief time
of freedom between the two imprisonments. Elfriede describes the difficult
visits she made to Johann in the prison camps.*

Visiting the Prison

Elfriede Steffen

Several days after the arrest of my husband in 1963, I left my
children in the care of a neighbor lady and set out in search of
him. Everything was completely unfamiliar to me. It was the first
time I was in such a large city. Where would I even begin to ask?
I walked up to a taxi driver and said, "Please take me to a prison.
My husband has been arrested." He drove me to the door of a
prison, and I paid the fare.

Once inside I asked, "Is there an inmate here by the name of
Johann Steffen?"

The desk attendant checked the roster and answered, "No. Go
to the next prison," and gave me the appropriate address.

In order to get there quickly, I asked a policeman the way and
added, "It's a political prison."

He obligingly explained how I could get there in the quickest
way and through which door I must enter. At the prison, I received
the information, "Your husband and the other man from your
church who was arrested the same day are here. You're permitted
to bring them food and also clothes."

Tired, yet happy at heart, I went home. Now at last I knew

---

1. An old city in Kazakhstan. In 1993, the spelling of the city's name was officially changed to *Jambyl* or *Dzhambyl*, and in 1997 the city was renamed *Taraz*.

where our husbands had been staying, and that Anna and I could even bring them something to cheer them.

When I arrived home and went to get my children at the neighbor lady, a woman informed me, "There was a man here who was sent by the examining magistrate. He was to register your belongings and confiscate anything valuable. This man said he had been present when the house was searched, and that there was nothing of value there—only a woman and three little children. The neighbor women confirmed this with their signatures." Thus, nothing was seized.

One evening Nikolai Kusnekow, our Russian neighbor, came to visit us. Nikolai worked with Johann in construction work. While at our house, he wept bitterly over our family's sad state of affairs.

He told us he'd been summoned to Johann's trial to testify against him. He had emphatically refused, whereupon they had made threats against him. His answer to them was, "Do with me what you will. I can say nothing bad about Johann concerning his work. On the contrary, he's a good worker, even when we others sit down and smoke a cigar and drink beer. I will never testify against Johann."

Our Turkish, Russian, and Greek neighbors came to visit us as well and showed empathy in regards to the arrest of my husband.

Christmas 1963 and January 1964

This was a very sorrowful time at our house. The children just couldn't understand why their father didn't come home for so long. Time and again they laid the pillow on his bed and said, "Papa shall come to sleep here." Then they lay on the pillow and cried.

Over and over again, I had to think of Johann's admonition not to lose courage or else I wouldn't be able to bear the hard times.

Early in the morning on December 25, 1963, the first day of Christmas, I opened the front door. Someone had left something on the doorstep: two packages of food and clothing for the children. No one had announced himself as the benefactor. May God bless those dear Christians who so kindly provided for us. In this way God abundantly used other believers to encourage the poor and sorrowful ones. We also received help from many Christians of other villages. God allowed these afflictions, but He also helped us bear them.

In January 1964, posters were hung everywhere. The council used this method to inform the public that a trial was to take place in the lecture hall in which two believers would be sentenced. I supposed it was my husband and Anna's husband, Alwin Klassen, and that they would be brought here from Alma-Ata on January 13.

Johann had been arrested in October 1963. At that time, it had not been very cold yet, but now winter had begun and it was bitterly cold. He would be suffering from the extreme temperatures in the prison here. Therefore, in the evening I packed some clothes and food.

The next morning, January 14, I got up early while the children were still fast asleep. Deep snow had fallen during the night. I packed the clothes, a lined jacket, boots, and other items into a waterproof bag. Then I prayed to God and trusted Him to help me, that I might be permitted to deliver these things to Johann.

With the bag on my shoulders, I waded through the deep newly-fallen snow. All was still; no one had yet been out to break any tracks in the streets. Here and there a light shone in a window. A dog barked, and the crunching of the snow gave me an ominous feeling.

I proceeded through town until I reached the police station. Standing outside the guardhouse at such an early hour preparing to knock made time stand eerily still. "Ever bravely forward," was my firm resolve.

The door of the guardroom was unlocked. I knocked the snow off my shoes and approached the guard on duty. He had laid his head down on his hands and gone to sleep. Very softly I said, "Good morning."

He raised his head, rubbed the sleep from his eyes, and groggily asked, "What do you want here so early in the morning?"

"My husband will stand trial here today," I told him. "He doesn't have warm enough clothes. Would you please give him these packages of clothes and food?"

"I can't take care of it without the judge's consent," he replied.

Whereupon I said in return, "I have nothing forbidden here in my bag. Please be so kind as to fulfill my request."

He looked at the clock, and then came over to me, took the

bag with all its contents, and carried it into the cell. There he woke Johann and said, "Your wife has brought you these clothes. Quick, get changed."

In a short time he was back. He had given Johann everything that was in the bag and had brought back the clothes Johann had been wearing.

I thanked him heartily for his kind act and then left quickly. No one must be permitted to find out what had happened, or the warden would be in serious trouble. I thanked God for this answer to my prayers. My cares for Johann in this respect had been removed.

When I got back home, the children were still asleep. But now they had to rise, eat breakfast, and be taken to the neighbors so I'd be able to get to the trial on time.

I was thirty-three years old at the time. My mother wasn't present to stand by me. She was so far away, and how could she attempt such a long journey in winter? Yet I knew Mother was praying for us in Issyk and was concerned about us.

The Trial in January 1964

The lecture hall, where the trial was to be held, was filled to the last seat. Believers and unbelievers alike had come. My heart was nearly broken. I wept silently, and my feet could barely carry me anymore. But when I looked at the two men, the courageous soldiers of the church of Christ, God gave me the strength to endure that day.

When I arrived back home, the house was ice-cold. I quickly kindled a fire in the stove for the children, so they wouldn't have to sleep in cold beds. We'd all eaten at the neighbors. God had given us such good neighbors, who shared our sorrows and helped us in our need.

After the children had gone to sleep, and the many questions concerning my husband had ceased, I also fell into a deep sleep after having said my evening prayer.

The next morning I again rose early, this time building a seasoned fire in the stove so the house wouldn't be so cold that evening. The second day of the trial passed. Tomorrow the sentence was to be handed down.

The third day we took the children along to the trial, so they could see their father one more time. While the sentence of five years in the work camp was being read, little Mariechen ran forward and threw her arms around her father.

The guard looked quickly around him and asked, "Where did you come from, little one?" And Maria had to go back to her seat. At the time, she had just turned five.

After the trial we were allowed to talk with Johann in the police station. The grounds for the sentencing of the brethren were that no Christian meetings were permitted in homes. (Yet there were no churches where we could worship.) So they were both taken back to the prison in Alma-Ata.

Anna Klassen and I were allowed to pay our husbands one more short visit at the prison in Alma-Ata. Then we waited for letters from them after their arrival at the work camps.

Be still, fear not; bravely go on your way!
For Jesus goes with you; He goes the way before you.
    Only Him you must trust; He brings you to the goal
    In spite of storms and billows, though many they may be.
O keep trusting, O keep trusting, O keep trusting in God.

How Can I Continue Without My Husband?

Tante Mariechen invited the children and me to live with her in Tajikistan, but Johann and I objected to it. If we did that, I, along with the children, would have to work on the cotton plantation and have to travel much farther to visit my husband in the camp.

VISITING THE CAMP AT OTTAR

Johann was sent to the camp at Ottar. In his letters, he wrote that I could come visit him, but that the camp was in an out-of-the-way place in the steppes. This was in 1964. A brother in the church volunteered to accompany me on a visit there. I was so glad that I didn't have to travel alone in such unfamiliar territory. Our daughter Maria was five years old, and I took her with me.

Our train arrived at our appointed station in a little town, and we got off there. Then we had to travel about five or six kilometers into the steppe, by truck. Since there was no water line to the camp, water had to be obtained at this station. There was a water pump with which the water was pumped into a big tank on a truck. We were allowed to ride with this truck, all sitting cramped together on the seat beside the driver.

At the camp, we discovered the miserable living conditions of the prisoners. The camp was only now being established. Some of the men lived in houses, others in tents. The camp was fenced on all sides with barbed wire and guarded by soldiers with dogs.

To our good fortune, Maria and I secured a reunion with Johann, who lived in a tent. For two days we could be together. All this time, the brother who had come with us had to wait outside the camp in the living quarters of the workmen.

Our homeward trip turned out to be very difficult. Our train seldom stopped at the little station where we'd gotten off, so we had to seek out the next nearest station in the city of Ottar, which lay twenty kilometers away through the steppe. Fortunately, an automobile traveling that way took us along to the Ottar station. From there we took the train to Alma-Ata.

Four months later (still in 1964), I was allowed to pay Johann a second visit. Between these two visits, Johann had become acquainted with a fellow prisoner, a Chechen from Issyk. This man wrote to his wife, also a Chechen, and Johann wrote to me, that we wives should become acquainted. One day this woman, whose name was Anna, came to visit me and greeted me very pleasantly. We discussed the possibility of traveling together to visit our husbands.

Finally, the time came when we could prepare for our trip. Anna, my three-and-a-half-year-old son Peter, and I would go. I was familiar with the route this time, and we got off again at the tiny station.

There at the station we discovered a small kiosk that sold food. This was a rare occurrence, because at the time conditions were very poor, and food was scarce. We bought several kilograms of sugar and wheat grits and were very thankful for our good fortune.

From there on, we again rode with the same water truck as we had the other time.

That evening Anna received permission to see her husband. However, I was denied permission since I had come a week too early. The four months weren't up yet.

We needed a place to spend the night. In the meantime, another woman visitor had come, and a room was assigned to us outside the camp. At least we were under a roof. We closed the doors and barred them with an iron hook to ensure our safety.

All three of us were tired out from the day's journey, little Peter most of all. I had the added bitter disappointment of not being allowed to see my husband, and the thought that I had made the trip here in vain. Anna also came and joined us later. I prayed, and then we lay down to sleep.

It was already late. In the next room were men who were temporarily doing group work in the camp.

Suddenly there was a knock on the door and a request that we open and let them in. At first they asked kindly, trying to persuade us. Then they used threats, and finally with cursing and yelling they stormed off. Every last one of them was drunk. At last, the night became still, and we were able to get a bit of sleep.

The next morning we again had to look about for a way back to the station at Ottar. Today there was no vehicle leaving from camp. However, at noon two trucks loaded with wood drove into camp. Anna went straight to them to inquire as to whether we could ride along to Ottar.

The driver answered that they were from Alma-Ata and that we could ride along all the way there. I cautioned Anna that it was somewhat risky to ride with them for such a long distance, and that I was fearful of trying it. So we agreed to ride along only as far as Ottar.

It was already five o'clock in the evening by the time we left—Anna in the one truck, and Peter and I in the other. We drove off through the steppes.

After a while I noticed that the drivers had turned off of the main road and were headed for a ravine. And all about us not a soul was to be seen. Here, in such a lonesome, desolate place, mischief could easily happen, and my mind panicked. A great fear gripped me, and I prayed earnestly to God that He would protect us.

Anna, on the contrary, was in good spirits. She had told me earlier already that she carried a knife to defend herself if she needed it. This did nothing to quiet my fears, so I cast all my fears before God, firmly resolved to trust in Him alone.

Then we saw that the men had hidden wood here—stolen wood. When they had finished loading it, we drove on. My thankful prayer ascended to God.

Arriving in Ottar, the men drove up to a service station. I tried to get my bearings and decided that since there was a railroad track nearby, there must also be a station somewhere close by. "Come, Anna, we'll go to the station and take the train," I urged.

But Anna protested, "These aren't bad men. I've already spoken to them, and if we continue with them, we'll arrive in Alma-Ata about ten o'clock tonight. Then we can spend the night with my relatives."

I didn't want to do that, but Anna remained unyielding, and she pleaded with me not to leave her alone. So we continued our journey by truck.

When it was already evening, the men drove into a village and sold the wood. Late in the evening, we arrived in Alma-Ata. We got off at a bus stop and paid for our trip.

There we stood with our baggage and the food we'd purchased. Anna said to me, "Elfriede, you stay here with all the things. I'll be back once I've found my relatives." Peter and I sat down on a bench, and Anna left us.

I waited and waited. Fortunately for Peter, he soon went to sleep. Fewer and fewer buses came, and still fewer stopped.

Finally, a woman came along, and I asked her how I could get from there to the train station.

She explained it to me, but it was inconvenient with the changing of buses and the fact that the bus routes would soon be discontinued for the day. She left on the next bus, and I continued waiting and Peter kept on sleeping. An uncanny feeling stole over me. My fear increased as the lights in the tall buildings went out. Would I have to sit here like this for the rest of the night?

I stood up, tied the baggage into two bundles, and awakened Peter. I was prepared to take the next bus arriving at the station.

Finally the bus came. I was just ready to get on when a married couple stepped out of the bus. "Are you Elfriede?" they asked me.

"Yes," I answered, taken completely by surprise. Quickly they helped me board, and the bus drove off. On the way, they told me they were Anna's relatives and had come to get me. At the next stop, we got off and proceeded on foot.

To me it was becoming increasingly strange and eerie. We were already at the edge of the city, in complete darkness, and there were no longer any streets. Walking on a footpath, we passed a pond. Frogs croaked their nighttime song, but otherwise there was an unearthly silence.

Finally we approached a house, and I heard Anna talking. On the one hand, I felt relieved, but on the other—to spend the night here with the Chechens? I tried to bolster my courage, but I was overwhelmingly tired.

Anna greeted me, and I informed her, "I was just ready to leave. You stayed away so far into the night."

"Oh, but don't leave," Anna replied.

Our host had two wives. They gave us tea to drink, bread to eat, and water to wash ourselves.

The one wife led Peter and me through the house. As we passed a room, I could hear people sleeping inside. She said, "This is where the children sleep." She lit a lamp in the adjoining room and showed me to a bed for Peter and me. I thanked her, and then I knelt and thanked God in prayer for keeping us thus far and requested that He would also guard us through this night. We went to sleep quickly, for the house was peaceful in the night stillness.

God's Protecting Hand

All at once I awoke. What was that? Two arms were reaching cautiously toward little Peter. I could make out a man standing beside the bed, prepared to take Peter away from me. Filled with fright, I asked, "What do you want? Let the child sleep!"

Softly he said, "*Sh-sh-sh*! I only want to take the child away to make more room." He said more, but it was clear to me what he was after.

"If you don't go away right now, I'll scream and die for fright right here on the spot!" I threatened. Thereupon he quietly went out again. In this way, God protected me from that horrible man. And he was the host of the house, a Chechen.

Slowly I was able to quiet down after this scare. The worst part was that, at the time, I was expecting our fourth child. Sleep was gone, and I could only wait for daybreak to come.

When I heard the first crowing of the rooster, I knew it must be nearly morning. When daylight broke, I awakened Peter. We knelt and thanked God for protecting us through the night, and I besought Him that He would also be with us during that day.

When it was fully daylight, and I heard Anna talking in the next room, I knocked on her door, entered and said, "Anna, I want to go home."

"Well, but you've slept well?" she questioned.

I repeated my urgent desire to go home. So we readied ourselves for the winter journey of traveling the last fifty kilometers to Issyk by bus.

After breakfast one of the wives of the house accompanied us to the bus stop. Now, by daylight, I could see how far out of the city we really were. I never told Anna about the incident of that night, but I never again traveled with her.

Later, I sold our house with the intention of moving to my mother's. However, that fall when the government in Moscow changed hands, it was announced that Christians would be released from prison. So I remained in Issyk. The Fasts, a Christian family, took us into their home. I was able to go to work since two Christian sisters offered to keep the children during the day. I worked at a nursery, and thus God saw to our needs, both for a dwelling and in providing care for the children.

During that time, our fourth child and third son was born, and I named him Helmut.

The Fast family was very good to us, lending emotional support and caring for us so that I didn't have to live alone in a house somewhere. During the day, the two believing sisters, Helene K. and Lydia K., carefully tended my children.

In January 1965, my mother came from Korkino and lived with us. Since we had such little room, she was allowed to sleep at the neighbor's house. We all lived together in harmony.

Helmut was a very sickly child. The doctors, as well as I, went to great pains to try to help him. Finally, after several months he grew stronger. Then my mother looked after the children, and I was able to go back to work.

A New Beginning in Issyk

Meanwhile, many Christians had already been released because an amnesty had been proclaimed for them by the government in Moscow. There was a legitimate hope that our brethren would be released as well.

One March morning in 1965 we had just sat down to breakfast when—behold! there came Johann walking up the street! "Papa's coming!" I yelled, and we all sprinted to the door. Each wanted to be the first to welcome him. Only little Helmut lay in the baby coach and wasn't aware of what was going on.

Our house in Issyk, 1966.

That same day Johann's fellow church brother also returned home. A feast of thanksgiving was held in the church, and we praised God for the safekeeping and release of the Christian brethren. At this point, the fellowship of believers was close in spirit and knit together in unity.

Now we had to find ourselves a bigger home again. Since I did garden work, it was easy to find a building site. First, we built a small temporary dwelling; then we planted our own vegetable garden. Afterward we built the permanent house.

The church established a Sunday school consisting of various groups that met in homes.

In June 1966, our fifth child, a son, David, was born. We were thankful to God for our five children, who grew up to be a joy to us.

It was a hard year. Johann worked at a building site. After his day's work, he had to work on our own house. And finally, there was also the work of the church. When David was two months old, I returned to work. My mother was at our home with the five children. With God's help we were able to manage, and late in the fall of 1966, we moved into our new house.

Then came another beautiful Christmas. Poems and hymns were diligently learned in the Sunday school. The children looked forward to these pleasant times. Meanwhile, our three oldest children were attending the children's class.

The long-awaited Christmas Eve finally arrived, celebrated by young and old alike. It was a blessed evening for everyone.

If Christmas fell on a weekday, everyone had to go to work because, naturally, this holiday wasn't recognized by the state. Tighter controls were also applied, as to where children's classes and believers' meetings could take place. Our children had to endure many difficulties in school.

Mother's Death

In 1967, my mother became seriously ill. She had long been suffering from fluid on the heart. Already by late fall, she was confined to her bed, but she lived to see the Christmas and New Year's festivities.

I asked whether I should write to her sons, requesting that they come see her once again, but she said, "No, I long for those who are already in heaven." Her longing was for the heavenly home, and on January 5, 1968, she quietly fell asleep, her earthly journey ended. She was buried on January 7. My brothers and relatives had come, and many other people also went to the cemetery to pay their last respects to her.

My mother was a faithful Christian and also a loving "grandma" to her grandchildren. She taught them passages from the Bible as well as poems. She loved to tell the children stories, and she also helped them with their schoolwork. She took pleasure in singing, and many a hymn still makes me think of her. During her life, she copied many hymns, one of which was the following:

> The most beautiful hymn on earth
>   Remains with me all my life,
> The hymn that my mother
>   Sang in my youth.
>
> *Chorus:*
> My mother dear, my mother dear,
>   I think of you when this song I hear,
> No gold, nor any precious stone,
>   Can replace my beloved mother dear.

After my mother's death, I could no longer go to work because the children had to be cared for at home. Therefore, we borrowed money and bought a cow, but we needed hay for the cow during the winter. One day, quite unexpectedly, a truck with a huge load of hay drove up to our home, and the men unloaded the hay into our barn. At first, I didn't know if the hay was ours, or if it was the neighbors', but Frau Peters, our neighbor, said, "The hay is yours."

"Thank you," was all I could say.

And so, God again cared for us through other people. By November of that year, we had paid off all we owed for the cow. We were thankful for all of God's blessings; we were debt-free and had enough hay for our cow. Milk was an inexpressibly valuable commodity for our large family.

Dark Clouds Arise Again

That same month, November of 1968, oppressive sorrow again came upon us. Johann had just gone to work, and I was at home with the children. Since we had no water line along the street, I had to fetch water at a pump. On the way home, I suddenly noticed fresh tire tracks in the snow. Fear gripped me.

When I arrived at home, a police car stood before our house. In the yard were men who proceeded to search the house. The examining magistrate was among the group. They were looking for Christian literature. What they found, they took with them.

This time they targeted our children. We were no longer allowed to take them along to our services, nor could Sunday school be held.

In school, in the presence of the examining magistrate, many children were asked, "Where are your children's classes held, and who is your teacher?" Our children were going to school at the time, so Maria was also questioned by her teacher.

But Maria just kept quiet and didn't answer a single question. Her teacher wrote a favorable report for her saying, "It's a good thing that Maria says nothing, but simply keeps silent with that line of questioning."

Maria and the children of other Christian parents no longer had the courage to continue going to school. Consequently, the parents presented a joint petition to the school directors, requesting that their children no longer be called up for questioning.

Meanwhile, more and more of our church members were being questioned. Two brethren, one of them Johann, were arrested and then released again pending a trial.

My husband and Alwin Klassen were sentenced in April 1969.

Several schoolchildren were ordered to appear in court and testify that the two had taken part in Christian instruction classes. The children, however, didn't go. They didn't want to testify against the believers. They had enjoyed the children's classes and loved the Lord Jesus. Johann and Alwin K. were both sentenced to three years in captivity and sent to the concentration camp. The brethren were firmly convinced that it was God's will to provide the children's Christian teaching.

"Suffer little children to come unto me, and forbid them not: for of such is the kingdom of God" (Luke 18:16).

This placed heavy responsibility on us women because Anna and I were both left behind with five children. We needed a double portion of our earlier strength to raise the children alone. All the responsibilities and cares now rested entirely on my shoulders again, but God saw our needs and granted us His rich blessings.

It was a great relief that we now had a cow as well as the garden next to the house. The children and I worked industriously to gather in the garden vegetables and care for our small farm, which consisted of a cow, a calf, and some chickens. We also received assistance from the fellow believers in the church and even packages from German Christians. For these we thank God to this day and for all those who helped us.

Soon after their sentencing, our husbands were sent to separate places in the camp. We could send them as many letters as we wished. However, we could only visit them four times a year.

Every time I went to visit Johann, I took one or two of the children along so they could see their father and talk with him. While I was away from home on such a visit, the sisters in the church helped with the household duties.

My health began to decline. I suffered from heart spasms and low blood pressure and became so weak that I could no longer stand to do the housework. During this time of physical affliction, the neighbor women came and helped out. Yet through God's grace my health improved again.

> And if He leads on paths that are rough and steep,
> Yet they are ways of wisdom, and for my salvation.
>> Through suffering to joy, through darkness to light,
>> Jesus leads His own, therefore be not afraid!
> Keep trusting, keep trusting in God!

In Issyk, Elfriede Steffen at home alone with the children, while her husband is in prison again, 1970.

ENCOURAGEMENT FOR THE MOTHERS

One day my sister in the faith, Katharina E., and I discussed a plan: we wanted to deliver greeting cards to the older people—sixty years and older—wishing them a happy birthday. We went ahead with our plans. On each person's birthday, we congratulated them with either a card or a bouquet.

One day I was on the way to fulfill such an errand. On the way home I met a sister and we visited awhile. She told me of the miserable situation of her family. I visited another sister who also complained about the burdens of her everyday life. Comforting her the best I could, I went on my homeward way.

Soon I met a third woman. She was standing on the street, looking about her as if she were waiting for somebody. As I drew nearer, she beckoned, "Come here!" With a sorrowful-looking face she said, "My heart is weighed down so heavily with all the burdens and cares in our family."

Back home I pondered over these sisters' situations. What was God trying to tell me through the conversations with these three women? Two of the women had large families. Apparently, they were often tired and despondent.

That Sunday in church a hymn was announced entitled "Motherly Love." I noticed how the hymn touched the hearts of the mothers. Many a tear flowed.

Now I understood what God was telling me: the mothers needed to be comforted. An idea entered my mind, *Why not proclaim a "Mothers' Celebration"?* I visited my friend Katharina E. and told her of my experiences, my conversations with the women, and my idea of having a celebration for the mothers. She said she had also thought of trying something like that.

We began to formulate plans as to how to handle the matter. Katharina went to the ministry and asked for their consent.

We then copied poems and children's songs, distributed them, and practiced these with the children's group. The youth group decorated the walls of the house, where the service would be held, with bunches of flowers and Bible verses such as, *"Honor thy father and thy mother, that it may be well with thee."* Everything looked very festive!

The long-awaited Sunday finally came. It was in mid-summer. The preachers chose their theme to fit this Mothers' Celebration, and the choir sang many hymns suitable for the occasion. The day was a great surprise to many and a wonderful blessing to all. Katharina and I thanked God that He had so wonderfully heard our prayers.

This is one of the poems quoted that day:

> We need mothers,
> Mothers who show love to the weak,
>> Who exercise understanding, patience, and meekness,
>> Who prove the spirits and grieve not the Spirit.
>
> We need mothers who wait and trust,
> Who in conflict and distress look only upward,
>> Who let nothing divert their faith and goals.
>
> We need mothers who tend to wounds,
> And bring sick souls to the Great Physician,
>> Into whose hands, with pains and burdens,
>> Sons and daughters flee for refuge and rest.
>
> Who, as mothers, understand and sympathize,
> And can separate the true from the false.
>> These are the mothers, who on earth,
>> Are needed more than ever in the last days.
>
> If you still have a mother,
> Then thank God and be content.

Not everyone on this great round earth
Is granted this great good fortune.

If you still have a mother,
Then love her with all your heart,
Before the chilly river of life
Drives you into a strange country.

In these years, we sisters in the church also did much praying. Often we'd meet once a week for united prayer. The church also continued holding services, youth classes, and children's classes.

Johann's Homecoming

In the three years that Johann was in camp this time, it was at least easier to visit him than previously. He was in Dzhambul, and I could travel there from Alma-Ata by train, leaving in the evening and arriving in Dzhambul the next morning. In the city lived one of Johann's aunts and her daughter, who kindly took us in. The camp was also in the city.

Later his aunt moved to another village, but there was a Christian church in Dzhambul. So we were accommodated by a Christian family named Skomjakow and also by the D. Löwen family. The distance to the camp wasn't far, and I saw God's leading in this need. To this day I'm thankful for that leading, and for the warm reception I received from these Christians. On every visit to Johann I took one or two of the children along so we could rejoice together. I could also see that the other prisoners were truly fond of Johann.

Finally, in April 1972, I was allowed to bring Johann home from the camp! I made the trip alone. Three whole years had gone by in which we could be encouraged only with letters and a few visits. Great was our joy over his release and the reunion. Through God's love and grace, we had been preserved in faith and trust.

When we arrived at home, the children were overjoyed at having their father home again! The church thanked God for His great mercy in keeping the brethren in the faith, and after a long wait, bringing them back home.

But our tormentors continued to watch closely where we Christians met. There were intervals when persecution abated somewhat. At those times, Christian holidays could be celebrated and baptisms performed. People came to the living faith in Jesus Christ. The church met in three separate homes, which were filled to overflowing.

In 1974, we were permitted to erect a large tent in which to hold church services. Willing hands made the work fly, as young and old pitched in and helped with the building, and by December the job was completed.

Then the dedication service was held. The Christmas service was conducted in the tent and was attended by children and adults alike. Many visitors also showed up, and on Sundays the building was crowded. Many of those present were converted and came to a living faith in God.

7. Arrested for the Third Time

(1966–1976) In this chapter Johann writes of his third prison sentence, this one for three years. He was offered an early release if he would promise not to preach when he got out. He refused, of course.

The church then had four years of relative freedom, but all the while the authorities threatened to stop church services. Johann was called for questioning numerous times and threatened with arrest. This again took place for the fourth time, as described at the end of this chapter.

Before the Examining Magistrate

Johann Steffen

In 1966, we learned that a new law was soon to go into effect. Christians would be fined fifty rubles each if they met for worship and preaching services without permission. It was recommended that at least one member of each district church make a trip to Moscow. Consequently, in May of that same year, hundreds of believers converged on Moscow.

And what became of it? Did anything change? No, thereafter the persecutions began anew. Nor was our village of Issyk spared. Once again we were called before the authorities. We were sternly forbidden to meet for worship. Often their agents even attended our meetings.

Families in whose homes services were held were punished severely. The government directed us to the registered churches, desiring that we attend those.

This continued until November 1968, when abruptly seven house searches were made at the same time, our house being one of them. Because I was out with a work crew at the time, I wasn't home. Therefore, the police took other brethren with them, some of whom weren't released.

When I returned home later, the examining magistrate informed me that I was to appear before him for questioning whenever I was summoned. Soon I was summoned too. At once he laid a paper before me, which I was to sign.

"What's in this paper?" I inquired.

He read it to me. I was to be a witness for my brethren whom they had put in prison.

"I'm not prepared for that," I declared. "And if I do testify, it will be as one who is also accused."

Immediately he tore up the paper and filled out another with my statement on it. Then he forbade me to leave my home until the trial.

When the questioning session was ended, I was again summoned so I could become familiar with the charges. In addition, the examining magistrate told me, "All the others have been found innocent except you and Alwin Klassen."

I was thankful for the fact that the other brethren and sisters were not brought to trial. The examining magistrate was a Kazakh, a good man. During our imprisonment, while awaiting trial, many people were summoned. Schoolchildren were called before the school director (the examining magistrate was also present) and quizzed about the Sunday school—whether they attended and who taught the classes. It was a grievous time for the grown-ups, but no less so for the children.

In April 1969, we were sentenced. Alwin Klassen and I each received three years in a concentration camp. The proceedings stretched out over three days, from April 23 to 25.

Again a propaganda film was shot. (This film was then shown in our country for several years, including in the schools our children attended. One evening when the children came home, they told Mother, "We saw our father in the theater today," because watching the film was mandatory for all of the students.)

Now my wife was left behind with five children. The three oldest already attended elementary school, but the two little ones were still at home.

In Prison in Alma-Ata

After our sentencing we were committed to the prison in Alma-Ata. There we two brethren were again separated.

When I entered the cell, it was so full there was no room for me. In order to accommodate my belongings, the other prisoners had to move closer together. The cell was built to house eighteen men and had nine double beds. I was the forty-ninth prisoner in the cell! When we lay down to sleep at night, the table had to be carried out into the corridor.

In the Camp at Dzhambul

A month later I was transferred to the camp at Dzhambul, (now Taraz) where I served out my three-year sentence. For the fourth time in my life, I had to endure the rigors of camp life. During this time many difficulties arose, and because I seldom received a leave from camp, life at home was also quite miserable.

About that time, our address became known in Germany. At Christmas, for the first time, my family received a package from there. Oh, what great joy it brought! From then on, packages of clothing, food, and other necessary things arrived again and again.

Every time I received the news from home that another package had come, I could again travel my lonely way with renewed courage and thank God for His love and care for the family. When I had been arrested in 1963, the church had not yet been large enough that it could adequately help all the families hit by the persecution. Later, more brethren were arrested, so that, all together, eight families were affected.

At that earlier time (1963), Elfriede had been forced to go to work to earn a little, much-needed income. Every morning she had taken the three children to a sister in the church. They'd stay there for the day, and she would pick them up again in the evening. This was very difficult for her. Therefore, I was glad that this time she could stay at home.

While I was in camp at Dzhambul, a boarding school building was being constructed in town, and it was urgent that it be completed on time. When it was finally ready for occupation, the government requested that the camp excuse several of the productive workers from their penalties—release them outright, if possible.

One day four workers, myself included, were summoned before the camp administrator. Two of us were Germans, one a Russian, and one a Kazakh. We were to go outside one at a time.

When the first, the Kazakh, came in again, it was the Russian's turn. While he was inside, the Kazakh related how the interview had gone for him. He had been told, "Your sentence was ten years and you haven't even served a third of it, so we can't do anything for you."

The German was next. The Russian had the same story to tell. He had eight years to serve, and since he had served less than a third of them, they could do nothing for him either.

Finally it was my turn. Inside the building I was asked, "How much of your sentence have you put behind you already?"

"A third," I answered.

"Good! Then you may go home because the government has requested that good workers be given an early release. But do you promise not to preach anymore if we send you home before your time is up?" (The officer knew the reason I was in camp.)

"If I had made that promise before the court," I responded, "they wouldn't even have sentenced me. Such a promise is out of the question."

"In that case, you'll have to serve out your entire sentence in camp," he said crisply.

"Well and good," I said. Back in the barracks I asked the German, "What did you say to them? Your sentence was for three years, and you likewise haven't served a third yet."

"I told them my wife had handed in a request in Alma-Ata and that there they had reduced my sentence by two years. Therefore, I had only three more months to go. I had received a confirmation of this from my wife several days before. Whereupon they declared, 'You may politely sit out those three last months.'"

According to that, two of us still had too much time to serve; one, too little; and the fourth wouldn't promise what they desired. So all four of us had to stay in camp.

Released—Home at Last!

But my three-year sentence finally ended. I was freed on April 25, 1972. My wife was already waiting outside the camp gate when I finally came out in the afternoon, this time without a guard.

On the way home, my wife recounted how persecution was still raging in Issyk. Everywhere, churches were being searched. Whenever a worship service was tracked down, the worshippers were severely punished.

But at home the children were eagerly awaiting us, and we had a joyous reunion! My homecoming was also celebrated in church, and God be praised, everything took place undisturbed! But persecution continued. From time to time the authorities came, harassing us, and threatening us with arrest.

When we held the harvest thanksgiving service in the fall of 1973, they sorely harassed us. We ministers dared not show ourselves in public. The observances were held in the open. We succeeded in not meeting up with the authorities because it was right over lunchtime. Yet among ourselves, we thought that someone would likely end up being arrested. But God kept His protecting hand over us and didn't allow it to happen. We could all remain at home with our families.

On our way home from the celebration, my wife said to me, "If they take you prisoner again this time, my ailing heart won't take it anymore. But," she immediately added, "keep on quietly performing your church duties." At that point God alone knew how much she'd still have to go through.

Some of the church brethren told me that ministers who had been arrested a number of times had finally moved to new locations. "What good will that do?" I questioned. "If I continue to carry on my ministry at the new place, they'll get me there too."

Then an idea came to me. Since the Germans had already begun to return to Germany, perhaps we could try it too. Maybe, just maybe, they'd let us cross the border. If the council of the brotherhood raised no objections to our changing our residence, we would try it.

We did have friends in Germany, so I wrote a letter to the government, sending along everything that was required. At that time, this part was quickly accomplished, yet I knew only a few received permission to leave the country.

I told my wife, "I have the visa already, but I still haven't talked to the church to see if they agree to the move."

At the next church service, I informed the brotherhood of our intentions and asked if they were in agreement with such a step. With the exception of three brethren who abstained from voting, the church was in agreement.

We filled out the application and submitted it in 1974, but we received no exit permit. Instead we got a refusal, and so we didn't move.

Before the Government Council Once More

In the fall of 1974, I was again called before a member of the city council, who asked me two questions. The first question concerned the registration of churches. "Have your churches registered," he said, "so that I don't always have to keep an eye on them?"

"Our written petition has been submitted for some time now," I reminded him, "Please examine it and give us an answer on it. Our petition is in conformity to the Word of God. Divine service is to be carried out according to the Bible, not according to the whims of the government."

Here I might briefly clarify why we as a church had earlier agreed to be registered. In 1969, the brotherhood, by the resolution of the church council, had recommended that the churches register themselves on the premise that church and state are separate. *"Render to Caesar the things that are Caesar's, and to God the things that are God's"* (Mark 12:17). On this basis we had submitted our petition.

Now I asked the officer for permission to put up a tent in the garden of one of the brethren, for the purpose of holding services until they give us an answer to our petition. He agreed to this request and gave his permission for the erection of a tent, though it was only verbal. But that was enough for us.

The officer wasn't alone. A member of the security council was also present. The municipal officer had certainly not expected things to take the turn of events they were now taking. Then he came to his second point, which was much more important than the first: Helmut Schmidt, who was then Chancellor of Germany, would be coming to Moscow in October. During that time, none of us were to be seen in Moscow. That had been his main concern when the officer called me before him.

I answered him, "I'm positive that none of us will go there." After I had emphatically confirmed this statement, I was allowed to leave the room.

Construction of the Church Tent, and Its Results

"We have permission to put up a tent," I announced to the brethren. Plans were immediately drawn up and building materials purchased. There were also church members who were willing to donate a plot of garden space where church services could be held.

On November 2, 1974, after a prayer service, work was begun at the building site. First we had to dig out the fruit trees. Then work on the building was begun. All of the brethren who were able helped equally, whether young or old. All worked happily until late in the evening. Even just seeing the work in progress already, brought tears of joy to one's eyes and filled one's heart with prayers of thanksgiving. The government let us build without interfering, and they also knew where we were building.

The tent was ready to be dedicated by December 7. On that Saturday evening the whole church, plus many visitors, gathered together. The church was dedicated with God's Word, prayer, and the singing of spiritual hymns. It was a not-to-be-forgotten evening. From that time on, we could meet for worship in peace and quiet.

However, the government didn't stand idly by for very long. On February 21, 1975, I was again summoned before the authorities. The officer said, "We hear you've built a tent for worship services. That tent must be torn down by tonight."

"Such a thing will never happen!" I protested.

Thereupon he said, "Not a trace of it may be seen by Monday morning."

I answered, "We will not tear it down."

"Then we'll start to harass you and bring you to trial again," he replied.

"What you did in the 1960s, you can't do anymore in the 70s," I pointed out to him.

Uneasiness clearly showed on his face as he said, "We will tear it down."

"You cannot tear it down," I countered. "If you do, we'll give up our citizenship."

After these words the conversation ended, and I left the room. On February 26, six of our brethren were summoned. The whole governing council had come together. After a long discussion, they permitted us to continue holding services as we had been doing. This was again only a verbal consent, just as we had earlier received only a verbal permission to build.

On March 20, the authorities summoned twenty of the brethren to the town hall. There the attorney for religious matters, his assistant, and several others were present. They told us, "A registration such as you desire isn't possible. Attend the registered church in Issyk. We'll give you one month's time to talk it over with the church, and then we want to hear of your decision."

After a month, we notified them, "The church has resolved that everything will remain as it is at the moment."

Immediately they threatened us, but we kept on meeting, and no one harassed us. In July, officials of the city government again came and examined the building plans, but the church services weren't disturbed. That summer we were able to hold a beautiful baptismal service in which thirty-nine believers were baptized.

In September, we celebrated the harvest thanksgiving service. The whole day was spent in preaching God's Word, reciting poems, singing by the choir, and enjoying a noon meal. A large number of visitors showed up. The tent was too small, so some people sat outside in front of open windows.

Three government representatives were there. One of them was the mayor! But they were very friendly and didn't harass us the least bit. Interest showed on their faces as their eyes took in the room decorated with fruit, flowers, and Bible texts.

But then on October 8, I was again summoned before the town government. The attorney for religious matters and his secretary were present. The attorney didn't say much. He only said, "You've played with us long enough! I'll give you a week's time to consider whether or not you'll go to church in Issyk and register the way the government wants it, and not the way you want it. If you haven't acted by that time, we'll come and tear down your tent. If you want to revoke your citizenship, well and good. We'll then bring several of you to trial, so the rest can see how the matter stands." After this short discourse, I was allowed to leave.

Consequently, we called a meeting of the church members. The church decided unanimously to refuse registration. We would firmly resist a registration by which the government would end up ruling the church. And the government wouldn't consent to a registration such as the church wanted.

We made our position clear in writing: "If you tear down our tent and arrest one or more of us, we'll be forced to revoke our citizenship and investigate possibilities of leaving the country, because there's no religious freedom here."

This written declaration, signed by eighty percent of the

church members, was submitted to the government. The church hadn't made a light matter of it, but had spent a whole day in earnest prayer for help to arrive at a decision. After that, things were calm and God continued to bless wonderfully. In this time, many people were converted to the Lord Jesus. Praise and thanks be to God for His goodness!

But it didn't last long, for whenever God's people are greatly blessed, something usually intervenes from another quarter. The government was merely waiting for an opportunity to take drastic measures. And that opportunity came.

LONGING TO EMIGRATE

Already in 1974, many Germans had been becoming rest-less and were wishing to return to Germany, especially the non-believers. They even gathered in front of the town hall to submit their request. This was understandable, considering they had endured severe hardships in Russia, especially after World War II. In the last thirty years many fathers had had to leave home and give up their lives in prisons or concentration camps! Who wouldn't have a longing to leave such a country?

And now, although the worst times of Stalin and of the war were over, no relief appeared to be in sight, especially for Christians. To be sure, the government permitted a few to emigrate to Germany, but by far the greater majority were denied exit permits. As a result, the people became restless. Many Germans were prepared to revoke their citizenship and move to Germany just as soon as they had permission to do so.

There were also a few members of our church who were thinking of giving up their citizenship in order to succeed in getting to Germany sooner. These people were counseled in church. A brother was even invited to come and explain to us believers what should be our attitude concerning this question. Many questions were brought up at the meeting when this brother was present. One sister remarked, "But we're Germans and would so much like to go to Germany, where our ancestors came from."

"That's true," the brother acknowledged, "but don't forget, you're also God's people, and not all things are proper for the people of God. Make an application according to the requirements of the law and wait patiently until permission comes."

In spite of this, several of the members submitted their

papers declaring that they wished to be relieved of their Russian citizenship.

One Sunday forenoon at the church service, I was called outside. There I saw the mayor. He came toward me and said, "So now it's clear what you teach here. Your believers submit their identity cards and want to go to Germany. Well, we'll make a quick end of the whole matter."

I kept still and thought, *In such a case, all one can do is wait.* Then he left.

Afterward, several of the brethren discussed the matter, and one remarked, "We can form our own opinion of what's in store for us now."

In late June I was summoned before the government. A brother accompanied me. Upon arriving there, we met another church brother who likewise had been summoned. This other brother was one who had submitted his exit papers.

Now it became clear what was going to happen. The government would play us against each other. The officer began by questioning the brother. "Why and for what purpose did you submit your exit papers?" Then he turned on me accusingly for allowing such a thing in the church. "We'll close the tent and deal with you as we did earlier."

"If you do that," I protested, "the whole church will have the right to revoke its citizenship."

The Government Takes Action

After that, we left. In a few days, they actually came and sealed the doors of the tent. Thereafter we held our services outdoors on the lawn.

The first Sunday in July, the church observed Holy Communion. People who had earlier come to the faith were baptized. It was a beautiful day filled with richest blessings. Again we had visitors from the government, but they only looked on. They could see that worship services, though held out-of-doors, were still being kept.

ARRESTED

After that, the government could no longer stand idly by, and I was arrested on July 12, 1976. When I came home from work, my wife told me, "A police officer was here today and said you were to report to the police as soon as you came home from work."

Just then a brother who had a car came to visit us. "Please, take me to the police station right away," I requested.

"But eat your supper first," my wife pleaded.

"I can do that afterward," I answered, and so the brother drove me directly to police headquarters and waited outside in the car until I should return.

But his waiting was in vain, for they didn't let me come out again. I had to stay there without any supper. But that wasn't the worst part of it. The worst was that I was in prison again.

The brother waited a long time for me. When he finally inquired what was keeping me, he was told that I'd been arrested. He went home and notified my wife and the rest of the believers about what had happened.

Late that evening they brought another newcomer into my cell. This fellow told me (all the other cellmates were already asleep) that the street in front of the police station was swarming with people. *That's the believers from our church,* I thought. And so it was—and they stayed there all night.

Now the government reached a different decision. The next morning they brought me out and said, "We're going to take you before the judge who will sentence you to fifteen days' arrest."

Some of the Christians, including my wife, still stood outside, so I told them, "I have to appear before the judge." In a short time we were back, and I told my wife, "I have to serve fifteen days and fifteen nights."

But the government did all this merely as pretense, to quiet the believers so they wouldn't demonstrate again as they had. After this they took me to a neighboring city, and after that interval, they transferred me back to Issyk again and declared that I was under arrest and would be brought to trial.

Later, the question occurred to many of the brethren, as well as to me, whether it had been God's will that so many Christians had spent the night demonstrating before the police headquarters. Wouldn't it have been better to do as Moses once commanded God's people: *"The LORD shall fight for you, and ye shall hold your peace"* (Exodus 14:14)? Or as when the Apostle Peter was put in prison, and the whole church came together to pray? The believers at that time had done the only proper thing: they came together to pray. Acts 12:12 says, *"Where many were gathered together praying."*

And what was their answer? Peter came out of the prison.

Often we Christians are so hasty in our zeal, that we don't do what God would have us do. We'd rather strike with the sword, as Peter once did. It was Peter's blind passion that the Lord Jesus didn't like to see.

Thus it was with me also. When the government had summoned me and demanded that the tent be torn down, I had said, "Then we'll revoke our citizenship." I had believed myself to be in the right, for hadn't they earlier given us verbal permission to build the tent? But in God's Word we read, *"Charity vaunteth not itself, is not puffed up"* (1 Corinthians 13:4).

We ever need to learn. *"The Spirit . . . will guide you into all truth,"* the Lord Jesus said to His disciples (John 16:13). The people of the world can see how united the Christians are. If they throw one of them into prison, all the others fight for him. But how does God look upon such a fight? It's good for us if we let ourselves be taught and led of God.

A Prison in Irkutsk

The wooden covers at the windows allow the light to come into the cell while preventing the prisoner from looking out the window.

A Prison in Slavgorod

Top: Watchtower;   Bottom left: Prison courtyard;   Bottom right: Wing of the prison.

A PRISON IN SLAVGOROD

Top right: Cell door with peephole and hatch;

Bottom: Cell with lavatory;   Top left: Inside the cell.

CHILDHOOD HOME

In April 1993, I visited my childhood home.

Top: This is where our house stood.

Center: Many times we went swimming or fishing in this stream.

Bottom: The once beautiful church house in Schönsee.

8. Arrested for the Fourth Time

(1976–1985) Johann recounts his fourth prison sentence under the Communists, during which he was treated a bit better than during his earlier terms. Johann learned how to relate to the officials in order to get them to respect him. He learned which things and situations to avoid in order to stay out of trouble with the prison guards. His responses show a very astute understanding of human nature, even that of hardened guards and prisoners.

He writes about the issue of church registration. This was a very divisive issue among the Baptists (the Mennonites were not recognized at all, but the Baptists were if they were registered). Some felt that registering was a form of obedience to the government, if they could do so conscientiously. Others felt it was a compromise, a denial of fidelity to God, to even consider registering. And, as Johann relates, the thinking changed with time.

Those who did not register were more prone to do things underground and made less effort to comply with government regulations concerning the church. This explains how the non-registered brethren set up a secret printing press without Johann's knowledge. They, as a registered church, would probably have avoided such illegal activities. Johann ended up going to prison over the issue.

In Prison Again at Alma-Ata
Johann Steffen

The same day my fifteen-day sentence ended, I was brought to the prison in Alma-Ata. There I again began the hard life that goes with the loss of freedom. When I didn't return home after fifteen days, my wife went to the police to inquire after me. There she was told that I was already in prison in Alma-Ata and would be brought to trial. I was confined to cell number 19, which was filled to capacity but not overfilled.

I Believe in Nothing

From time to time I was called for questioning. The interrogator, whose name was Siminkauwitz, was not a good man. His view was, *I'm going to make an end of the Christians in Issyk. I have always marveled that Christians can believe everything written in the Bible. I believe in nothing.*

"I've never yet met a person who believes in nothing," I countered.

"I'm telling the truth," he retorted. "I truly don't believe in anything."

"Are you a Communist?" I ventured to ask.

"I most certainly am," he answered.

"Then don't you believe that you'll build up communism?"

"Yes, that I believe."

"So—you do believe—you just don't believe in God!"

"You won't get to see Germany," he declared.

After that I kept quiet and thought to myself, *This is not the main issue. Someone else will have the final word on this matter.*

Yes, Siminkauwitz wanted to make an end of the Christians in Issyk; but as it turned out, the Lord made an end of him, because he died very suddenly. The policeman who was present and heard him scream just before he died, said, "See! It's evident that the Baptists have prayed to God, and He has taken him away."

When I was released in 1981, I went to the cemetery and sought out Siminkauwitz's grave. For a while, I stood before the grave in deep thought, *He heard the Gospel so many times. How sad that he didn't find the way to God.*

My trial was held in Alma-Ata on October 28 and 29, and November 1, 1976. The district attorney made a speech and spoke very scathingly of the believers. "The Christians raise their children to be intellectual cripples," he said, among other things. He recommended five years in concentration camp under strict conditions.

When he had made an end of his tirade, I said to him, "It's not correct to say that we make cripples of our children. We bring them up solely in the principles of the Bible. How many children, on the average, do the non-believers have? One or two—three at the most. Where are all the rest of the children? You kill them already in the womb before birth because you don't want to have them. And you want to spiritually kill the children of the believers.

The grave of Siminkauwitz (1937-1977). He tried to convince himself, "I believe in nothing." How sad!

We Christian parents won't condone something like that."

Sentenced

After a recess, the sentence was read: Five years! This was in agreement with the recommendation of the district attorney.

On the evening of December 22, a number of other prisoners and I were transported to camp by train. I was in the same compartment with several men who had become acquainted earlier. One of them sat next to me and asked, "Do you have your sentence with you?"

"Yes, I do," I replied.

"Let me read it, please," he requested. This was nothing new to me, for it had been requested time and again, especially by thieves.

When he had read it, he called to the others, "Be quiet and listen! I'll read his sentence to you. You've never met a person like him before." Then he read the whole thing aloud. Such a lively discussion immediately followed the reading, that the long ride to Aktyubinsk,[1] near the Caspian Sea, didn't seem long at all.

---

1. Located in western Kazakhstan, *Aktyubinsk* was called this Russian name until 1999, but now it is called *Aktobe*, its Kazakh name. Johann called it *Aktubinsk*, the German name of that time.

In Prison in Aktyubinsk

In Aktyubinsk they again put us in prison by groups. We were admitted to a small cell that was already way overcrowded. As always, the one who was boss on the train appealed to the boss of the cell. The cell boss was easy to recognize. He sat at the head of a bed, and his chest was black with tattoos of lions, snakes, eagles, and the like. The "train boss" groveled up to him, and they conversed for a while. Then the cell boss said to the newcomer, "Appoint two of those who came with you to put the cell in order."

It was so extremely cold outside that the toilet pipes had frozen. Therefore, when the toilets in the upper story were used, the sewage gushed out of the pipes on the ground floor, even though they were stopped up with rags. Now I was anxious to see which ones he'd appoint, realizing it could fall to me. But he named the two others, and they cleaned up the cell. We were let out of the cell only in the morning and evening to relieve nature. The time in between was torturous for us.

After the two had made order in the cell, the chief called me to him. The other man had told him about me, and he wanted to read my sentence too. When he had read it, he said, "The government hasn't yet been able to break you people. Us, I daresay, it has broken." By "us" he meant the bands of thieves, which I'd already learned to know in the years 1950 to 1955. He meant to say that there were only a few left of those who were judged thieves according to the law. He counted himself as one of them. Then he said, "But you—stick to your beliefs!"

We arrived at the prison on Christmas Eve, December 24. This caused me to meditate sorrowfully, *Many families will be keeping Christmas with their children, but Father is missing at our house. How often we've already been separated over such holidays! And how many more such days are still to come?* I thought back to the beautiful Christmas Eves when the carolers had come to the windows and sung Christian hymns. Here there wasn't even room to sleep comfortably.

Yet it was much better than twenty-six years earlier when I had also been in prison, but that time not for Jesus' sake. Then, God had chastened me in love, so that I'd repent (Revelation 3:19). This time I suffered because I had become His child and wanted to live up to His commandments.

In the Camp at Uzen

We had already spent a week at the prison. During that time, the toilets had been repaired, so that the cell became more bearable.

In the first week of January 1977, we were moved to the camp in the city of Uzen.[2] This was a very wretched camp. The government sent here only prisoners whom it wanted to punish severely. We arrived in the evening but were still permitted to bathe that evening.

Next morning, as was the custom, we had to individually report to the camp leaders. When I entered the room, two officers were sitting there. One was the assistant administrator, and the other, the security officer. As I spoke about my family, the assistant administrator suddenly barked, "Before us stands a hardened criminal. Keep a close watch on him! I want to be informed of his every step." After work details were assigned, we prisoners were directed to our various cells.

When we returned from work at night, we were always searched to make sure no one had brought any forbidden item, such as a knife, into camp. Almost every evening the officers stood before us.

One evening, when the assistant administrator was present, the security officer, who was given charge over me, wanted to show he was informed of my every step.

For several evenings, I had noticed that a number of prisoners were singled out and taken to a small house. *What happens to them in there?* I wondered. Now I was destined to find out because the security officer called for me too.

When I entered the little house, I saw that everyone had to undress and submit to a thorough search by the guards. So I removed my clothes and waited.

When the entire brigade had passed through the camp gate, the two officers came over to where we were standing. Then the assistant administrator said, "You don't need to ever send this one here again. He won't carry any concealed item because he's a believer." The former had merely wanted to demonstrate that he was keeping close watch over me as he had been told to do. But that was the wrong thing to do. At any rate, in the four months I spent at the camp, I was never again sent to the little house.

---

2. Located at the Caspian Sea; close to Novy Uzen, or Zhanaozen.

In early 1977, it was so cold at the camp that the heating system in the barracks froze. Because of that, we had to sleep with our clothes on, but it was still bitterly cold.

At that time, my wife came, bringing along one of our children to visit me. She had first gone to the prison at Alma-Ata to deliver a package for me, only to discover I was no longer there. Upon asking where she could find me, she was directed to Uzen on the Caspian Sea. So she set out on the tiresome and difficult 3,000-kilometer[3] journey.

Quite unexpectedly she now suddenly stood before me. We were allowed to be together for a few days, and a small electric heater was even set into the room for us. It was a very happy several days!

I was at this camp for only four months, since my relatives had submitted a petition to the government that I be transferred to another camp.

In the Camp at Shevchenko

So in May I arrived in Shevchenko,[4] where conditions were much better. Here we could even take a bath weekly. In the four preceding months in Uzen, a bath had been possible only three times. As a result, we had been sorely tormented by lice. I served the balance of my five-year sentence in Shevchenko, finishing it in July 1981.

When I arrived at the camp in Shevchenko, I had to work in construction. Here, too, the prisoners were not unkind to me, except for one, who was very antagonistic toward me. We had to plaster a three-story building on the outside. When that was done, we worked on another job not far away.

At noon, after we had eaten our lunch, we'd go into one of the rooms of the house to rest until our lunch break was over. One day when I came out to go back to work, someone threw down part of the scaffolding, and it landed about one meter in front of me. It didn't hit me, but I wondered who had caused this near hit.

Several days later, after we had returned to camp from work, we saw one of the prisoners come out of the toilet and go to the guard.

---

3. 1,865 miles.
4. *Schewtschenko* (German); now called *Aktau*; located on the eastern shore of the Caspian Sea.

This guard soon came back with two other guards, and they went to the toilet (the camps always had outdoor toilets). When they came out, they carried a prisoner who was dead—beaten to death! Later we found out that the dead man was the one who had been so fiendish to me.

I thought to myself, *If he was the one who threw something at me from the scaffold, then the others saw him do it.* The others were all gracious with me, so it looked as though they had taken revenge in this way.

After several months some of us, myself included,

Picture of Johann Steffen. In the camp at Schewtschenko, 1979.

were transferred to another workplace, a factory where concrete blocks were made for building projects in the city. In the room where we put on our work clothes, there were always several men smoking. Therefore, I was always the first to come out and go to my section of the workplace.

One morning I had been working for a good while, and the others still hadn't appeared. All at once, a man walked past and asked, "Old man, don't you know we don't work today?" I was silent and pondered why the prisoners wouldn't be working today. Noontime came and I went for lunch and then back to work again.

From earlier experience, I knew what the prisoners would do to one who worked when they didn't work. In the afternoon, the factory leaders passed by with the leaders of the camp and saw that I was at work. What would happen now?

That evening in the camp they called us together and began to revile the prisoners and make threats against us. The next morning, everyone was back at work again. One of the prisoners came and told me that a fellow prisoner had seen me working, had gone to the brigadier, and informed him that the Baptist was working. The brigadier had only replied, "Let the Baptists work." Therefore, I received no ill treatment over the incident.

When we were brought back from work in the evening, we were always searched outside the gate. The next evening I saw the secret police talking with our warden. When the guard had searched me, I entered the camp, but there the warden stopped me and ordered me to come to his office after supper. "Very well," I answered.

After supper I went to him in his office, and he began to discuss the previous day's events with me. He wanted me to document that none of the prisoners had worked yesterday, save me.

"You tell the secret police who ordered you to do this," I told him, "that the camp leaders themselves saw I was working and the others weren't. Why should I have to write it down also? I will not write it down." Now the government wanted me to write such a statement, then they'd read it to the other prisoners. If I had done such a thing, what would the prisoners have done to me? This goes to show how God was with me and sheltered and kept me.

EAVESDROPPING

The camp authorities here were not cruel to me, but the government authorities of Alma-Ata, or more correctly, the security officers, continued to do their work. Usually when my wife came to visit, we weren't allowed to see each other the first day, even if guest rooms were available. I clearly understood why—they first had to install their eavesdropping equipment.

One evening in March, when my wife was there waiting to see me, some of the other prisoners and I were summoned over the loudspeaker to appear before the guards. There we were searched and instructed to wait. We waited and waited, but nobody appeared.

Finally, the woman who customarily brought us to the guards came in. "How much longer must we wait?" we asked her.

"I don't know. You'll have to ask the camp administrator," she answered and left again.

It was clear to me that the others all had to wait on account of me. As we waited, nine o'clock came and went. Ten o'clock would be bedtime. Suddenly the woman reappeared and commanded us to follow her.

I had entered the room where my wife waited for me, and we had greeted each other. I asked her, "Why did it take so long until we were allowed in here?"

She answered, "We were already in the rooms when the woman who had admitted us came and said, 'You'll all have to come out; you can't meet your husbands until tomorrow.' Thereupon most of the women began to scream and threaten to complain to the supervisor tomorrow morning."

"How did you get into the room at all?" I marveled. "Did the woman tell you to come in, or did you come in without being told?"

"No room was occupied," she replied, "therefore each woman chose a room for herself."

Now I understood. Someone else was using the room intended for us! That was where the eavesdropping equipment had been installed. They had definitely used the waiting time to install a small hidden microphone outside our window. All this didn't disturb us, however, since we knew what we could safely say. What we didn't dare say aloud, we wrote on paper.

"Did you receive the Christmas letters from me and the children?" my wife asked me.

"Yes," I answered out loud. I wanted to determine whether they were listening in on us. "At Christmas half of all the letters in our barracks were for me. I mean—I got many letters, not only from you, but also from the other Christians."

At Easter I received only the letters sent from home. That was proof that they'd been listening in on us during my wife's visit in March. They wanted to show me how many "half the letters" was!

Now I wrote a letter home, informing my wife that the government had listened in while she was there to visit me. I wrote that at Christmas I had received many letters, and at Easter none had been let through except those that had come from home. I informed her that it would go likewise with the letters I wrote from camp.

The security officers got the message. Sometime later I was given all my mail. Such were the difficulties we encountered all the time, but we could confidently bring them all to God.

Every morning before we went to work, we had to put on our work clothes in a separate little dressing room. Since much smoking was done, the room was always filled with tobacco smoke. One day an officer came in, accompanied by a security official, and said to me, "Steffen, can't you make order in here? Why, it's impossible to breathe!"

I answered him, "Because I always kept order of things while I was free, I was arrested—this is already the fourth time."

The security officer was laughing as he left the room. True, they wanted to see order, but not the kind of order God likes to see.

MORE CHALLENGES

Later I was told my foreman had had to stay home and that an interrogator had come to hold a discussion with him. *I'm sure he came because of me,* I immediately thought.

Afterwards, I too, had to stay home, and the examiner asked me various questions. *What's the meaning of all this?* I asked myself. That evening I was called before the public prosecutor who likewise asked me a number of questions. I began to see that matters didn't look favorable for me.

At that time the government tried to pin more punishable deeds onto the believers whom they didn't want to release. That way, they could sentence them to additional time. Apparently, this is what they were trying to do with me, although it was still quite some time until my sentence would end. Why were they starting it already? And what could I do about it?

One day I said to a fellow worker, "Listen, I need a photograph of myself. How can I manage it?"

"I'll discuss it with a photographer I know well," he said. One day he came to me with the words, "Come with me; I'll take you to the photographer."

I didn't tell a single person why I wanted the picture. When it was developed, I sent it out of the camp, and it was relayed on to Germany for me.

After the picture had been printed in various foreign newspapers, there was a change in my living conditions. One day I didn't have to go to work; instead, I was told to seek out doctors who had come from Alma-Ata. These doctors asked me, "What ailment are you suffering from?"

"I'm not sick," I said in reply, "only weak from the meager food." From then on, I was left alone until I was released in 1981.

MY EARLIER DREAM

As I reflected over the past, I recalled a dream I had already dreamed back in 1943. I hesitated to mention it because people often say, "Dreams are like bubbles." And truly that is so in many cases. But this dream meant a great deal to me, for in it my whole life was shown to me.

The dream came to me one summer night in 1943. All the people of our village were running toward the west. "Where are you hurrying to?" I asked them. The answer I received was, "Don't you know the Russians are returning? And we want to flee to Germany with the German troops."

Then I started running too, though not very far. I turned into a yard and hurried toward the stable. There I wanted to hide behind a well. There are many such wells in stables in the Ukraine. But then I thought, "This is unsafe; the Russian soldiers will surely find me here." Then I ran to the horse's stall.

Suddenly two Russian soldiers entered, and as if someone had given me away, they headed directly toward me. They seized me and threw me down on the ground beside the well. They proceeded to saw off both of my legs and both arms. Then they also started to saw off my head. When they had cut it about halfway off, the one said to the other, "That's enough; we'll let him go."

After they've sawn at me five times, I thought, *they'll let me go. Being sawed five times represents being tried and sentenced five times.* The first time, when I had been brought from Poland to Minsk, I hadn't been given a trial. Therefore, I didn't count that time. When the one Russian soldier said to the other, "That's enough; let him go now," I thought, *And where to?* Then I realized it could mean only one way—the way to Germany.

At the moment, I found myself serving my fourth sentence in the work camp, and so I could still expect a fifth prison term. In my story here, I'm relating some of the events ahead of time. I had to serve out my entire five-year sentence. Afterwards, I was released again.

After I was home again, I traveled to Dzhambul with several brethren. One of the brethren from Alma-Ata said to me, "Now, Brother Johann, surely this was the last time in prison for you."

"No," I replied, "I still have to go to prison one more time, and this will surely be the hardest term." Then I related my dream to the brethren. And that's exactly what took place, too.

EASIER WORK?

At camp, the other prisoners wanted to help me obtain easier work, but I continually turned it down. I'll give several examples here to show that a Christian could not work at just any job. A fellow worker said to me, "Johann, the man who works in the public bath will be released in a few days. We'd like for you to work there because the work is very easy there. One needs only to tidy things up."

"I can't do that," I protested. "You know the government has strictly forbidden that the baths be opened before four o'clock in the evening. Yet some of the prisoners would already like to bathe right after lunch. And because there's a factory close by, and many of the men do very dirty work, it's arranged that they can take a bath every day. If the baths are opened earlier and the government finds out about it, the manager of the bath will be reprimanded or perhaps even punished. On the other hand, if he doesn't let the prisoners in earlier according to their wishes, it goes even worse for him. As a Christian, I can't put myself into such a position." Similar jobs were occasionally offered me. To be sure, the prisoners wanted what was best for me.

One day just as we returned to camp from work, the officer in charge of those who were allowed to work without a guard asked me, "How much of your sentence have you already served?" I told him. Then he commanded, "Come to my office after supper to write out a request, so that I can send you to work without a guard."

What should I do now? I really didn't want to go to work that way, for it often brought great difficulties with it, especially for the Christians. But I couldn't explain that to him, so I went and wrote my request, and he accepted it.

The next workday I said to my brigadier, "Please listen quietly to what I have to say." Then I told him what had been requested of me the day before, and how I didn't want to go to work in this manner. "Now," I pleaded, "would you please go to the factory boss and explain to him how matters stand? A month ago, they took one of your trained workers and sent him to work outside the camp without a guard. Now they want to take the second one. Without trained workmen, how will you get your quota filled?"

Consequently, he went to the director and informed him of everything. The director immediately called the camp administrator. The request for a transfer was turned down, and I was permitted to retain my previous job. But the brigadier was astonished. He couldn't understand why I didn't want to work outside the camp. All the others snatched at the chance to work outside the camp without a guard.

"But you know the problems," I told him, "Fellow prisoners ask you to bring in something from outside camp. That's strictly forbidden. The guards take away many privileges if they find such smuggled articles. Can't you see what's at stake here? As a believer, I can't do such a thing." Now he understood my motive, and I was allowed to work in the factory until my day of release came.

Released—Home Again at Last!

On July 25, 1981, my wife and my sister Margareta came to accompany me home from camp. We boarded the train that evening, and after a three days' journey we reached home.

On August 1, we were able to meet undisturbed for a service of thanksgiving. This service took place in the yard of one of the brethren. On the following Sunday, we were able to hold a worship service. How aptly the songwriter described such an experience!

> He knows, my Father above does know
> What kinds of storms will trouble my journey;
>   Yet He is able to still the storms,
>   And change darkness into day.

Then our work at home began, and it wasn't exactly a small job either. Our daughter Maria planned to get married August 30, and Willi, our oldest son, barely a month later on September 27. On September 26 of the following year, Peter, our second son, got married.

In those first months there was little time left to think back over all that lay behind me. It was only forward! In our garden we had set up a tent in which the first two weddings were held. We did the same thing a year later for the third wedding, and the government caused us no trouble.

After my release in 1981, I was frequently asked how my fellow prisoners had behaved toward me, considering that I was a child of God. "Not unkindly," I could honestly answer.

"Why, then, did they beat another brother so unmercifully?" asked one of the brethren.

"In which camp did he serve?" I asked in return. "When was he beaten, in prison or in camp?"

He answered, "It happened as he was being transported from one camp to another."

Then it became clear to me. I asked, "What kind of work had he done in camp?"

"He was employed in distributing food in the kitchen," he answered me.

"Well, then he can be thankful to God that they didn't kill him. You see, if one does only the most inferior work in camp, it will go well with him. But the other prisoners reckon those who work in the best positions as informers to the government. Therefore, I never wanted an easier position, so the prisoners couldn't think such things about me. That brother should have been aware of this since it wasn't his first time in camp."

But the government also possessed a peculiar method for tormenting prisoners or even breaking them down completely. These prisoners were simply placed in a different prison cell from time to time. The other prisoners became aware of this, and believe me, they did find out. They found out everything because whenever a newcomer arrived, he was asked from what cell he came and how often he had changed cells. If he had moved frequently, they often became suspicious that he might be an informer, and they'd gang up and beat him.

In this way Brother Dückmann from the Omsk area was once moved from cell to cell, and the prisoners beat him very severely. But through God's grace the brother survived this ill treatment. The government dealt this way with him until he was finally put into a cell in which the cell boss was still one of the genuine thieves. This fellow quietly heard him out and saw that the government was trying to break him down. Furthermore, he gave strict orders that no one dared hit him anymore, and he also sent a letter from the brother to his relatives.

When his relatives received the letter, they promptly went to the prison administrator and informed him what the security guards were doing with their husband and brother. The government was astonished that what went on inside the prison had leaked out to the public. But, sad to say, such things did occur. They later tried to do the same thing to me.

REGISTRATION OR NON-REGISTRATION

As a church, we were able to hold our meetings in Issyk undisturbed at that time, aside from the fact that a few brethren were summoned from time to time. At such times, the issue of church registration was always brought up. Once two government agents from Moscow and Alma-Ata even came to see us. Four brethren were summoned.

At that time, much slander was directed at me, especially by a woman of Issyk, the mayor's assistant. "You hold the church in your hands!" She made many other accusations. She also declared that the church leaders had promised that the church would be registered "when Steffen comes home." Yet, during the time I was in camp, the brethren of the Russian Council of Brothers (Baptist Council of Churches) had changed their stand on church registration. In 1969, they had appealed for registration on the condition of *"Render to Caesar the things that are Caesar's, and to God the things that are God's"* (Mark 12:17). Ten years later, they were unanimously opposed to registration.

After this summons, we brethren called a meeting and asked the others, "Did you promise the government that the church would register?"

"No, we promised nothing," they replied. "We only announced that we'd make a decision after your return home."

And that's exactly what we did. We thought the matter over for a while, prayed about it, and resolved to register the church only if all the members were agreed. A meeting was called, and it was announced that we were ready to register under the conditions set forth by the Council of Brothers in 1969. All were agreed to this proposition. With this stipulation, the declaration was submitted in the fall of 1983. In January 1984, we received the official notice from Moscow: "The church in Issyk is registered."

In the fall of 1983, one of the Christian families had moved to Germany. One of the brethren bought their house with the idea that church services could be held there. A tent was erected in the garden for the purpose of holding a wedding. Later, the church also held its services in this tent. A heating stove was set inside for the winter. In this manner we were able to continue holding our worship services in peace.

But after our church was registered, our dispute with the brethren of the Council of Brothers began. They came to us time and again and accused us of taking this step after they had, as a body, advised against registering.

"How are we supposed to understand and respond to your interpretation?" we protested. "In the early sixties, you demanded that a church leave the brotherhood if it registers itself, thereby aligning itself with the Moscow Union. Then you demanded a registration that wasn't allied with the Moscow Union. And now you again demand no registration at all. What will your next written proclamation sound like? Besides, we haven't joined the Moscow Union,[5] nor have we promised the government a say in our church matters."

More House Searches

Nevertheless, a secret printing press was operating in Issyk without the knowledge of the church leaders. This did not continue, however, without dire results. On a Saturday evening, November 24, 1984, two of the Issyk brethren had their houses searched. One of them was at home and was arrested immediately. The other and his wife were away, but someone else was at home, so the search was initiated.

The following Sunday in church, I recognized Brother Heinrich Wolf outside. After the service, I learned that the government was searching his house, and they had found a cardboard box of Christian literature.

When my wife and I returned home from church, I asked her, "What should we do now?"

"I'll go and testify that the books belong to me; he should not go to prison because of me." My wife agreed, so we prayed about the matter, and I left.

As I entered their yard, a man stood there. "Where are you going?" he demanded.

"I need to go into that house," I answered.

"That won't do," he informed me. "A house search is in progress there, and no one is allowed to enter."

---

5. Likely the *Moscow Union* refers to the All-Union Council of Evangelical Christians-Baptists (AUCECB), the large organization of officially registered churches, while the *Council of Brothers* refers to the Council of Churches of Evangelical Christians-Baptists (CCECB), the organization of Non-Registered Baptists. Unfortunately, there seems to have been a miscommunication and misunderstanding.

"I know," I told him, "and for that very reason, I need to go in."

Then he let me pass. When I entered the house, a policeman already sat at the table writing up all the literature that lay on the table. Beside him stood a man in street clothes, apparently another security officer. The church brother sat on the sofa, his wife and children beside him. I immediately recognized my own box of books on the floor beside the table. I said to the policeman, "The books in that box belong to me." He didn't even glance up at me but just kept on quietly doing his written work.

But the man who stood by asked, "Who are you? Where do you live?"

I explained that I lived in the neighborhood and gave my last name, whereupon he went outside. Shortly, another man came in and asked me the same questions. I answered accordingly. Then he asked, "Does the material in the attic also belong to you?"

"I think everything that belongs to me is in this room," I answered, "but bring me something from the attic, and I'll see if it's mine."

Instead, he went out. Awhile later they called me from outside and announced, "We're going to search your house now too. Lead the way for these people standing here (one of them was a policeman)—full speed ahead to your house!"

When we arrived at our house, my wife was on her knees praying. When she had ended her prayer, the search began. They told my wife and me to be seated. Our son-in-law had just arrived; he was allowed to watch.

The security officer came to the chest of drawers in the living room where we sat, on which stood several Christmas cards with Scripture verses. He looked at them and when he opened one, it started to play. He acted very frightened, looked all about him, and wasn't at ease again until he understood that the card in his hand was the source of the music. We had to laugh. It was evident he'd never seen anything like it before.

A year earlier, the same thing had happened to us. My wife had received just such a card from Germany and had opened it. When the card suddenly began to play, she had asked, "Where is the music coming from?" I had to call her attention to the card in her hand.

Now this house search also drew to a close. The Christian

literature they found, they gave to a woman who wrote up every-thing. The two men left the house.

When the woman had written up everything, the policeman said to me, "Come with me." Immediately we thought, *Now it's off to jail again.* We went back to Brother Heinrich's house once more, where the search was still in progress. A group of young people from our church kept a vigil outside along the street.

When we entered the yard, I saw a huge heap of paper. Now I was compelled to look at what the brethren of the Council of Brothers (Soviet-Zerkwej[6]) had done. Without asking us (that is, the church leadership) for our approval, they had set up a printing press in Issyk. Now I was afraid I'd have to go to prison again.

The policeman turned to the officer in charge of the search and announced that he had brought me here. They were standing close enough that I could clearly hear what they said. "Let him go; if we need him, we'll know where to find him," the other replied. I was allowed to go home, but they arrested Brother Heinrich.

Under Arrest Again

I couldn't understand the entire matter. It is usually inadvis-able to pour gas on the proverbial fire, making matters worse by inviting trouble to places where there are already difficulties. And that was surely the case in Issyk, for there had already been three mass arrests and trial proceedings there. Now the two Wolf brothers were in prison, and time and again I was being summoned before the questioner. His main interest, naturally, was finding out how the printing press had come to Issyk.

This was how matters proceeded until May 14, 1985. That evening they arrested me when I returned from work.

Prison life began anew. I pondered many things. *Why did I have to go to prison so often?* I thought back to the time I had resolved not to renounce God, no matter what men did to me. I had told no one of my resolution, yet I knew God had heard. *Is this now the test to reveal whether I'm really steadfast?* I asked myself. This time would prove to be the most difficult of all my stays in prison and in the concentration camp.

—*Continued on page 159*

------

6. Russian term for the churches that are sometimes referred to in English as the Non-Registered Baptists.

9. Separated for the Fourth Time

(1976–1984) In this chapter Elfriede tells of her experience during the time period that Johann describes in chapter 8, his fourth prison sentence. Hers is a heart-warming and moving story of a heroic effort in trying to raise a growing family alone, of strenuous visits to Johann in prison, and of the care and support of a faithful brotherhood. The two oldest of the Steffen sons, Willi and Peter, grew to manhood during this time and were called for military service. The Baptists at this time did alternative service, such as construction work, and wore a uniform, but carried no weapons. The three oldest children—Maria, Willi, and Peter—all got married in 1981 and 1982.

Hard Times

Elfriede Steffen

In 1976, the situation again began to grow more tense. Already by July, the doors of the church tent had been sealed with lead seals. Again we had to hold our meetings outdoors on the lawn. Soon thereafter, my husband was again placed under arrest. Johann had been called to police headquarters on July 12, 1976. When he didn't return for a long time, we went to headquarters to inquire about him and were told he'd been arrested. The next day I went back to find out more about him. After a long wait, I was told he was under arrest for fifteen days. Dark clouds were gathering over both our church and our family.

On the morning of my husband's arrest, our house was so empty. On other days I was always making breakfast at this time, but now he was no longer here. This was the third time he'd been torn away from the family. I wept and prayed to God for strength and comfort for the future. Then I took a Scripture card out of the little box and read the verse from Proverbs 10:28 that was written on it: *"The hope of the righteous shall be gladness."*

This was God's answer to me. This was comfort from His own hand. First, we needed to wait patiently with hope; then the fullness of joy would come. I comforted myself with this promise. I had to learn to wait with patience.

At the end of the fifteen days, I again went to the chief of police for more definite information. From the chief, I learned that Johann was being held for trial and that an inquiry was to be conducted. I explained that Johann was totally innocent and asked why an innocent person could be held in custody.

His response was, "As far as I'm concerned, I'd be ready to release him, because people like Johann should not be here. There are enough troublemakers on the street; let them be put under arrest." Furthermore, he told me, "You have the full privilege to secure your husband's release through written requests." He said that everyone here in Issyk had refused to prosecute the case—the judges, the examining magistrate, and others. Therefore, a deputy named Siminkauwitz had been sent from Alma-Ata to act as questioner. He could be reached at the office of the district attorney.

Now I felt somewhat more informed, but I didn't immediately go to the district attorney's office; I wanted to wait awhile to see what would develop further.

A few days later, a car drove up to our house and stopped before the yard gate. Two men got out and approached the house. I was alone at the time. The one introduced himself as Siminkauwitz, the questioner; the other was the chauffeur. They wanted to conduct a house search with the purpose of looking for Christian literature. But he only looked about casually, and he examined our identification papers. The Bible lay on the chest of drawers, and he flipped carelessly through it. I requested that he leave me the Bible, and he answered, "Yes, I have no need of it."

After they were out in the yard again, I asked which articles he was citing as grounds for my husband's arrest, for the length of Johann's upcoming sentence hinged on that. He named several articles. I examined them and calculated that it would be a lengthy sentence of several years. "So long?" I questioned. "I won't survive this!"

"A woman like you will survive it," he replied. And the fact is, I did survive those five years. But Siminkauwitz, the questioner, died a year and a half later of a heart attack in January 1978. He was buried in the Issyk cemetery even though his family lived elsewhere. They came to Issyk for the funeral. Johann's trial took place in October. This time he was the only defendant. Later, two other brethren were also arrested. On the third day of the trial, the summons was handed down: five years in the concentration camp under strict supervision.

In December, shortly before Christmas, I discovered that Johann had been taken from the prison. Only after he was in the camp was he allowed to write letters to us. One time I traveled to Alma-Ata and asked for his new address. After repeated requests, I was told, "In the city of Novy Uzen."[7]

I went to the post office and obtained the correct postal code. Then I wrote a letter to the camp there, and only two days after his arrival, Johann already had my letter. Oh, what a joy this was to him!

On the other hand, I was hearing no news from him. This caused me great unrest and uncertainty as to his condition. Many alarming thoughts and concerns discomfited me.

Visiting Johann in Novy Uzen

So we decided to look him up. My son Willi and I, along with a woman whose daughter would host us for a night, set out on the long, tiresome journey in February 1977. This time we had a four-hour plane ride.

We arrived in Shevchenko early in the morning, where we took the bus into the city. We hunted up the Nikolajewa family who received us warmly into their home. We told them our reason for coming, and they thought it was still a fairly great distance to Novy Uzen. There were two travel options: bus or taxi. We figured the taxi would be too expensive, so we went to the bus station and asked, "When does the next bus leave for Novy Uzen?"

"Because of the bad weather, no more buses will run today," we were told.

Then a man approached me and asked, "Where would you like to go?"

"There are three of us who'd like to go to Novy Uzen," I replied.

"I can take you there in my car," he offered. We discussed the price. He asked five rubles apiece. Willi and I, if possible, wanted to spend two days at camp, but the other woman had to return the

---

7. *Nowo Usen* in German; the current name is *Zhanaozen*.

same day. The driver offered to take us to the camp and bring the woman right back again.

It wasn't easy to drive in such weather. The way led through a bleak, snowy wilderness. The asphalt road was covered with ice, and the strong winds made driving even more difficult. But God protected us, and we arrived safely at our destination.

I went straight to the camp office and asked, "Is there a man here by the name of Johann Steffen?"

"Yes," he answered, "but he's still at work."

I wrote up a request for a two-day visit, and we received permission for both Willi and me. The woman who had accompanied us returned to her daughter in Shevchenko with the kind driver.

We had to wait until four o'clock in the afternoon. Then we were given a room with two beds, a small table, and two stools. This was all well and good, but the water pipes were frozen. That was very bad! Also, the water in the radiators was frozen; they were ruined. The room was ice-cold, everything was frightfully dirty, and the smell was awful. How were we to cook our food when Johann came home from work, and then to live in this ice-cold room?

Finally, someone came, bringing us a pail of water and an electric heater. The heater was made of a big tile with a spiral heating element in the center. And wonder of wonders, it worked! Even the cord was all right. We were so thankful for it. The room soon became warmer, and we were able to cook.

In the evening, Johann was brought to us. We were overjoyed to see each other again. Until supper was ready, we seated ourselves around the heater, which served both as cookstove and heater. We talked about the happenings of the day and wondered why no news from Johann had reached us. He told me of his joy over the letter he had already received the second day after his arrival. We later found out his letters had been held here at camp, and not forwarded because he had written them in German. Then we ate our supper, and after having thanked God for His love for us, we lay down to sleep.

The next morning, the room was warm enough to melt the ice from the radiators. Water ran out of the broken radiator into the room. With that water, I could now wash the dirty floor. That day was Sunday, and the room was nice and warm.

On Monday, Willi and I took the bus back to Shevchenko, and from there we flew home to Alma-Ata.

Afterward, we wrote requests to Moscow that Johann be released. They wouldn't release him, but they transferred him to the camp in Shevchenko, which was a great relief to him. It also made it easier for us to visit him.

We were allowed to visit him once a year for two days and twice a year for two hours. If we went by train, it took three days to travel the distance. There were always many difficulties and unpleasant happenings during travel. Sometimes we'd have to wait for days before a room became available. There were plenty of vacant rooms. Nevertheless, we had to wait for our two-day visit. During those times of waiting, the Nikolajewa family always received us warmly.

MORE PARTINGS

At home it was somewhat easier for me than it had been during Johann's earlier imprisonments. The three oldest children went to work now, and the two youngest were in school.

Since the tent had been torn down, the church met in groups in the homes. The children's and youths' classes continued to be held, and the church was experiencing harmony.

"Commit thy way unto the LORD; trust also in him; and he shall bring it to pass" (Psalm 37:5).

The years passed, and the waiting grew harder. In May 1979, our oldest son Willi was called to military service. This was, for all of us, a sad time, in which we learned to trust in God still more deeply. At that time, Willi was already a child of God.

His faith was tested during this time, and he had to endure a great deal in the service. But we're thankful to God for faithfully protecting him. The second person had been torn from our family prayer circle, yet we remained united in prayer and intercession. We wrote many letters back and forth. The third hard blow for our family came in November 1979: our second son was called for military duty. It was a cold winter day when we accompanied him on his departure.

It was doubly hard for me to see him go because at the time Peter was still not grounded in the faith. At eleven years old he had made a decision and acknowledged himself a sinner. Yet, in the last years he had become indifferent. Therefore, as a mother, I had great concern for his soul, and his father wasn't at home.

But God heard my prayers and laid His delivering hand on Peter when he was in great peril of life. Once when he had some free time, he became lost in the great virgin forest of the Far Northeast. God led him and his friend back to their base again. Another time he was protected in a car accident, and a third time in a fire while he and his comrades slept. When he returned home, he said, "Mother, it was your prayers that preserved me."

"In the world ye shall have tribulation: but be of good cheer; I have overcome the world" (John 16:33).

God be praised! He directed so that both of our sons could work in construction when they were called, and they did not have to carry arms.

Visiting Johann

In March 1980, Maria, now twenty-one years old, and I wanted to visit Johann at the camp in Shevchenko. I bought plane tickets for the trip there and back.

The evening before our departure while we were still at home, a violent storm arose—first it rained, then snow mixed in, and finally a thick cover of snow blanketed everything. A Christian brother had promised to drive us to the airport at Alma-Ata with his car, at one o'clock in the morning. We waited, but in vain because he didn't appear. Finally, it was high time to leave, and still he wasn't there. So Maria and her girlfriend ran to his house to wake him. They knocked and called his name, but no one opened up. They were all sound asleep.

They ran to a relative of her friend, who quickly drove to our house. We loaded our baggage and were soon on our way. But the road was dangerous and slick on top of the loose, new-fallen snow, and our progress was very slow.

When we arrived at the airport, I hurried to the desk, but I was told it was already too late. The plane hadn't taken off yet, but the steps had been taken away. Nobody could board anymore. (Isn't this how it was with the ark? The doors were closed.) At any rate, we were left behind and had to go back home again.

The next day we went to Alma-Ata, returned our tickets, and bought others for the next flight. This was a mail plane, and we had to make two landings en route to discharge and to take on mail. Instead of the usual four hours, the trip took seven hours.

We finally arrived in Shevchenko in the morning, and the Nikolajewa family took us in as before. That same day, Maria and I went to the camp to apply for a two-day visit. But, as at all other times, we were put off even though there were empty guest rooms.

It was evening by the time we could return to the city from the camp. We went by bus, and we noticed a man watching us. Another man wanted to escort us to the house and offered to carry our baggage. I politely declined, but he accompanied us anyway.

The next day we returned to the camp, and again we weren't promised a visit until the next day. Finally, when almost evening, at four o'clock on the third day, we were given a guest room at the camp.

We were finally reunited upon Johann's return from work that evening, and we had a happy time together. It was going tolerably well for Johann at the time. We could share many happenings, pray together, and exhort each other with spiritual encouragement and comfort for the rest of our time of separation.

Our two oldest sons were in the service at the time, and it was a great relief to be able to discuss this and clear up family matters with him.

For two days I could be with him and prepare his meals because I had been allowed to bring him five kilograms of food. Then the difficult parting came. It wasn't easy for him either, knowing we were so alone on the trip, traveling as we were. But we knew we could and must trust God in all things, because He tells us to cast all our cares upon Him.

There was rain and a cold wind during our visit, and I caught a cold, but we survived. The worst part was that Maria had to return before I did. Her vacation time was up, and she had to go back to work promptly.

When my two-day visit was over, I went to the airport, only to find out that my ticket had run out. I went to the ticket office to return it and buy a new one for the next flight, though at a loss. However, I was told that there would be no seat available for the next ten days. That was much too long for me, so I decided to make the trip home by train. I decided not to go directly home, but to stop off to visit my brother in Korkino. My train would leave that evening.

On the train I became acquainted with a woman who was traveling the same route I was. This was very convenient for me because we had to change trains during the night.

At a small station, we had to update our tickets. The other woman stood in line while I guarded our baggage. When this was taken care of, we heard the announcement that our train would arrive late. So we had to wait. Then came the announcement that we needed to board on track number two.

While we were waiting, another train pulled in on track one. Now it stood there, making it impossible for us to get to track two. Fortunately, the conductor allowed us to board this wrong train and get out on the other side in order to reach our train. You can be sure we were quick about it too, but by the time we emerged on the other side, our train was already moving away slowly. In Russia each coach has its own conductor, and the one who would have been closest to us wouldn't open for us. Then another conductor called, "Come here." The ground was slick and icy. He stood in the doorway of his coach, and we handed our baggage up to him. Then he took my hand and pulled me up—and it was a long way up, with no platform there. Then he also pulled the other woman up as the train moved ever faster. We had taken a very dangerous chance. If the man hadn't assisted us, it could have turned out very badly for us.

We found our seats, but it was a long time before our thoughts could quiet down. We rode together until Chelyabinsk, and from there we went our separate ways.

I was given a warm welcome at my brother in Korkino. I stayed there several days and then continued by plane from Chelyabinsk to Alma-Ata, finally arriving safely at home.

Maria had also made it home safely. Her plane arrived right on time at one o'clock in the afternoon, and she rode directly to work. At the time, she worked the second shift in a shoe factory.

It's exactly the same in spiritual matters—without God's help, we'll never be at the right place at the time God wants us to be there. But it rests with us, whether we want what is God's will for us, and whether we're awake or are asleep in sin. If we're sleeping, a small delay brings with it many detours and great loss. Often, we don't recognize until later God's leading and His protection on the winding pathways of life.

The times of waiting, when letters failed to appear, were very difficult for me. Once it went two months until a letter arrived from Johann. In that letter he wrote that he wasn't receiving any letters from me. At those times, I wrote pleas to the camp administrators. As a rule, the exchange of letters would then return to normal because the letters had been detained in camp.

It was always a great joy when letters came from our two sons. This always renewed our courage and joy as we kept on praying for them. There were only four of us left in our family prayer circle, which we kept intact each evening.

"But they that wait upon the LORD *shall renew their strength"* (Isaiah 40:31).

Onkel Enns

An aged brother in the faith, Cornelius Enns, visited us many times during these trying years. His visits were short but always rich in blessings. He always read from the Bible or explained the meaning of some selected Bible passage. Other times he would tell about an answer to prayer that he had experienced.

Onkel Enns had also had to spend many years in prisons or camps. During that time, his wife was alone with the children. The grounds for his arrest had been that during the war years he had talked to others about God in the concentration camp. He had been sentenced to be shot to death. After he had spent quite some time on death row, he was allowed to write to Moscow, requesting a pardon.

Onkel Enns quickly wrote and submitted a petition, begging for mercy since he still had a family at home. In those days, there was little hope of a pardon, but he prayed the more earnestly to God, committing his family, and indeed his own life, to God's leading.

Sometime later, a number of prisoners were summoned from their cells, and his name was among those called. The prisoners stood in a long hall; all was still—deathly still.

Then names were called. One group had to pass out through a side door, the other through the door at the end of the hall. No one knew what was in store for him. Onkel Enns's name was also called; he was to go straight ahead through the door at the end of the hall. He reached a room where a prison official sat.

The officer asked him his name and invited him to be seated.

Then he explained: "A written order from Moscow has reached us. Your death sentence has been commuted to ten years in concentration camp."

This was totally unexpected for Onkel Enns. He could only stammer, "Thank you."

Afterward, he was led out again. God had heard his prayer of faith. Later he was sent to a coal mining camp, where he had to work hard and suffer great hunger. He became so exhausted that he often asked himself, *Will I ever see my family again?*

But God gave him strength, and after many years he was released and was able to return to his family. This is what gave him such a deep understanding of our situation. He prayed much and had confidence in God that the prisoners would be freed again. Onkel Enns remained close to us through fond memories.

In these years of waiting, we were not lonesome in our home. Maria had already confessed her sins to the Lord and was attending the youth class. During the winter, the girls' group met one evening a week in our home. Mending would be collected from large families for these evening gatherings. Stockings, children's clothes, and other things were mended, and new clothes were sewn or knitted. While the girls worked, one of them would read Christian stories to the others. Yes, those were blessed evenings.

Time slipped by, and the year 1981 drew nearer—the year when we had hopes for a reunion with our loved ones.

The Year 1981

Finally 1981 arrived, the year we had long yearned for. Joyfully we awaited the homecoming of our dear ones, Johann and the two boys. We planted the garden in April. In May, we renovated the house and whitewashed all the rooms with lime. Then I painted the doors and windows white. Willi was to return from his two-year service, and by that time everything must be in tip-top shape and looking festive. But for a short time, there was total confusion in the house, because all the furniture was pushed out of place.

On May 5, Helmut didn't have to go to work until the second shift. I had gone into the stable to feed the calf. When I came back out again, Helmut stood at the door, wearing a military cap and looking happily at me. "Where did you get that cap?" I asked, and quickly added, "But hurry up! It's time you are off to work," and went to the door of the house.

Suddenly Willi stood there before me! My joy couldn't be put into words. After two long years, our son was finally home again! The joy was very great for a mother's heart that, tested by sorrow, had anxiously and lovingly awaited her son's return.

Later I thought, *Just as unexpected and sudden as this will be the rapture of the saints from this earth. And the joy in heaven will be much greater still! There will be no separations or sorrows there, but we will dwell in rest and peace with all the other believers.*

Work inside our house progressed. There were also several repair jobs to be done on the outside. The children diligently helped with the work. Everything needed to be in good order, so that my husband would be thoroughly pleased when he would come home. By this time the garden was also blooming magnificently.

BRINGING JOHANN HOME

Finally, the long-awaited month, July 1981, came. All the preparations had been made. The plane tickets, from Alma-Ata to Shevchenko and back, had been bought. On July 24, my sister-in-law Margareta and I left by plane from Alma-Ata to pick up Johann in Shevchenko after his five-year confinement at camp.

We reached our goal safely. Everything had worked out beautifully so far. Johann was to be released on July 25. Then we planned to spend the night with the Nikolajewa family and take the plane home in the morning. Everything had been planned carefully and in detail.

But—the adversary wasn't asleep. When we arrived at the camp office on July 24, the camp official said, "You are not permitted to go by plane."

"But I've already bought the plane tickets," I protested.

"No," he said firmly, "I can't allow that."

"Why can't you do that?" I questioned.

"Johann might escape somewhere or other," he explained.

I answered, "My husband would never try to flee or escape."

Thereupon he said, "You two may fly home with the plane. Your husband will come on the train."

"I've waited five years for my husband, and we've made this long trip to bring him home from camp," I lamented. "And now he has to make this long, three-day journey on the train? I won't stand for it! Where my husband is, there I will be too!"

"Then you'll have to redeem your plane tickets and buy train tickets," he replied.

Pleading did no good! He remained firm. The other officers who were present and heard the conversation said, "All these years Johann has shown himself to be trustworthy, and he was also a good worker."

The camp official also confirmed what they said, "Johann was a dependable worker." He also mentioned other believers who had been in camp, naming Wiebe and Nikolaus Klassen in particular. "They were all good men. But you must go home by train, and the tickets must be bought through the camp."

Then I gave him money for three tickets. On July 25, we went to the office to inquire whether the tickets had been bought and when Johann would be released. Margareta and I had decided not to return the plane tickets yet. Just in case they deceived us and didn't give us our tickets, sending Johann off on the train anyway, we could still make it home sooner by plane. These men were not to be trusted.

Noon came, and still no one had brought us the tickets we'd ordered and paid for. Because it was Saturday, all the office doors were closed. Only one door stood open. Inside sat two men who were strangers to us. Once more we asked them about our tickets, and when my husband would be released.

"Oh, but he is free," they tried to make us understand, and acted as if they knew nothing more about it.

More time elapsed, it was already two o'clock when a man drove up in a car. He told us only two tickets had been bought, and we were to accompany him to the train station.

We refused, for we had ordered and paid for three tickets. So he drove away without us. Again we went to the men in the office. This time we were firmer with them, "We've come to get my husband. Why are roadblocks being laid in our way? If you won't let us all three travel together, we'll register a complaint about you all."

Immediately they made a telephone call and events were set into motion. A van and driver were placed at our disposal, and an offer was made to send soldiers along to guard us, but of course we refused the bodyguard.

Things moved in rapid-fire succession. First, the plane tickets were returned. Then we went to the Nikolajewa home to pick up our things. We quickly bought provisions for the three-day trip and finally came back to the camp.

When we arrived at camp, Johann was already out in the office. Finally, after all the agitation and the seemingly endless wait, we were allowed the joy of seeing each other again. What a joyful meeting!

There was little time left until the train departed, and it was quite a distance to the station. An officer accompanied us to the station on the bus, and from there to our coach. Only then did he give us our tickets. The train soon departed.

It was evening already, but only after we had ridden for some distance were we able to relax. Now we understood that God had evened out the way so that all three of us could make the homeward journey together on the train even though we had to ride for three whole days.

Next morning when the train made a stop, we went to the post office and sent a telegram, so the children would know we were coming home on the train.

We reached Alma-Ata at seven o'clock on the evening of July 28. Our children were waiting for us at the station, except for Peter, who was still in the service. Several brethren and sisters in the church were also there to greet us. When we arrived at home, more of the believers were there to welcome Johann home! Together a prayer of gratitude was offered.

Saturday evening, a thanksgiving service for the whole congregation was held at K. Wolfs. We thanked God together for His protection and for the reunion with Johann, and also that the church had been preserved through great tribulation and kept in the faith and the mutual service of the Lord Jesus. On Sunday the worship service was held without any interference.

WEDDINGS

My fiftieth birthday came on August 8. We celebrated it the next day, along with the engagement of our daughter Maria and Jakob, her fiancé.

They were married on August 30. The wedding was held in our garden. A tent was set up for the occasion, and Johann performed the marriage ceremony. It was hard for me to have my daughter leave home, but so it had to be, for they *"shall leave father and mother"* and *"they two shall be one"* (Ephesians 5:31). Jakob and Maria found a temporary home in our neighborhood.

The engagement of Willi, our oldest son, and Elsa took place on August 23. Their wedding, which was held on September 27, also took place in our garden. Johann likewise performed the ceremony for these two.

So Willi left home too. He and Elsa likewise obtained a temporary home nearby. It was a joy for me to see them so happy. We had now added two more children to our family. We were thankful that they were all children of God.

On December 12, 1981, Peter returned home from his military service. Our joy was great, for God had heard all our prayers and had brought everyone home safe and sound.

Peter then also came to faith in Jesus Christ and found peace for his soul. He was baptized in 1982. All were now home again, and the anxious waiting for our loved ones ended for the time being. We would not let our thoughts dwell on the uncertain future.

Peter and Anna celebrated their wedding on September 26, 1982. Again a tent was set up in our garden, and Johann performed the marriage. They also lived in the neighborhood.

During those years, we received many letters, along with parcels of clothing and food, from Christians abroad. A hearty thank-you to all who thought of us in that difficult time, and who prayed for our family and supported us. God bless you all for your love! We received so many packages that we were able to also help other families.

Johann went back to construction work, and he led the church in worship services and in other matters. Helmut and I also went to work, and David attended the tenth grade in school. Things went well for us at that time. The Sunday services were also not being disturbed so much anymore.

In 1983, the church again erected a tent so that the entire congregation could meet at the same place.

Delegates from the government came to our services only on Christian holidays, but they caused us no trouble. At any rate, we had rest for a few years.

In November 1984, David was called into military service. We accompanied him on his departure, and prayed that God would protect him while he was far from home. So there had to be another parting.

Four days after David's departure, the next harsh blow hit us. Quite unexpectedly, another round of house searches began—first at G. Wolf's, then at H. Wolf's, finally at our house, and still later in other homes. All kinds of Christian literature, including Bibles, were confiscated.

10. Arrested for the Fifth Time

(1985–1987) Johann's fifth prison sentence, for five years, began in May 1985. He considers this his most difficult sentence of all. By this time the prison gulag in the Soviet Union was dominated by criminals and thieves. Johann relates how they tried him out. But worse than that were the devious means the government authorities used to try to get Johann into trouble. They tried to get the other prisoners to misuse Johann, but instead they protected him out of respect for his character. This chapter is a commentary of God's grace in providing wisdom and protection to Johann.

In Prison Again in Alma-Ata

Johann Steffen

(Continued from page 142)

The next day, May 15, 1985, I was taken to the prison in Alma-Ata. Again, I was put into cell nineteen, where I'd been the last time.

After several days, a fellow prisoner Victor and I, with our belongings, were moved to the cellar, where usually only the most hardened criminals were kept. There were already two others in the cell: a small Russian and a tall Gypsy named Nikolai. There was sleeping room for only three people, yet there were four of us. They showed me to a sleeping place, and the other fellow had to sleep on the floor.

As always before, the question asked was, "For what reason have you been brought here?" I explained to them the reason for my arrest.

Thereupon the Gypsy said, "It won't be difficult for us here in the cell. Onkel Johann, where do you live?"

"About fifty kilometers from Alma-Ata," I told him.

Then he said (as thieves say), "I have feet, and what we need, we'll get." This meant that he had someone available whom he could send to our house and get whatever I wanted. They especially liked to have money brought so they could get someone to buy what they needed.

I immediately protested, "My wife's income is only twenty-eight rubles, so there's nothing to bring." These criminals had all they needed here in the cell: drugs to smoke, all the available intoxicating and narcotic pills, and other similar vices. Nearly every day, two people were sent out to buy whatever they were out of. In the fifties and sixties, such a thing would have been impossible. The other prisoners would have killed the culprits for trying to intimidate others.

DIFFICULT DAYS WITH THIEVES

One day, after they had again received something from the outside, the little Russian said softly to the Gypsy (I was close enough to overhear him), "Let me tell him to wash my socks." There was always one in the cell who dominated the others.

I thought, *If he allows it, it will lead to a tragic ending.*

Nikolai consented, and the little Russian said to Victor, who was also a Russian, but much stronger than he, "Wash my socks for me," at the same time showing him where the dirty socks lay.

"Very well," the other replied.

Is he in prison for the first time and doesn't know what he's bringing upon himself? I wondered. From many years of prison experience, I knew what the results would be. First, wash the socks, then the underwear, and finally, wait on the other whether you wanted to or not.

After Victor said, "Very well," the little fellow sprang up, ran to him, and began to beat him in the face.

Then the Gypsy got up and asked me, "What shall we do with him now?"

"Nikolai, I've sat in prison for many years," I told him, "but never before have I had thieves ask a Christian what to do. They themselves always knew what they wanted to do."

"I know that too," he answered, "but I'm asking you now because you know the laws of the thieves so well."

Whereupon I said, "According to those laws, he should have waited until he had washed the socks. So he is acting contrary to your law."

"But he said, 'Very well,'" the little fellow objected.

"By that, I didn't say I'd wash them," countered the one who had been hit.

Then things quieted down again. For if in prison one calls himself a thief, yet doesn't comply with the unwritten laws of thieves, he stands in danger of being punished in camp. Therefore, everyone tries hard to abide by these laws. It put me in a very dangerous position to protect anyone unless one of these laws was actually violated, which was the case just now.

If anyone wanted to be let out of the cell, he had to knock on the door. The Gypsy wanted to be let out, so he knocked. Often, some time elapsed until the guard came to unlock the door. A criminal's patience is often rather thin, especially if he has taken drugs. So he said to the little fellow, "They don't want to open up for us today. We'll show them. We'll slash our wrists."

A frightening feeling gripped me. *This will be worse than before if they carry out their threat.*

The little Russian brought a razorblade at once, gave it to the prisoner whom he had hit, and said, "You take the lead; be the first to cut your wrist." The other took the blade, but just sat there. "Have you ever cut your wrist before?" the little fellow asked.

"No," answered Victor.

"Then you don't know how to go about it. If you cut it completely through, no doctor will be able to help you anymore. Give me the blade; I'll cut it for you." He did, and the blood started to flow out. Immediately the others hammered frantically on the door.

The watchman finally came and asked, "What do you want?"

"A fellow has cut his wrist! He must see a doctor immediately!" came the answer.

"He's no child anymore. He should know what he's doing," replied the guard, and walked away again.

"Do you see what kind of guard we have today?" the Gypsy said to the little Russian. "We'll show him! We'll all cut our wrists."

"Yes," agreed the little fellow, "but not Onkel Johann."

I resolved in myself that I certainly wouldn't do such a thing. But if they did it to me, what could I do to prevent it? I prayed earnestly.

The little fellow brought out the razor blade again, which he had already hidden in the mattress. Who would be next?

At just that moment, the guard opened the door and asked, "Where is the fellow who needs a doctor?" My prayer had been answered; no one else did any cutting. The guard had first gone to find the doctor, which was why it had taken so long until he opened the door. Thus a hard day passed by.

That the next day would be an even more trying one; no one could have foreseen it at that point. In the forenoon, the little fellow left his cell after having knocked on the door for a short time. He returned, bringing along something to smoke as well as some tea.

Nikolai generally went out in the afternoon, which he also did that day. When he came back, he said, "Before the day is over, we'll make someone pay." Then he added, "It will soon be supper time, and we won't begin until after supper, so no one interrupts us."

What's up so soon again? I thought. Already my prayers went up to my Lord and Savior, that He would wonderfully direct all things to turn out for the best.

When supper was ended, the Gypsy stood before the door so no one could knock, and so the guard couldn't look into the cell through the peephole. Then he asked the little Russian what he had told the officer about him that forenoon.

"Nothing at all," the other replied.

"What do you mean 'nothing at all'?" protested Nikolai. "How could he know then what was spoken here in the cell?"

"What did the officer know?" returned the little Russian.

"Several days ago," Nikolai answered, "I related in the cell how I had given a guard twenty-five rubles to see to it that I got some pills. To this day I haven't received them. The officer reproached me for being so impatient. He said he simply hadn't had time to buy them, but he'd go tomorrow."

The little fellow answered, "I didn't tell him that."

Then Nikolai asked the one who'd been to the doctor the day before whether he'd told on him. He answered, "I was only with the doctor; I didn't see anybody else."

"Well, then who could it have been? Onkel Johann doesn't leave the cell, so it could have been no one but you." But the other again denied it. Nikolai was silent for a moment, and then said to me, "Maybe it was you after all?"

"How could that be, if I don't go out at all?" I questioned.

"I know that, but while we're sleeping, you could write it on paper. Then in the morning when they take us out for fresh air, you could let it drop. The guard would pick it up and know the information."

"Nikolai," I said, "first, I have nothing to write with; secondly, when they take us out, I'm the first to go out and the first to come back every day. You always come behind me. So then, if I dropped a paper, wouldn't you notice it?"

"True enough," he said, and turned to the little fellow again. "So then it could only have been you who passed this information on to the authorities." Then he looked at the one who had been beaten the day before and gave him a signal to beat the little Russian.

He fell upon the little fellow and began beating him with his hands. When the little fellow collapsed to the floor, he trampled him with his feet.

I was afraid that this time they'd kill him because such things often occurred in prisons. But when Victor became tired, he lifted the fellow he had beaten from the floor and set him upright again.

Then Nikolai asked me, "Now, Onkel Johann, what shall we do with this fellow now? Yesterday, the other fellow hadn't yet washed the socks, and you gave the correct answer. But after an act such as this, what now?"

I answered him, "I already told you that thieves never inquire of believers what they should do."

"I know, I know," he answered.

While they had been beating the other fellow, many thoughts had gone through my mind. *Yesterday I had stood up for the one, and they'd stopped beating him. But now, alas, what could I do?* And it was very risky to do anything because they usually left off abusing the beaten one and fell upon the one who interfered.

I asked the Gypsy, "Do you still remember everything I told you the night I was brought into this cell?"

"I do," he replied.

"I said then," I reminded him, "that wherever I was, the government would listen in on all that was said. You said that only a few days ago here in the cell you had spoken of the twenty-five rubles you'd given to the guard to buy you pills, and that it had been taking him so long. They eavesdropped on that conversation, and today they gave you their answer. Therefore, it looks as if one of us had informed them." All became quiet for a few minutes.

Then he said to the little fellow, "Pound on the door!" which meant, "See that you get out of here."

"Praise God!" I thought. "He can leave alive." He knocked at the door, and the guard let him out and put him into another cell.

Who, except God who gave them to me at the right time through His Spirit, would have known, the evening I entered the cell, that I would later utter such words? Otherwise, the little Russian might have had to die, whereas now he could stay alive. It is no light matter to relate such events, but still less easy to actually experience them.

In the following days I had many deep thoughts about how wonderfully the Lord always stood by my side as I faced the future. Just what would the future still bring?

BE NOT AFRAID, ONLY BELIEVE

Past events came back to my mind. In the winter of 1958–59, soon after our wedding, my wife and I had made two mottoes with sayings from the Bible. We had bought very small beads. Then, with the beads, I had shaped the lettering of the texts, and my wife had fashioned the flowers. Who would have thought then that these two Scripture texts would accompany us throughout our lives? *"Be not afraid, only believe"* (Mark 5:36) and *"Cast thy burden upon the LORD"* (Psalm 55:22). We hadn't seen into the future when we designed the mottoes.

But in the years that followed, we had many opportunities to learn not to fear and to lay all our burdens before the Lord—I in prisons and camps, in hunger and at hard work, and my wife struggling alone at home with the children, time and again. We learned that fear retreated when we rolled our cares before the Lord.

We later brought these two plaques along when we moved to Germany. Sometime later, a sister from Tokmok in Kirgizia had designed two other mottoes in similar fashion with the words *"The LORD is my shepherd"* (Psalm 23:1) and *"Pray without ceasing"* (1 Thessalonians 5:17). We also brought them with us to Germany. These Scriptures will accompany us until He comes again and receives us home from this earth. We need to pray without ceasing, and He will always remain our Shepherd.

Sentenced

The trial was held several days later. Just as in 1976, we were tried in Alma-Ata, presumably because the judges in Issyk refused to touch my case. All three of us received five years of confinement,

Be not afraid, only believe!   **Cast thy burden upon the Lord!**

but I under strict controls.

After the trial they allowed us to spend a short time with our wives. Then I was taken to another cell, in an area where those previously sentenced awaited the transport to camp.

Waiting to Be Transported to Camp

Two Russians were already in the cell when I arrived. The one immediately asked, "Do you have your sentence with you?" When I answered in the affirmative, he demanded, "Give it here to read." When he had read it through, he laughed and said to the other man, "Now we'll fare well because a pastor has joined us." Then he asked me, "Where do you live? How far is it from here?"

"About fifty kilometers," I replied.

Then the Russian said, just as the Gypsy had done before, "I have feet; we'll be able to get what we need. Five hundred rubles will do for a beginning."

I gave him the same answer I had given to Nikolai, "My wife receives only twenty-eight rubles for income. There's not much to be had."

He burst out laughing. "Here stands the pastor of a church with over 200 members. If each member gives only ten rubles, that's already 2,000."

"It's not like you think it is. I'm not supported by the money the members give," I told him. "Instead, I have worked just like everyone else, and we have lived from my earnings. Besides, my wife said she wants to go to Kirgizia to our relatives who live there. So there'd be no one at home, even if you sent someone there."

"We still have time," he asserted. "It's still a month until the transfer." After about ten days had passed, he laid a piece of paper before me, handed me a ballpoint pen and commanded, "Now write!"

I had had time to ponder what I would do. I had agreed with my wife that if she received a letter from me from prison, and it was written in Russian, she would know I had written it under pressure. In such a case, she was to give nothing to the bearer of the letter. If, however, it was written in German, she was to give him whatever the letter asked for.

So I began to write. I said to the Russian, "It will do no good to write 500 rubles. She won't be able to pay it anyway. It would be better if I write 150 rubles." He didn't answer, so I continued writing. I also gave the exact address.

He read the letter, and then went to the door and knocked. The guard opened, and he went out. When he returned, he said, "Everything is in order."

IN THE DEN OF LIONS

Two days later, they called him out of the cell. When he came back, he had money with him. I thought my wife must have forgotten our agreement. However, when she later visited me at the camp, I learned that she had by no means forgotten, but had asked herself what would happen to me if she gave nothing. And she was quite right in thinking so.

But the worst was still in store for me. It was clear to me that the Russian would take action just shortly before my departure for camp. As soon as this appointed time was announced, he would cold-bloodedly require me to write another letter and this time demand a large sum of money because he would still have to remain in prison. *If the Gypsy in the first cell was a bear,* I thought to myself, *this Russian is a lion.*

The days went by. One evening, another man was brought into the cell. When we were taken outdoors for fresh air in the mornings, he was always the last to leave the cell, and one morning he didn't return. The two others discussed possible reasons why he didn't return.

Suddenly the door was thrust open and "Lion's" name[1] was called. A little later the other fellow was summoned, and soon after

---

1. I call him that because I've forgotten his real name.

that, I too was called. I was directed into a room, and the officer in the room spoke abusively to me. "What's going on in your cell?"

"Nothing," I replied.

"What's this—nothing!" he bellowed. "Then why doesn't the other fellow want to go back to the cell anymore?"

"I don't know," I responded.

"What are the names of the other two in the cell?"

"You know that better than I do," I told him.

"So—you're going to act like a partisan, who also never says anything." I remained quiet. "And you don't know what I am referring to?"

"No, I have no knowledge of such a thing."

"The man who was in the cell with you knows it," he retorted. "He doesn't want to go back. He declares you struck him."

"That would not happen, that a believer would ever strike an unbeliever," was my answer.

Another officer came in, and the two of them went into the next room. When they returned, I was taken back to the cell. The two others hadn't been returned yet. I looked about the cell and saw that only my possessions had been rooted through. The others' belongings remained untouched.

Now I understood their plot: the authorities put my fellow prisoners in the adjoining room. There they could hear what I said about them, which would give them grounds for beating me in the cell. The government often used such methods, but my God was with me so that this time their plans were foiled.

After this happened, my cellmates acted as if nothing had happened. But I wondered what they would yet hatch up to use against me.

One morning after breakfast my last name was called. When I came forward, I found out I was to prepare for my departure. *Now, I thought, the hard moment has come.* But "Lion's" name was also called; he too was to get ready. *Praise God, I thought in silence. Now you won't have to write another letter,* I told myself.

We finished preparing ourselves and were called to be transported. Many prisoners were already waiting in the corridor. There the provisions were distributed, and we had to enter a waiting room to wait for a thorough search.

All at once my cellmate was summoned to appear without baggage. What did this mean?

When he came back, he told his companions, "I'm not going along after all. I have to go back to my cell." And he was led away at once.

I could hardly contain myself for joy as I beheld the wonderful ways of God. The "Lion" had had to come out with me, so he couldn't put pressure on me in the cell. And now, on the journey, I didn't have to be with him. What a wonderful God I had! He continually let me feel His presence and His might.

"Thou art the God that doest wonders: thou hast declared thy strength among the people" (Psalm 77:14).

ANOTHER TRAIN, ANOTHER CELL

We were transported to the train station and there put into a "Stolypin," or special prisoner coach, so named for a Czarist prime minister whose name was Stolypin. Then the train began to move, though no one knew where this journey would take us.

They brought another little Russian to me in the compartment. *What's the intent of this?* I asked myself.

In Zilinograt we were put into a transit prison. Earlier, we had heard how strict the guards were there. When we arrived in the evening, we had to stand in line. Whoever didn't stand exactly as he was ordered to, was immediately beaten. Then an officer came with our papers, called out the names, and told each one where he was to go.

When he called my last name, I stepped forward. "So you're a rabble rouser? Well, we're not afraid of such as you!" He took me and showed me to my place.

To another he shouted, "You escaped from the deportation camp. We'll show you!" And he directed him to the same place where I was. He was the fellow who had already ridden in the same compartment with me on the train. We were put into the same cell. There was no water in the cell, so he knocked on the door and asked if he could please move in with the others. His wish was granted.

In Alma-Ata the prisoners could talk together through the windows, but that was positively not permitted here. Once we heard frightening screams in a nearby cell. The guards were reviling and beating a fellow prisoner.

A few days later, our journey continued. Once again we had to appear for roll call. As the officer held my papers in his hand he said, "Here he is—the rabble rouser, who caused a disturbance in the cell."

"That's not true! He wasn't even in that cell," the other prisoners protested.

"Nobody asked you! Shut up, if you please!" he bellowed at them.

Then we were driven to the train and sent to the camp at Arkalyk.[2]

In the Camp at Arkalyk

When we arrived at the camp, we had to sit down and wait until the gate was opened. The officer who was in charge of us studied our papers. At the top of these papers was the name of the prisoner, followed by the grounds for his sentencing. Suddenly he called out my last name. I stood at attention, and he looked me over from head to foot but said nothing.

Afterward, the gate was opened, and we were led into camp and shown to our barracks. The little Russian, with whom I had already traveled, was again in the same barracks with me and on the same job. From the beginning, I was suspicious of him.

At first we worked together on a building site, but later he was transferred to a cabinet shop outside the camp. He had to pass through the gate to get there. One day in November, I was assigned to this work too, so we were reunited.

In December, a political prisoner came to our camp. He also had to work with us. His name was Janesch Albrecht. He was from Moscow, a member of the group around Sacharow.

Mid-month, an officer came and handed the brigadier an order to call all the prisoners of the work force together. When everyone was assembled, the officer asked, "Is Steffen here too?"

I informed him that I was. He had various newspapers in his hands. Now I knew what was coming: he would read my sentence in public. That's exactly what happened.

He gave the newspapers to the brigadier and commanded, "Now read!" All my sentences were mentioned, including the twenty-five years in work camp, according to which I appeared to be a very dangerous criminal. Several of the prisoners, and also the brigadier, already knew that I was a Christian, but the rest didn't

---

2. A city in the Kostanay Region of northern Kazakhstan.

even know me at this point. I could see the men asking each other who was being discussed. Those who knew me pointed me out to the others.

After everything had been read, the officer took back his newspapers and left. His work was done. Now the prisoners were to do with me as they thought best, whatever they pleased.

After most of the crowd had dispersed, and I too was again out at my worksite, two prisoners approached me and said, "Onkel Johann, have no fear that any of the prisoners will lay a hand on you. And if anyone does do anything to you, let us know about it. He'll stop it right then and there."

To be sure, the prisoners had clearly understood what the government was trying to do to me with this act. And now the government would find out that all the prisoners, even those who hadn't known me before, now looked favorably upon me. They all knew me now and always greeted me pleasantly.

The Red Armband

I deliberated what had happened and thought, *What will they dream up next?* The prisoners had already told me I need have no fear; how much more valid were the words of the Lord Jesus, *"Be not afraid, only believe"* (Mark 5:36).

It wasn't long until the government did think up something else. One evening, an officer summoned me. "Report to the guards. From now on, you'll always wear the red armband."

"I will never put on the red armband because I'm a Christian," I objected.

"It makes no difference to me that you're a believer," he returned.

Again I said, "I will not wear the red armband."

Because of this, I had to spend fifteen days and nights in the isolation cell. Right after that, I was taken out and put into cubicle number two, after I had removed my shoes and outer clothes. In there, the prisoners were allowed to wear only their underwear. Four other prisoners lay on the floor. They asked me, "For what reason were you brought here?"

When I had told them, they said, "You've done the right thing." In camp, the only ones wearing the red armband were those who had been deemed spies over their fellow prisoners. The prisoners never spoke well of such men. In fact, they were often even beaten to death. The thieves were especially bad for doing this.

Why did the camp administration try to compel me to wear the red armband? Because they had found out the thieves were on my side, and therefore no prisoner would harm me. Now they were attempting to put me in a bad light before the thieves, so they'd make an end of me. But God wouldn't allow that.

One evening, another prisoner was brought to the isolation cell. After he was finished answering questions as to what he was guilty of, he began to question me. "Are you a Christian?"

I answered in the affirmative.

"Are you a German?" he asked next.

Again I answered with a yes.

Finally he wanted to know, "Where did you formerly live?"

"In the Ukraine," I replied.

When he asked, "Did you also live there during the war years?" I knew who was giving him his orders.

When I honestly answered yes, he sounded even more interested. "Were there German troops in your area?"

When I once more said yes, he asked me, "What did Hitler actually want?"

"That he didn't tell me," I answered.

Then he asked, "Do you Christians celebrate May 9, the day of the victory over Hitler?"

"No," I replied, "we believers have other holidays of our own."

The other prisoners listened. They too immediately understood for whom he was working. He was sent by the government to torment me. In prison, if prisoners don't want a certain man with them, they say, "Knock on the door!" Suddenly someone said to the questioner, "Pound on the door, so they put you into another cell."

"Will the guard do this?" he asked in return.

"Yes, yes, just go ahead and knock," he was answered. So he knocked, and the guard took him away. Thus, God held His protecting hand over me this time also, as David says in Psalm 7:10: *My defence is of God, which saveth the upright in heart.*

My punishment in the isolation cell lasted until March 8. During the last days, the cell was packed full. At the last, there were twenty-three men in the cell. In the evenings, many experiences were related. I was frequently asked to speak from the Bible. One evening as I spoke and they all listened intently, the door was suddenly thrust open and a government official stood there. "Even here you practice your propaganda, Steffen!" he accused.

The prisoners yelled, "Shut the door! This is none of your business."

He obeyed. Then the prisoners said to me, "Onkel Johann, tell us some more out of the Bible." I gladly fulfilled their wish. But when we lay down to sleep, I was fearful that now the government would try another tactic against me.

When my isolation time was ended, I was let out. I immediately went to the bathhouse and washed and shaved because in isolation one is neither allowed to shave nor to wash. When I stepped into the barracks, an officer immediately came and demanded, "Put on the red armband and go to your work."

"I have just sat out fifteen days because of this," I protested.

"That makes no difference," he retorted. "If you don't obey, your wife won't get visiting privileges. She's already been waiting here for three days."

I had already known for some time that my wife and son were there. I said to him, "I will not wear the armband. You may make of it what you will."

With that, he disappeared. As I mentioned previously, I worked outside of the camp. The next evening, as was our custom, we awaited the announcement of visitors. I went outside and waited for the announcement over the loudspeaker. I would have also been able to hear the call in the barracks, but there the prisoners were often so noisy that the loudspeaker couldn't be heard.

The announcement came, but my name wasn't called. I assumed they had made good on the officer's threat.

The next morning I went to work as usual. There the fellow who always called the prisoners to work in the morning sauntered past me and said very softly, "Today you'll get permission to see your wife."

"Thank you," I replied.

He whispered the message in passing because he was a prisoner himself, and had to be careful that no one overheard him and reported it to the camp leaders. Then, without a question, he would have lost his job. He had learned I was to get this permission because he worked for the camp administrator, and he wanted to pass on the happy news to me. How happy and thankful I was!

VISITS AND WEARINESS

In fact, I was summoned that very afternoon and was permitted to spend a day with my wife and son. My wife related how long she had had to wait until our meeting was finally possible.

Later the political prisoner and I were assigned to work with the homosexual prisoners. Their work consisted of cleaning the toilets in the camp. In the winter, when the toilets were full and frozen over, this was hard work. Often one had to go at it with a crowbar. We refused to do this work, and remained in the barracks. The next day, we stayed there too. The government sternly demanded that I get to work. If I continued to refuse, I'd be put into the isolation cell. Again I prayed earnestly to God.

I wrote a letter to Germany, describing what all the government had done to me, and what it was further planning to do to me—including the fact that I had to clean the toilets with the homosexual prisoners. I had the letter smuggled out of camp, and it actually reached Germany.

Two days later, they summoned us and announced that we didn't have to clean the toilets. Instead, we were to clear away snow in the camp and keep things tidied up everywhere. Albrecht and I did the work together. In the summer, the barracks needed painting, and there were other jobs to be done in the camp.

That summer a committee came from Alma-Ata to inspect the camp. Because we worked in the camp, we were able to see them. Later I asked a man from our barracks who had also been in the isolation cell, whether the lice had also bitten him so badly in there.

"No," he answered, "a committee from Alma-Ata was here. They ordered that the lice be exterminated."

I thought of my letter, in which I had specially mentioned the plague of lice in the isolation cell. This letter was published abroad, so it also came to the attention of the Soviet authorities.

The camp leaders never summoned me about this letter, but they ordered the little Russian to find out how I was able to get letters out of camp. I learned about it through fellow prisoners who told me how he questioned other prisoners, especially those who were extra friendly to me. I didn't take it too seriously, but only thought, *You poor fellow, you won't find out how I do it anyway.*

Nevertheless, it was a difficult time for me so that, just like many men of God, I was often weary of life and would rather have died. Many times I asked God to let me die. I no longer desired freedom, nor to see my family again, but rather to be with God. But God did not answer this prayer. I was to go home again, and even reach Germany, the land the authorities had declared I'd never see.

In the summer of 1986, our son Helmut and his wife Rita, together with my wife, came to visit me. They had been married in May. Now they wanted to see me. Before the officer allowed me to join them, he said, "You are permitted to speak only Russian. Otherwise you can't be together for two hours."

"I understand," I replied. When I entered the visitors' room, they were already seated at the one side of the table. I was to sit on the opposite side. Shortly thereafter the officer left the room. I wondered about that, thinking, *No doubt he has something in store for me.* But he came back and sat down with us.

When our time was up, I asked the officer for permission to pray with my family and give thanks to God. He reflected over it, and finally gave his consent. We all stood to pray, and once again the officer went outside and soon came back. Then we said our farewells and parted.

The officer led me outside again. Then there followed a thorough search. I had to undress, and he even looked into my mouth. Now it became clear to me why he had gone out and come back several times; he figured that during those intervals my family members would slip something to me. Then they would have had grounds for punishing me again. But, of course, there would have been many other possible ways to sneak something into the camp.

In the fall of 1986, Albrecht and I had to work on a building project. The building was to be finished quickly, namely by New Year's Day, so 400 men were ordered there. Winters in Arkalyk were very cold and also often stormy. In fact, the wind could be so strong that it tore down electric lines. When that happened, we sat in the barracks by candlelight if anyone happened to have a candle on hand. If not, then all was dark. Even in the canteen, only a small oil lamp burned. When we came home from work, everything was dark.

Once we arrived at camp in the evening during such a storm. The 400 men were searched one by one at the camp gate. We were the very last, and therefore were very late getting into camp.

We went directly to the canteen to eat our fish soup, which was our evening meal. While we waited for our soup, Albrecht said to me, "I'd never have thought we'd have to endure something like this."

"This isn't nearly as hard as in the 1940's when hundreds died of hunger and hard work," I replied. "Today nobody dies from hunger anymore."

"That's right," he relented. "You've already been through much."

In January 1987, my wife came to visit me, bringing along our youngest son David. He had just been released from military service in the fall. Again they sat for two hours at one side of the table and I at the other. This time a woman was present. As usual, all conversation had to be in Russian. I asked my son, "How did it go with you?"

He gave a detailed account of his experiences in the service.

Then I told him, "You still have a serious step in life to take."

My wife immediately understood and said, "He's already taken that step."

"When?" I asked.

"During the prayer week at New Year's," she replied.

These glad tidings calmed my concerns and fears in regard to the years in camp that still lay ahead of me.

When the allotted visiting time was ended, I joyfully returned to my barracks and thanked God that all our children had given their lives to Him. I could hardly understand why many Christian fathers could be home with their families all the time, and yet not all the children would come to the faith. And of all people, we were allowed to experience such grace. Yes, God had heard the numerous prayers for our family that had ascended to Him from many Christians.

Soon to Be Free?

When we returned from work on February 12, I heard over the radio that the Supreme Soviet had declared amnesty for 140 political prisoners. Afterward, we went for supper. In the canteen I hunted up Albrecht. We no longer worked together at that time. I asked him what was new, and he replied, "Nothing."

Then I said, "I received a telegram from Moscow—you're free!"

His eyes grew large, and he pleaded, "Please don't joke with me this way."

When I told him what I'd heard over the radio, he said, "Well! Then we'll be going home."

"Not I," I returned, but I thought of the fact that political reasons were also cited in my sentence. After supper we left the canteen. He went directly to the office, meaning to ask whether he was already excused from work tomorrow. I advised him not to go—things wouldn't move ahead that fast—but he went anyway. The next morning I saw him going to work again.

When we returned from work in the evening, one of the other prisoners came running toward me and said, "Your friend is already sitting in the train, headed for home." They had brought him from his work, given him his papers, and let him go.

I went into my barracks. There on my bed I found a note he had left behind, informing me that he'd gone home.

Two weeks later, I received a letter from home. In it my wife had written, "Heinrich Wolf has been released. We're now waiting for Gerhard and for you."

Why did they release one of us three brethren and not the other two? I asked myself. All three of us were sentenced under the same code.

One evening a fellow prisoner came and handed me a letter, with the remark, "It came in the mail. Because there was no address on it, we read it to find out whom it was for." It was written in Russian and contained only words from the Bible. By this they knew for whom it was intended. The name "Johann" did not appear once in the letter.

TROUBLE AT HOME?

I took the letter, and when I saw whom it was from, I rejoiced, for it was from a brother who lived close to Issyk. Yet when I read it, I was filled with fear and apprehension. He kept comforting me with the words that the Lord Jesus would stay close to us even if we could no longer see our loved ones.

At the end, he wrote that he had been in Issyk. He also begged pardon for the poor handwriting since it was already late at night when he had written it.

What was I to think? My wife had heart trouble—that I knew. The doctor had even marveled that, with her weak heart, she had survived the severe strains she had had to endure. I had now been here for nearly two years, and the brother had never written to me before. *What might be the reason for this letter? And right after he has been in Issyk?* I asked myself. Because he had mentioned the thought several times that there would be a reunion in heaven if there were none here below, I could think of only one thing—my wife had died.

I received that letter on March 10. I got no further letters from home. My fellow workers could quite obviously see my dejected mood. "What's wrong with you?" they inquired. I briefly related my concerns to a few of them. One can hardly imagine how earnestly I entreated God during that difficult time. The time in which I was tormented in prison had been hard—but now?

The days passed very slowly. Since I still received no letters from home, it kept getting harder all the time.

THIRTIETH ANNIVERSARY

On the evening of March 16, four long-term workers were informed over the loudspeaker that they were to report at a new workstation in the morning. I was among the ones called.

What would I do now? I had left my work clothes at the place where I'd been working up to now. I hunted up the other three. They fared no better. They had also left their clothes at the old workplace. They decided that since they had had to switch job assignments so often already, they would go to the old place again in the morning.

"I can't do that," I told them. "I've been in the isolation cell, and by no means do I want to go there again. I'll report to the new workplace and hope you won't be angry with me about it."

"We won't hold it against you," they answered. "We know how the government has treated you in the past."

So on the morning of March 17, 1987, I went out with the other work crew. When we arrived at the workplace, I sought out the brigadier and asked, "Where shall I work?"

Immediately he inquired about the other three. "There were four workers assigned to me."

"The others went to their old workplace," I told him, "because their work clothes are there—and mine, besides."

"You may rest yourself today," he informed me. "There's little you could do by yourself, and besides, you don't have the proper work clothes."

Not having to work wasn't bad, but since the building was to be finished as quickly as possible, many civil authorities and also some of the camp officials were there. And now, not to work but to walk about, and that in clothes not suitable for construction work, must surely make one conspicuous. I didn't wish to be anywhere that the authorities or camp officers were, so I walked about from place to place. This was more strenuous than working would have been. Even in the toilets, I stayed there until someone else came in before I went out again. I thought back to our wedding day exactly thirty years ago. *What kind of an anniversary celebration was this?* I had to sneak about, even in the toilets, to escape the eyes of the officers!

Finally lunchtime came. We ate our lunch in the trailer. After lunch break, the brigadier said, "You may stay in the trailer so you're not so conspicuous." Apparently, he had taken notice of my plight that forenoon. I was glad of it, and this day, too, came to an end.

After supper I was summoned over the loudspeaker to come to the workers' office. The man next to me at the table said, "The three others who didn't go to work with you have also been called." I went immediately.

At the office, I found out I wouldn't have to work the next day. I could stay home. I saw two of the others who had been assigned to the new job disappear down the corridor.

I headed back to my barracks. As I drew near, I saw a group of men milling about. This caught my attention, even if it didn't necessarily mean anything special. Before bedtime, many of the men wanted to get a bit of fresh air. When they saw me coming out, several of them excitedly came and said, "Tomorrow you're going home!"

"Where did you learn of this?" I asked in return.

One of the men who had been called to the office because of the job, had heard of it there, and had spread the news right away. Another lamented that if only he were a Christian, he could have his freedom too—but not as it was.

Everyone in the barracks already knew about it, and so I gave away whatever I didn't need and quickly lay down to sleep.

But I couldn't sleep. My thoughts were with my wife. When Brother Heinrich had been released, she had written to me. At that time, they hadn't released me. But now, when my wife was apparently dead, they let me go home. Instead of rejoicing, I couldn't sleep.

Next morning when I was called, I was commanded, "Hand over everything that belongs to the camp." After that, I was given my papers, and I was released in the afternoon.

FREE AT LAST!

This time, too, an officer accompanied me, but not to the train station—this time we went to the airport. There I was seated on a plane, and about two o'clock at night I reached Alma-Ata. I wanted to get home quickly, so I went to the taxi stop. I gave "Issyk" as my destination to the driver.

"I'm not allowed to drive to Issyk," was his answer, "but I can take you to Talgar."

That will get me closer to Issyk, I thought; so I agreed, and he took me there. I paid him, and he left me standing at the curb. *Surely someone will give me a ride to Issyk,* I thought hopefully. But it was already eleven o'clock. The last bus had gone long ago. And long as I waited, nobody stopped to give me a lift. This was understandable because I was still dressed like a prisoner, and who would want to give such a person a ride?

I walked about for a while. Finally I went to the bus station, hoping to spend the night there. However, the doors were locked, so I sat down on a bench outside and waited. Then I got up and walked along the street again. Maybe this time someone would stop and pick me up. But again no one stopped. Again, I milled around for some time and then decided to attempt to sleep on a bench. But March was much too cold for this.

Suddenly I heard someone sweeping with a broom. "What time is it?" I asked him. He didn't know, so I lay down again, thinking, *If they only knew at home that I'm here, they'd surely come for me.*

Then I heard a vehicle approaching. It stopped, and the driver began talking to the man who was sweeping.

Then the driver turned to me and asked, "Where do you want to go?"

"To Issyk," I answered.

"To Issyk?" he echoed. "If you pay me three rubles, we'll drive to Issyk."

We made a deal, and I climbed into the cab of his truck, in which another passenger was already sitting. *What kind of people am I sitting between? And that, at night?* I thought.

Along the way, the driver said to the other man, "We're coming to a shop. Go talk to the watchman; maybe he has something to smoke." So the other fellow climbed out, and when he returned, he had cigarettes. Now they wanted to smoke but had no matches. They asked me, but I didn't have any either.

What kind of men are these? They do not have anything. With whom have I set out on this journey? I thought and prayed silently to God. We stopped at a service station where they got matches. Then we continued driving, and they smoked.

After a while the one remarked, "Issyk? Not three rubles, but five, and we'll take you there."

"Yes, I'll pay five rubles," I answered.

Then he asked, "Is your wife at home?"

"There'll be somebody at home," I replied.

"Well, then we'll also get something to drink—brandy, or something like that."

"We don't drink brandy," I told him, "and we keep nothing like that in the house."

"Are you a Baptist?" the other asked.

"Yes," I replied. Then the tone of the conversation changed. In Issyk, I gave them the five rubles and also some candy I had with me, and they continued on their way. "Praise God!" I sighed. Again He had heard my prayers.

11. Johann Is Unexpectedly Arrested Again

(1985–1988) Elfriede recounts her experiences during Johann's last imprisonment. (Johann's account is in the previous chapter.) Contrary to Johann's fears, Elfriede had not died but was alive and well when he came home from prison. Finally, after years in a work camp as a youth, and five prison terms totaling eighteen years and spanning his whole lifetime, Johann was free. They were able to move to Germany soon thereafter.

More Arrests

Elfriede Steffen

First the two Wolf brothers were placed under arrest. Then on May 14, 1985, a man came to our house and said to Johann, "Come with me to the police station; they're waiting for you there."

"You've come to put Johann in prison," I protested.

He replied with a strong "No!"

But I didn't believe him. "Put on warm clothes," I told Johann. "They're sure not to let you come back so soon." Out on the street, the police van was already waiting for Johann.

We waited for quite some time, but Johann didn't come back. So we went to the police station to inquire after him. The police sergeant looked at us quietly and said, "He has been arrested."

I was very agitated and said to the policeman, "You cheats!"

I was immediately sorry that I, as a Christian, had used such a strong term, and the next day I went back and apologized.

On May 15, I again went to the police station to deliver some food to Johann. There I went to the examining magistrate and asked him, "May I give my husband Johann the food I've brought for him?" He gave his consent, and I was allowed to talk to Johann for a few minutes.

"I'll do everything in my power," the examining magistrate declared, "to see that your husband doesn't get more than three years. If I had my say, he'd be acquitted."

"He who does good, will receive a blessing," I replied. "It says so in the Bible."

"Yes," he agreed, "Our Koran says so too. My parents are getting up in years," he added. He was obviously of Asiatic nationality. "Pardon me, please. It's hard for me to conduct these proceedings against Johann, but the judge has the final say."

I answered him, "As a Christian, I can forgive you."

The trial was held in the court of Alma-Ata in June 1985. The judge was a Kazakh woman. The accused ones were the two Wolf brothers and Johann. All three were sentenced to five years in a concentration camp. Without trust in God, I don't know how I could have gone on living. I besought God for comfort and strength, and He granted me both. *"They that wait upon the LORD shall renew their strength"*(Isaiah 40:31).

WHY?

A few days after the trial, we wives traveled to Alma-Ata with clothes and food for our husbands. This was an especially hard day for me. For the fifth time, Johann was in prison, and again I stood before the high iron gates for hours—waiting, waiting, until I could deliver something to him. The worst part was that again he had been torn away from his family and church, whom he loved so fervently.

The question arose, "Why?" Not quite four years of freedom, and now already five more years of separation.

We were allowed to visit him only three times a year. Added to that, David was called for two years' military service. But the Lord Jesus is *"the same yesterday, and to day, and for ever"* (Hebrews 13:8). He gives strength and comfort to the weary through His Word.

"Rejoicing in hope; patient in tribulation; continuing instant in prayer" (Romans 12:12).

From time to time, we inquired about our husbands at the prison. We weren't allowed to write letters to them. In July, we received the message that Johann had been transferred to Arkalyk.

Immediately I sent letters to the camp, so that in his first days, Johann already received comfort through letters. Through other Christians, we obtained the address of a family in Arkalyk.

There were only two of us left at home anymore—Helmut and I. In September, for the first time, the two of us went to camp to visit Johann. First we hunted up the K. family, who lived in Arkalyk. We were very warmly received there. This was always the case when we went there. We recognized it as God's marvelous leading. We will never forget this dear family.

Helmut and I were allowed to visit Johann for two days. The climate in Arkalyk is not agreeable; the winters are bitterly cold, and the other seasons are very stormy. All this made me feel so sorry for Johann. Again, he had to live among such rough people in the barracks.

The church services in Issyk continued to be held in tents. Meetings were undisturbed, the children had their children's classes, and the youth had their youth classes. God blessed these gatherings. All was well, except for the fact that three brethren, Johann and the two Wolfs, couldn't be there.

In May 1986, Helmut and Rita celebrated their wedding in Shymkent.[1] It was a Christian wedding—they were married in church. The couple then lived in our house.

We regularly received letters from David, who wrote that it was going well with him. And when he ended his two years, in November 1986, we celebrated a happy reunion and gave thanks that he had returned home from military service safe and well.

On New Year's Day 1987, the young people had a program of poems and hymns from God's Word. At this meeting, David committed himself to God and found peace for his soul.

On January 10, the two of us traveled to the camp for a two hours' visit with Johann. Johann rejoiced to see David again after a two-year absence and to learn that he had become a child of God.

Amnesty for Political Prisoners

In February, David heard a special announcement from Moscow over the radio: 140 political prisoners were to be granted amnesty.

"Oh, I hope my husband and the other believers are among them," I said hopefully.

"We'll wait and see," David replied.

The next evening we heard the same announcement again. "Yes," I repeated, "I firmly believe this is also an amnesty for the prisoners from our group." And actually, a few days later, on a

---

1. *Shymkent* or *Chimkent* (English), *Schymkent* or *Tschimkent* (German; original usage); the third most populous city in Kazakhstan.

Saturday, H. Wolf returned home. He was the first one to be released. Now Helene and I hoped that our husbands would soon come home too. Every day the expectations rose, but it was all in vain. February passed, and they didn't return.

We wives therefore submitted written petitions to Moscow to President Gorbachev. My five children and I, as well as Helene Wolf and her relatives, had signed these letters. And we besought God to grant freedom for our husbands.

And our prayers were answered. On March 18, I was reading a book. While I read, I was twice reminded to pray for Johann, which I also did. I didn't know that he was already on his way home.

Early the next morning, the barking of a dog awakened me. *Who's coming so early in the morning?* I wondered. Looking out the window, I was able to make out Johann, Willi, and Elsa approaching our house.

Oh, how my heart was flooded with joy at the homecoming of my dear husband and our beloved father! We called the rest of our children to us and thanked God for His great love and mercy, which He had once more revealed to us.

In April 1987, my brother and his wife from Germany visited us. The joy at being reunited with my siblings was very great.

In May 1987, we applied for an exit permit to Germany. We had to wait a long time until we received approval. During this period of waiting, two of our children with their families emigrated to Germany. This meant more partings again.

Almost a year later, in March 1988, our permission to emigrate came, and on April 12 we, together with our youngest son David, took our leave from Issyk. Two of our children had to stay behind. This meant being parted again, and this time also from the church.

We arrived in Frankfurt on April 14, where we were heartily greeted by our children and many other acquaintances from our church who had moved earlier. In November, our children who had needed to stay behind, also came. Now we were all united in Germany.

Our youngest son married Elsa Balzer. But our greatest happiness and deepest pleasure lay in the fact that we could all be of one mind concerning the faith. We give God the honor and glory for this.

And when one day on earth
    My pilgrimage is ended,
Then I will be safe
    Forever at Home.

In the light of eternity
    I will understand
Why I had to travel
    Upon such ways down here.

12. Home Again at Last

(1987–1988) This chapter begins with Johann's arrival home in the early morning of March 19, 1987, after his release from prison the day before. Johann gives his perspective of the following months until their emigration to Germany in April 1988.

Is Mother Well?

Johann Steffen

How would I find things when I got home? My son Willi lived about seventy meters from our house. I went to his house first and knocked at the window. He didn't even ask who was there but instantly flung the door open. "Papa!" he exclaimed, and we greeted each other affectionately. Then we went inside.

His wife had also gotten up at once, and we likewise greeted each other. "Do sit down," Elsa said.

"I will," I said. "How is it with Mama? Is she well?"

"Yes, Mama is well," replied Willi. A great stone rolled off of my heart, and I seated myself. I looked at the clock. It was just a little before five o'clock in the morning.

Then I requested of Willi, "Please, go and start up the water heater; I'd like to bathe before Elsa has breakfast ready." After I had washed and we'd eaten breakfast, we headed for our house.

As we neared the house, the dog barked loudly. My wife awoke instantly and came to the window. Then she cried, "David, Papa has come home!" She scurried about, looking for the key. When she had unlocked the door, she said, "I figured it was Papa," but she had not spotted me right away. How great was her joy then, when she actually saw me!

It was almost seven o'clock by now. I told my sons, "Run, quickly, and tell your brothers, Peter and Helmut, and their wives, and also my daughter Marie and her husband." They all lived fairly close by in the neighborhood. When they arrived, we greeted each other and thanked God together. Then those who

G. Wolf, J. Steffen, and H. Wolf with their wives after being released from prison in 1987.

had to work left for their jobs.

I told my wife, "I hardly slept at all last night. I'll have to get my rest first of all. So for the time being, tell no one of my homecoming."

On Friday evening, March 20, we held a thanksgiving service at church. In the forenoon, my wife and I went to the city to report that I was home. There we met our son-in-law Jakob. "Gerhard Wolf has come home too," he informed us. So that evening we three brethren were together again.

The service was held in the tent. Many people had gathered for the evening. It was a beautiful gathering, and the Lord richly blessed us.

When the group was dispersing, as we heartily greeted each other, a sister asked me, "Are the hard years over now?"

"Who had the hardest lot—you or I?" I countered.

"What do you mean?" she wondered.

"Why, you have fourteen children," I answered. "How much work and care do you have with them? That certainly isn't easy!"

REMINISCING OVER CAMP LIFE

Later, I reminisced over my years in camp, taking count of the time I was allowed to have God's Word with me. At Dzhambul, I succeeded in taking a Gospel along into camp. For one year, I was able to read in it. Then it was found during a search and confiscated. In Arkalyk I was able to own a Bible for eight months. The rest of the time, I was without a Bible.

As I recalled all my years in camp, I marveled how, especially in the hardest times, God stood at my side with His protecting presence. Just as with Daniel in the lions' den, so during my last imprisonment in Alma-Ata, they threw me into prison and indeed into the dungeon with the murderers—the Gypsy and the little Russian, whom I might call "lions."

Likewise, in Arkalyk they put me into the dungeon and put their agent in with me, who tried to draw the other prisoners to his side so they'd do with me what the government wanted them to do.

What did Daniel say when they had cast him into the lions' den and the lions couldn't harm him? He said, *"My God hath sent his angel, and hath shut the lions' mouths"* (Daniel 6:22). Who was this angel? It was the Lord Jesus. Also, when the three young men, Shadrach, Meshach, and Abednego, were in the fiery furnace, who protected them? It was the same Lord, for the king said, *"Did not we cast three men bound into the midst of the fire?"* *"Lo, I see four men loose, walking in the midst of the fire, and they have no hurt; and the form of the fourth is like the Son of God."* Then Nebuchadnezzar said, *"There is no other God that can deliver after this sort."* Thus, it happened just as the three young men had said, *"Our God whom we serve is able to deliver us from the burning fiery furnace, and . . . out of thine hand, O king."*

It was exactly the same for me. Who was it that did not permit the prisoners to do to me what the government desired? It was the Lord, who was able to come through the locked doors. He would not let the prisoners torment me. Instead, I was able to speak to them from the Bible in prison. To the Lord be thanksgiving and honor!

PREPARING FOR EMIGRATION

This time when I was released, I did not again assume the leadership of the church. The two years in which I had had to endure so much had undermined my health. I informed the church brethren of this, and the brother who had taken over the duties in my absence continued in this position. Besides, in May

The second meetinghouse in Issyk (photo taken in 1993).

I turned sixty, and I considered myself too old for such a position of responsibility. At that point we also applied for an exit permit to Germany.

In the summer of 1987, the church tore down the tent and built a new one. The old tent roof was made of cloth; the new one we covered with slate. The building was nine meters by fifteen meters (thirty feet by fifty feet), almost as large as the one built in 1974.

By that time, about a third of the church had emigrated to Germany. In April 1987, a new wave of emigration began. When a visa was issued, one had to wait only three to four months for the exit permit. Often it came even sooner.

After a similar period of waiting, we went to the authorities in Alma-Ata and inquired about the approval of our application. But we received no positive answer at that time.

In February 1988, we traveled to Alma-Ata again to inquire how things were progressing. Almost nine months had passed since we had inquired the other time. When we called on the head officer in Alma-Ata and gave our names, the official said, "Please, go out again. You'll be called back in later." He also left the room and went to one of his co-workers.

After a while he called for us. His co-worker sat behind the desk, and he stood beside it. The assistant was the one who spoke. "There's no permission for your two sons, but you two may emigrate." Thereupon the head officer said in Russian, "Naturally there's nothing confirmed yet." They conversed further in the language of the Kazakhs, which we couldn't understand. Then the assistant announced, "The decision isn't final yet, but you may slowly begin to prepare for your exit."

"Then our son who lives with us may quit his job?" I proposed.

"No," he said firmly, "Slowly get ready to leave, as I said before. Come back again after the holidays—after March 8 would be best."

We returned on March 10, 1988, and were finally given permission to leave. We had to wait almost ten months for the permit. From then on, we made preparations in earnest, and on April 12 we set out from Issyk, arriving in Germany on Thursday, April 14, 1988. Our relatives and acquaintances awaited us there.

13. In Germany

(1988) Johann reminisces about his life and his prison experiences. He turned sixty-one years old in May 1988 and was ready to live out his retirement years in Germany among family and friends.

Home at Last

Johann Steffen

We had now arrived in the homeland that our forefathers had left 200 years earlier. Yet how will it be when one day our Savior comes and receives us into our long-awaited eternal home, where cares will be no more? It won't be long anymore until we'll be where *"God shall wipe away all tears from their eyes; and there shall be no more death, neither sorrow, nor crying, neither shall there be any more pain: for the former things are passed away. . . . Behold, I make all things new"* (Revelation 21:4-5). But, in order that we may be there, God's Word says, *"He that overcometh shall inherit all things; and I will be his God, and he shall be my son"* (Revelation 21:7).

On the Saturday after our arrival, a reunion of former Issyk residents was held in Paderborn. We were all able to attend. After such a long time, it was so nice to meet all these people who in earlier days had suffered with us in Russia. The thought came to my mind, *How lovely this is! We've just arrived in Germany and already we've met all these acquaintances and relatives with whom we lived in Russia, and with whom we shared joys and sorrows. How much lovelier will it be in heaven, when we're reunited with all the true believers?* I thought of my mother, who had so earnestly prayed for me that I would accept the Savior. Surely, it would be indescribable joy!

On Sunday evening, some of our relatives brought us back to Friedland. On Monday, we had to tend to our new paperwork. A week later we traveled to Rastatt, where our daughter lived. She had been allowed to emigrate eight months before we did. The church there was small, and there were few people whom we knew. We had to get used to our new surroundings.

Johann and Elfriede Steffen in Germany, 1988.

And Today?

Yes, the battle in the spiritual life goes on here in Germany too. It only shows another side of itself. Here there is great freedom and wealth, and both bring dangers with them. In Russia, the devil came as a roaring lion; here he comes as an angel of light. It is especially hard for the young people to stay in the true faith. An elderly brother, who had spent twenty years under arrest for his faith in the Soviet Union, read a passage from the Bible and admonished the church, "We as a church cannot tolerate that the youth are becoming so worldly!"

"Close your Bible!" was the response he got. And this happened to an elderly, tried-and-proven brother. This happens today in various churches—where spiritually-minded brethren are not understood. It is sad that in the churches and in homes of Christians, modem trappings, such as rock music and television, are making inroads. Who is happy about this? Naturally, only the devil. Many more sad things could be related about the times we're in today, but I would like to say only one thing more: "If our Lord and Savior says, *'I come quickly,'* may we be able to say, *'Amen. Even so, come, Lord Jesus'*" (Revelation 22:20).

After we had lived here for a longer period of time, and I had had time to think back over the past, it occurred to me how wonderfully God had guarded and preserved us in the past decades. Just as it says in Psalm 57:1: *"Be merciful unto me, O God, be merciful unto me: for my soul trusteth in thee: yea, in the shadow of thy wings will I make my refuge, until these calamities be overpast."*

To be sheltered under the wings of the Lord Jesus is marvelous. We were allowed to experience this in our lives when I was in the prisons and in camp, and my wife had to carry on alone with the children. Praise God for His great love to us!

14. Postscript

Revisiting the Ukraine

Johann Steffen in April 1993

With joy and sincere thanks, I wish to inform you that recently my long-desired wish has been fulfilled. After forty-nine years, I was permitted to hunt up my hometown, Wernersdorf, in the Zaporozhe[1] district of the Ukraine. It was from there that we had departed for the West in September 1943, during the war years. As I had stated earlier, we were taken to Russia after the war, and not until 1988 were we allowed to emigrate to Germany.

In March 1993, I was able to accompany a group of Christians[2] on a bus tour of Belarus[3] and the Ukraine. On this tour, I succeeded in reaching my old home village. I was overjoyed to again set foot on the place where I had spent my childhood years up to age sixteen, and many happy memories were awakened in me.

On the other hand, I was disappointed at the devastated appearance of our village, which had once been beautiful Wernersdorf, with its well-kept brick houses. The houses in the village had been torn down after the war, and the materials used to repair the war damages of the city of Tokmak, about fifteen kilometers away. Since the Germans had all left by then, Ukrainians were now living in Wernersdorf. They lived in the remaining houses and had also erected some new buildings.

I took a number of pictures of Wernersdorf, that show the village's present-day condition. The place now goes by the name of Pribereschne.

---

1. *Zaporoshje* (German); also *Zaporizhzhia*.
2. Christliches Hilfswerk TABEA e.V of Swisttal-Heimerzheim, Germany, organized this trip to sites where relief had been given. Several representatives of Christian Aid Ministries traveled along since CAM was supporting TABEA. See also Appendix D.
3. Formerly known as *White Russia*.

The village well is a sorry sight today. In my childhood, it was enclosed with a wooden casement.

The town well was a sorry-looking sight. During my childhood, it was enclosed with a tidy wooden encasement. When I looked into the well, I saw by my reflection that there was indeed still water there. But there was no bucket, so I was unable to draw and to drink of the delicious water once again.

In Wernersdorf I could find few people with whom I was able to talk. I spoke with a few people and gave them children's Bibles and a few sweets.

On the return journey, I passed through the neighboring village of Schönsee. There I was able to get an impression of the current condition of the church house there.

The Mennonite Church at Schönsee. It was built in 1909.

The once beautiful church as it appears today.

At home, it was once beautiful;
The fields, the river, and the hills—
    I especially like to think of them—
    The gardens and meadows in the distance.
The song that often resounded at home
Still echoes in my heart today.

We children often played on this stone. This was not far from my parent's home.

Visit to Wernersdorf

In the old Ukraine, lies demolished Wernersdorf,
It is wholly like the ruins of a sheep torn by wolves.
    All around is devastation, almost nothing is recognized;
    All the dwellings have been plundered, and are empty of all humans.

After fifty long years, Johann is traveling toward that place,
To see exactly how it looks and how things really are.
    Full of hope, they board a bus here, with folks from far and near—
    Germans, Swiss, and Canadians—and Johann, too, is now along.

After long and tiresome driving, over mountains, through the valleys,
Finally one could see a glimpse of the beloved Rosental.[4]
    Wernersdorf, its former name, where Johann spent his childhood,
    Where he fondly sat on his parents' laps and laughed for joy.

Oh, what fright! now only ruffians are living here and there,
Nowhere are there trusting smiles, and nowhere any joyful song.
    Only old gray stones remaining, which both a quiet witness bear,
    That not far from here once stood our house—that is clear to me.

Just look—there is the well that always quenched our thirst,
Though now pitiful and deserted, still the water gleams below.
    Sadly, I could not refresh myself with that clear water,
    For there was no bucket there to bring the water up.

And the streets, in their despair, with only here and there a house,
Full of longing, I kept looking. What good can come out of this?
    Suddenly—could I believe it?—I saw the Molotschna Creek,
    Where we often fished and swam with great delight.

Also several the lovely trees, which used to give us shade,
Still are standing—what a wonder—firmly grounded in their places.
    Home, where are you? Is there really nothing left here?
    To still the ardent longing, and the weary ones find rest?

God be thanked, there is a home, that has been prepared by God,
Where cares will all be lifted; there, no mocking and no scorn,
    There in heaven's eternal gleam, where the heart is never burdened.
    It is through Jesus, our Savior, that a home is given to us.[5]

—Johann Braun

---

4. *Rosental* means "Valley of Roses."
5. This poem was not a part of the book *Im Schmelztiegel*; Johann sent it to Frank Weaver with a letter.

15. Epilogue

Today we are in Germany, but our thoughts often wander back to the USSR.[1] We often remember the years we spent there and the many people we learned to know.

There were good times and also hard times. Through the hard times, we were brought closer to God and surrendered ourselves to His will. Because of that, we can attest to the great love God has for us mortals.

We now experience many joys, and realize that all those years of suffering were not in vain. Through letters and the news, we learn of the freedom granted to the Christian faith in the former USSR, of the churches being built, of the unhindered preaching of the Word of God, and of the many people coming to the saving faith in the Lord Jesus. Christian books are distributed in large quantities, and God grants His blessing to this.

We are ever thankful to everyone who prayed for us. We also pray for you.

Written out of love,
The Steffen Family

---

1. The Union of Soviet Socialist Republics (also known as the Soviet Union) existed from about 1917 to 1991. Sometimes it was simply called *Russia* since that was the largest of the fifteen republics.

The Steffen family in Germany in 1992.

The children of Johann and Elfriede Steffen in 2019.
Compare to the picture of Elfriede and the children in 1970 (page 105).

Appendix A: The Mennonite Experience in Russia

The story in this book takes place in Russia.[1] Two stalwart, courageous, and dedicated believers, Johann and Elfriede (Wall) Steffen, spent most of their lives under communism. Because Johann and Elfriede do not explain why, and by whom, they were persecuted, here is an explanation of that era and the prevailing political and social conditions is in order.

Russia is the largest country in the world. For a long time, Russia had vast areas of uninhabited land scattered throughout its 8,358,567 square miles. In the late 1700s, the czars of Russia made a concerted effort to attract settlers from western Europe to settle the more fertile of these lands. The Russian government offered many incentives, such as free transportation from the borders, loans, perpetual exemption from military service, free exercise of religion, and the right to proselyte. The southwestern area of Russia—Ukraine—was one of the prime areas for settlement. It was inhabited by nomads and Cossacks when it came under Russian control in the 1700s.

Mennonite Settlements in Russia

Between 1764 and 1767, one hundred settlements of non-Mennonite Germans were founded along the Volga River in south-central Russia.

The first Anabaptists to move into Russia were Hutterites.

---

1. The name *Russia* is used in different ways. Russia was the largest of fifteen republics that comprised the communist Union of Soviet Socialist Republics or Soviet Union. The USSR (existing from 1917 until 1991) was often called *Russia* since it was the predominant republic. Other republics of the USSR that are important in this story include the Ukrainian, Kazakh, and Uzbek Republics. The Russian Empire, or Imperial Russia, a huge Eurasian empire that existed from 1721 until the beginning of communism in 1917, preceded the USSR.

To escape persecution in Transylvania, they moved into an area northeast of present-day Kiev, building communes at Vishenka and Radichev. In 1842, they moved south to Molotschna,[2] close to the Mennonites. From 1874 to 1877, all these Hutterites moved to Canada and the United States.

In 1786, the Russian Viceroy Potemkin contacted Mennonites living in Prussia (present-day Poland), offering them lands in Ukraine. The Russian Count Rumiantsev knew some of these Mennonites and desired them as settlers.

The Mennonites were numerous in Prussia—so numerous that whole areas sent no men to the military. Since they did not take part in government and other civic activities, they were grudgingly tolerated and sometimes oppressed. The atmosphere was conducive to relocation.

In May 1787, the Prussian Mennonites sent Jacob Hoppner and Johann Bartsch to inspect the land. They met with Catherine II and she invited them to settle in what is now Ukraine. In 1788, a total of 228 families moved to Ukraine and founded the Chortiza Colony, called "Old Colony" because this was the first of their settlements in Russia. From 1803 to 1806, after another invitation from the Russian czars, 365 Mennonite families moved one hundred miles further south and founded the Molotschna Colony.

By 1835, there were sixty Mennonite villages in Ukraine, with a total of 1,200 families (around 6,000 persons). By 1859, the Mennonites numbered 34,500 persons.

The colonies were not without problems. After several generations, all the land was owned by a third of the families. Only this third had civic and economic rights. The landless two-thirds had no such privileges, and many were poor. Later this was corrected by mutual aid efforts.

In the late 1800s, the Russian leaders imposed universal military conscription and a program of Russification of all foreign settlers. This caused a mass emigration.

From 1874 to 1880, one third of the 54,000 Mennonites in Ukraine left for northern United States and Canada. Some, like Elfriede Steffen's grandparents, moved east into Kazakhstan and nearby regions.

---

2. *Molotschna* and *Chortiza* (or "Chortitza") Colonies were located in what is now the Zaporizhia region of Ukraine.

Communism and Two World Wars

The population in Ukraine rebounded and grew until there were 120,000 Mennonites by World War I. Meanwhile the Bolshevik Revolution of 1917 had taken away all semblance of religious and economic freedoms. Life was forever changed for the Mennonites.

After the war, over a third of the Mennonites lived outside Ukraine—in the Far East and Siberia. The outlook for religious freedom looked very bleak.

When it became possible, from 1922 to 1927, about 23,000 more Mennonites left Russia for Canada and South America (Paraguay and Argentina). Times were hard and several famines swept through the land.

When World War II came to Russia, the Chortiza Colony soon found itself in German-occupied territory. They could relate to the German soldiers and for a few years enjoyed religious and cultural freedom under their protection.

But when Hitler's armies were driven out of Ukraine, the fate of the Mennonites was jeopardized; therefore, the entire population of Mennonites evacuated with the German army to the general area of Poland where they had come from 150 years before. This was the fate of Johann Steffen's family, as he relates in the first chapter.

After Hitler's defeat, the fate of the Russian Mennonites became very tragic. Of the 35,000 Mennonites who had returned to German lands in 1943, two thirds of them were forcibly exiled to Siberia and the Far East.[3] This was the background for Johann's experiences in labor camp and set the stage for a life of persecution.

The Mennonites who had moved to the Far East (Kazakhstan and Uzbekistan) fared slightly better since they were away from the front. Johann eventually moved to this area, which at the time was most tolerant of the Mennonites. However, the religious persecution by the Communists soon reached them also.

Mennonites and Baptists in Russia

In this book, Johann frequently identifies himself as Baptist. How did the majority of the Mennonites come to be considered

---

3. Some of the rest managed to migrate to Canada and South America.

Baptists during the communist times?

The beginnings of the Baptists, both in England and in Russia, have long been associated with Mennonite influence. A common factor for both groups in Russia was the German Pietist movement of the 1800s, especially the "Stundist" movement of the Württemburg Pietists.

In 1845, a Pietist Evangelical Church was established near the Molotschna Mennonites by Eduard Wüst. There, as well as in northern Russia, the Stundists organized times of Bible study, prayer, and worship. Their thrust was that Christians should spend an hour each day in such religious activity; hence the name Stundist, from the German *Stund* (hour).

The "revival" which followed played a large role in the formation of the Mennonite Brethren Church in Russia in the 1860s. The Mennonite Brethren made immersion the compulsory method of baptism, thus aligning themselves with the Baptist practice.

The Stundist movement spread through Russia and drew together the evangelical groups—the Baptists, the Evangelicals, and the Mennonites, as well as sectarian groups like the Molokans and Dukhobors.

Since 1943, these groups have been united as the All-Union Council of Evangelical Christian Baptists. The president of the first Council, Jakov Zhidkov, was of Molokan background.

In 1920, a mission called *Licht im Osten* (Light in the East) was started by Jacob Kroeker, a Mennonite minister in Germany. They spread Bibles and devotional literature throughout Russia. The Baptists, as well as Mennonites, were active in the work of the mission. After World War I, this mission sent trained workers into camps of Russian prisoners of war in Germany.

Thousands of prisoners were converted, and when they returned to Russia, they gave significant impetus to the growth of the Baptist and Evangelical groups.

The persecution experience after the Revolution and during the world wars also tended to draw groups together. Believers of various groups found themselves together in prison or labor camps, and were drawn together as believers.

Many of the places to which the Mennonites were exiled had no Mennonite churches. Sometimes they started one, if possible. Other times they attended Baptist and Evangelical churches if there were any in the area.

In 1956, when the first Baptist delegation visited the United States after communism, they used the analogy of Christ reigning on a mountaintop to explain the merging of the Christian groups. Since a mountain is smaller at its top, the closer the believers were to Christ, the nearer they came to each other. The further they drifted away from Christ, the greater the distance between the Christian groups. Persecution drew believers closer to Christ. They related that in Russia the believers were uniting, not dividing, as they were in America.

As the Baptists organized, they obtained some concessions from the government, especially if they registered. The Mennonites were never recognized by the government and received few such concessions. Consequently, the Mennonites found a measure of tolerance by joining hands with the Baptists. The merger of the two resulted in a Baptist church with many "Mennonite" convictions and practices.

The core issue in this development was the registration issue, as Johann relates toward the end of his story. Registration meant reporting to the government and restricting church activity, but it also brought some tolerance and leniency on a personal level.

Those who did not register felt it was a compromise to restrict church activities, to refrain from Sunday schools, and to not take children to worship services. When government agents infiltrated some registered churches and reported the activities to the authorities, the issue intensified. Some church leaders were actually Communist agents.

The registered groups were, as a rule, against Bible smuggling, underground printing presses, and other "illegal" activities. The unregistered groups were not trying to please the government, so they saw these activities differently. Johann reflects on this in the eighth chapter.

The bottom line was that although registration and refraining from obviously "illegal" activities spared the registered groups some persecution, both the registered and unregistered faithful paid dearly for their faith.

Yet the churches grew and remained vibrantly active—a tribute to the enabling grace of God and the commitment and faithfulness of the saints.

The lives of Johann and Elfriede are a confirmation that the "blood of the martyrs is the seed of the church."[4] One senses God's sovereign care for His own when reading this compelling autobiography.

—*Edward Kline*
(Translator and editor of the English edition)

---

4. Attributed to early Christian writer Tertullian.

Appendix B: Timeline of Johann and Elfriede Steffen's Lives and Related Events

This autobiography includes incidents in a span of over one hundred years, ranging from the Mennonite migration to Central Asia in the early 1880s, to the Communist Revolution in Russia, World War II, the perse-cution of Christians in the Soviet Union, and the migration of ethnic German Christians from the Soviet Union to Germany. This timeline will help the reader to synchronize the separately described experiences of Johann and Elfriede with events of their time and Mennonite history.

1880 Elfriede Wall's ancestors left their home on the Volga River, took a long journey eastward, and settled in Asia.[1] [39]

May 1884 German Mennonites settled Uzbekistan (Asia), built a new village, and named it Ak-Mechet.[2] [40]

July 10, 1903 Elfriede's mother, Emilie Schmidt, was born. She enjoyed a pleasant childhood and youth in Ak-Mechet. [41]

July 11, 1903 Elfriede's father, Hermann Wall, was born, in Kirgizia. [42]

---

1. For more complete account, see Fred Richard Belk, *The Great Trek of the Russian Mennonites to Central Asia, 1880–1884*, Studies in Anabaptist and Mennonite History, No. 18 (Scottdale, PA: Herald Press, 1976).

2. This small group followed the egocentric, fanatical "prophet" leader Claus Epp, but many followers became disillusioned and forsook him and his failed prophecies. See Franz Bartsch and Cornelius Krahn, "Ak-Mechet (Uzbekistan)," *The Mennonite Encyclopedia*, vol. 1 (Scottdale, PA: The Mennonite Publishing House, 1955). Or Franz Bartsch and Cornelius Krahn, "Ak-Mechet (Uzbekistan)," *Global Anabaptist Mennonite Encyclopedia Online*, 1955, accessed Dec 1, 2020, https://gameo.org/index.php?title=Ak-Mechet_(Uzbekistan)&oldid=146352.

Also see Herman Jantzen, *Journey of Faith in a Hostile World* (Bloomington, IN: iUniverse, 2008). This book details how many Mennonite settlers fared when they first arrived in the East and settled in Alma-Alta.

1914–17 World War I.

1917 The Communist Revolution in Russia.

May 11, 1927[3] Johann Steffen was born in the Mennonite village of Wernersdorf, Ukraine. [11]

June 8, 1927 Elfriede's parents were married. [44]

1929–1930 Russian dictators took control of the local government in Kirgizia and related areas. Nearly all the property of the Germans was seized and put into a collective.

1931 Elfriede's father and her uncle David were drafted into the military, but were allowed to do alternative service for conscience's sake. [44]

August 8, 1931 Elfriede and her twin brother Siegfried were born. [45]

Winter of 1932 Six-year-old Johann's father was taken away, thieves plundered the village homes, and there was a general famine (the Great Famine, or *Holodomor*). [11–12]

May 1934 The fiftieth anniversary of the Ak-Mechet settlement was celebrated. [46]

Early 1935 The men of Ak-Mechet were arrested and taken to a camp in Urgench. Later all the women and children were taken to Urgench, and then to Tajikistan.[4] [46–48]

1936–38 Great Purge (or Great Terror), a time of intense repression and persecution in the Soviet Union. [61]

August 20, 1937 Elfriede's uncle David Wall was arrested and disappeared. (Years later during President Gorbachev's term, the family wrote to the Kremlin in Moscow and learned that David had been shot on October 5, 1937.) [56]

November 10, 1937 Elfriede's father died at age thirty-four. [51–53]

September 1939 Hitler's invasion of Poland, typically considered the beginning of World War II.

1939–40 Situation temporarily improved in the area where Elfriede lived. [60]

---

3. This date is not stated in the book. Johann gave it to Frank Weaver.
4. Today the Ichan Kala Museum in Khiva, Uzbekistan, commemorates the Mennonite experience in Ak-Mechet, in collaboration with the Kauffman Museum (affiliated with Bethel College), North Newton, Kansas.

June 22, 1941 Nazi Germany invaded the Soviet Union with over 3,000,000 troops, one of the largest military operations in history. [13, 61]

September 11, 1943 Due to the westward retreat of the German troops, Johann Steffen left Wernersdorf, a village in the Molotschna Mennonite Settlement in the Zaporozhe district of the Ukraine. Through great hardship he reached Warthegau, Poland,[5] in February 1944. [14]

1943–44 In Asia, Elfriede's area of Uzbekistan, most women from ages eighteen to fifty were taken to work camps. [62]

1944 Johann worked in Krutschwitz, Central Poland, on an estate, and then in Schretersburg,[6] digging military trenches for the Germans. [15, 18]

1944 Later the Russians imprisoned him in a camp near Minsk until the fall of 1945. Later, he and his friend Heinrich spent two more years together in Minsk in the Russian prison. [16–18]

May 9, 1945 Russia's official Victory Day for defeating Germany in World War II. [67]

February 1, 1947 The ship *Volendam*, with 2,303 refugees, was the first major transport of refugees to leave Europe after World War II.[7] These Mennonites had escaped into Germany or Holland, and the Mennonite Central Committee helped them resettle in Paraguay. In contrast, over 20,000 of their fellow Mennonites were forcibly exiled to Siberia and the Far East.[8] Johann never got farther west than Poland.

---

5. Benjamin W. Goossen, *Chosen Nation, Mennonites and Germany in a Global Era* (Princeton, NJ: Princeton University Press, 2017). See pages 166–173, section entitled "Mennonites in Wartheland," for a description of this unique Mennonite settlement.

6. German "Krutschwitz" is Polish *Kruszwica* today. German "Schröttersburg" is Polish *Plock* today.

7. Peter J. and Elfrieda Dyck, *Up From the Rubble* (Scottdale, PA: Herald Press, August 1991), 207.

8. John A. Lapp and C. Arnold Snyder, eds., *Testing Faith and Tradition, A Global Mennonite History* (Intercourse, PA: Good Books, 2006), 209–210. Tragically, many Mennonites no longer believed in nonresistance during World War II, and fought in the German Nazi army against the Russians, who had persecuted them so harshly.

Late February 1947 The Russians released Johann, age twenty, from Minsk. [19]

March 6, 1947 Johann arrived in Krasavino, his new "home" in the Vologda region. [19, 23]

May 31, 1947 Johann's sister Anna died of hunger and exertion. [24]

September 20, 1947 Elfriede's mother returned home from the work camp after being separated from her family four years and eight months. Elfriede was eleven when her mother left and sixteen when she returned. [68]

December 20, 1948 Johann Steffen's mother died as a result of hunger and weakness. [25]

August 20, 1950 Johann was arrested by the victorious Russians and imprisoned because he had helped the Germans. He was stripped of his citizenship for five years and sentenced to twenty-five years in the labor camp. [26, 28]

1950 Elfriede received her first Bible; they could now buy Bibles from a church in Dushanbe. [70]

March 5, 1953 Joseph Stalin died. [32, 71]

1953 Johann committed his life to Christ in a Russian prison camp in Siberia. [32]

January 1955 At the age of twenty-three, Elfriede moved north (close to the area where her mother had been in camp) and lived in Korkino[9] with relatives. [72]

Thursday, February 24, 1955 In fulfillment of his vision, Johann was released from a Russian prison camp in Siberia. He actually left on Sunday. [34]

Early March 1955 Johann arrived in Karpinsk with relatives, and after two months moved to the region of Kostanay (north Kazakhstan). Many Mennonites had moved to Kazakhstan. [35]

Summer of 1956 Johann was baptized; Elfriede was baptized the same year. [35, 74]

---

9. Korkino is located on the eastern slope of the southern Ural Mountains, twenty-six miles south of Chelyabinsk.

November of 1956 Johann met Elfriede at a friend's wedding in Korkino. [74]

March 17, 1957 Johann and Elfriede were married in Korkino. Johann was almost thirty and Elfriede was twenty-six. They lived in Kostanay briefly, but Johann had to leave April 1 on a work gang that had been organized for two months' service, cutting timber in the forest. [36, 75]

January 1959 Johann and Elfriede's first child, a daughter Maria, was born. [76]

September 1959 Johann and Elfriede moved south to the warm region of Alma-Ata, to the city of Issyk, close to where Elfriede had spent her youth. [76]

January 1960 Johann and Elfriede's second child, a son Willi, was born, and about the same time Johann was called to be a church leader. [76]

February 1961 Johann and Elfriede's second son, Peter, was born. [77]

1961 Formation of the "Non-Registered Baptist" churches in the Soviet Union.[10] [89, 139]

September 1963 Johann was ordained bishop. [78]

October 24, 1963 Johann and a brother in the church were arrested (his second arrest, but the first for Christian work). [81, 87, 93]

January 14–16, 1964 Johann's trial at Issyk. [84, 94]

1963–1965 Johann's imprisonment at Alma-Ata, and then in a prison camp in Ottar (five-year sentence but early release). [87, 91, 93]

1964 Elfriede visits Johann in Ottar, traveling with a Chechen lady, Anna. [96–100]

1964 Johann and Elfriede's fourth child (third son), Helmut, was born. [100]

January 1965 Elfriede's mother came from Korkino to live with Elfriede and the children. [100]

---

10. Some Baptists with Mennonite roots were a part of registered churches and some were a part of non-registered churches. Today the latter typically are more comparable to conservative Mennonites in belief and practice than the registered ones are. There are regional variations.

March 6, 1965 Johann's release and joyful homecoming. [88, 100]

June 1966 Johann and Elfriede's fifth child (fourth son), David, was born. [101]

January 5, 1968 Elfriede's mother died. [102]

April 1969 Johann's third arrest. This second imprisonment for his faith was spent mostly at Dzhambul. (As a youth Johann had been in a labor camp, but these were prison camps.) Alwin Klassen and Johann each received a three-year sentence on April 23–25. [91, 103, 107, 111]

April 25, 1972 Johann was released from prison. [112]

November to December 1974 A tent was constructed to be used as a church. [114]

Early 1975 Authorities harasses the Christians at Issyk. [115]

July 12, 1976 Johann was arrested the fourth time (third time for his faith), tried at Alma-Ata on October 26, 28, and on November 1, Johann was sentenced to five years in a concentration camp. [118, 127, 143]

January 1977 After a brief imprisonment at Aktyubinsk, Johann was moved to the camp in Uzen and then, in May, to Schevchenko. [128–130]

February 1977 Elfriede and their son Willi visited Johann in Novy Uzen. [145]

May 1979 Their oldest son Willi was called to military service. [147]

November 1979 Their second son Peter was called for military duty. [147]

March 1980 Elfriede and their daughter Maria visited Johann at the camp at Shevchenko. [148]

July 25, 1981 Johann was released after his five-year confinement at camp. [137, 153–155]

1981 The oldest children married: Maria on August 30 and Willi on September 27. [137, 155]

December 12, 1981 Son Peter returned home from his military service; he then also came to faith in Jesus Christ and was baptized in 1982. [156]

September 26, 1982 Peter's wedding. [137, 156]

January 1984 The church at Issyk was registered. [139]

November 1984 David was called into military service. There were house searches in Issyk due to underground printing activity. [140,156]

May 14, 1985 Johann was arrested the fifth time, tried in June, and sentenced to five years (his fourth sentence for his faith). On May 15, he was taken to the prison in Alma-Ata. [142, 159, 181]

May 1986 Son Helmut's wedding. [183]

January 1987 Elfriede visited Johann, bringing along their youngest son David, who had been released from military service in the fall and became a Christian in New Year's Day. [175, 183]

February 1987 There was an announcement from Moscow about amnesty for one hundred forty political prisoners. Elfriede and her children submitted petitions to Gorbachev. [183–184].

March 18, 1987 Johann is released from prison the day after their thirtieth wedding anniversary. [177–179, 184]

April 1987 A new wave of emigration to Germany began. [190]

May 1987 Johann turned sixty and considered himself too old to be the church leader. [189]

May 1987 The Steffens applied for an exit permit to Germany. [184]

Summer of 1987 The church tore down the tent and built a new one. By this time about a third of the church had emigrated to Germany. [190]

March 10, 1988 Johann and Elfriede were finally given permission to emigrate after waiting almost ten months for the permit. [184]

April 12, 1988 Johann, Elfriede, and their youngest son David left Issyk to emigrate to Germany, arriving there April 14. [184]

October–November 1992 Johann and Elfriede visited the United States and spoke at the Christian Aid Ministries Open House and various churches and schools.

March 1993 Johann traveled to Belarus and the Ukraine with a bus tour sponsored by TABEA [Tabitha], a German Christian relief organization. He left the group for a few days to visit his boyhood town of Wernersdorf. [200]

December 10, 2005 Elfriede Steffen died, at seventy-four years old.

April 21, 2013 Johann Steffen died, almost eighty-six years old.

—James K. Nolt

Notes on the Outline

Dates are given with our best discernment; there were some ambiguities we needed to navigate. A few dates were added from other sources, such as from letters Johann Steffen wrote to Frank Weaver, to help give historical context.

German names are given in some footnotes to tie this work to the original German, especially since some names were difficult to translate, and some places had name changes through the years.

Bibliography

Bartsch, Franz and Cornelius Krahn. "Ak-Mechet (Uzbekistan)." In *Global Anabaptist Mennonite Encyclopedia Online*. 1955. Accessed Dec. 1, 2020. https://gameo.org/index.php?title=Ak-Mechet_(Uzbekistan)&oldid=146352.

Bartsch, Franz and Cornelius Krahn. "Ak-Mechet (Uzbekistan)." In *The Mennonite Encyclopedia*, Vol. 1. Scottdale, PA: The Mennonite Publishing House, 1955.

Bartsch, Franz and Richard D. Thiessen. "Epp, Claas (1838–1913)." In *Global Anabaptist Mennonite Encyclopedia Online*. April 2005. Accessed Dec. 1, 2020. https://gameo.org/index.php?title=Epp,_Claas_(1838-1913)&oldid=145013.

Belk, Fred Richard. *The Great Trek of the Russian Mennonites to Central Asia, 1880–1884*. Scottdale, PA: Herald Press, 1976; Wipf & Stock Pub., Oct. 17, 2000.

Dyck, Peter J. and Elfrieda. *Up From the Rubble*. Scottdale, PA: Herald Press, August 1991.

Goossen, Benjamin W. *Chosen Nation, Mennonites and Germany in a Global Era*. Princeton, NJ: Princeton University Press, 2017.

Jantzen, Herman. *Journey of Faith in a Hostile World*. Bloomington, IN: iUniverse, 2008.

Lapp, John A. and C. Arnold Snyder, eds. *Testing Faith and Tradition, A Global Mennonite History*. Intercourse, PA: Good Books, 2006.

Sawatsky, Walter W. "All-Union Council of Evangelical Christians-Baptists." In *Global Anabaptist Mennonite Encyclopedia Online*. 1987. Accessed Dec. 1, 2020. https://gameo.org/index.php?title=All-Union_Council_of_Evangelical_Christians-Baptists&oldid=141017.

Sawatsky, Walter W. "Council of Churches of Evangelical Christians-Baptists." In *Global Anabaptist Mennonite Encyclopedia Online*. 1987. Accessed Dec. 1, 2020. https://gameo.org/index.php?title=Council_of_Churches_of_Evangelical_Christians-Baptists&oldid=86947.

Appendix C: Johann and Elfriede Visit America in 1992

David Troyer, the director of Christian Aid Ministries (CAM), visited Christliches Hilfswerk TABEA e.V, a mission in Swisttal-Heimerzheim, Germany. TABEA was supported by Christian Aid Ministries and was providing help to the Russian Christians and others.

While at TABEA, David met Johann Steffen at work, packing parcels to send to various parts of the former Soviet Union. A few evenings later, he had the opportunity to hear Johann give his life story at a local church. *This is a story that needs to be heard back home in America,* decided David.

So it was arranged that on October 31, 1992, Johann and Elfriede could be present at the annual CAM Open House held at the Ephrata warehouse. They spoke in German, and through an interpreter, they shared their experiences. Johann had been preaching the Gospel in communist Russia for twenty-eight years;

Johann is sitting in the front of the left-hand section and is wearing a nametag.

he spent eighteen years in prison and labor camps; and his wife, Elfriede, raised their five children in very difficult circumstances.

In 1992, Johann and Elfriede were first-time visitors to America. They could not speak or understand any English. On their flight, they were traveling with their friends and fellow minister, Nikolaus and Maria Klassen, who had already made several trips to America. But the Klassens were scheduled to visit the Mennonites in Mexico, while Johann and Elfriede were to be our (Frank and Laura Weaver's) guests for two weeks. Jon Stoltzfus and I took the Steffens to various churches and schools, interpreting as they told their story.

Laura and I were both raised with Pennsylvania German as our first language. I had studied High (Standard) German and was a novice interpreter. When Laura talked Pennsylvania German, Elfriede said, "Ich kann dich versteh." ("I can understand you.") They got along really well. One afternoon Elfriede asked Laura, "Sell ich de bluma geese?" ("Shall I water your flowers?")

The first Sunday, Jon Stoltzfus and his wife took the Steffens to the church service at Pequea Amish-Mennonite where Johann spoke, with Sam Kauffman interpreting.

On Monday evening, Laura and I took them to David and Alta Hoover for a German hymn singing, which was attended by many Groffdale Conference Mennonite folks. They sang out of the *Unpartheyisches Gesangbuch*, which they use in their church services.

On Tuesday at 8:30 AM, Johann gave a talk at Faith Mennonite High School. Late in the afternoon we visited Clay Book Store and had supper with Preacher Lester Sauder and his wife Anna, along with several other friends who appreciated the German language.

On Wednesday, we were at Gehman's Mennonite School. Johann gave his talk, and then the teacher gave opportunity for the children to ask questions. There was a good response.

We then took Johann and Elfriede to David and Alta Hoover. They had their horse and carriage ready for the trip to their Bishop Aaron Sensenig for lunch. Johann and Elfriede sat in the carriage and asked to have a picture taken so they could show it to their grandchildren at home.

David had suggested that I should come along to interpret, but Aaron said, "Mir brauche net an interpreter. Mir sind Deutsch." ("We don't need an interpreter. We are German.") They are

Johann and Elfreide at Gehman's Mennonite School (above) and in carriage (below).

accustomed to using German Bibles and songbooks in church, but in conversation, they talk in the Pennsylvania German dialect. David told me, "Be ready; we may call you." Sure enough, after lunch David called me, "Come on over; they want you to interpret for them." When I got there, I found a dozen of the Groffdale Conference ministers and their wives ready to hear his story, and asking many questions about church life in Russia.

Wednesday evening, Johann gave his story at Fairview Street Mennonite Church.

On Thursday, we took the Steffens to Preacher Amos K. Martin for lunch. In the afternoon, a dozen Weaverland Conference ministers and their wives came to hear Johann's story. Bishop Joseph O. Weaver was ninety years old. Johann was sixty-five and remarked on the good health of the elderly bishop. Joseph mentioned letters and conversations with German refugees of years ago. There was a sense of deep mutual respect at these meetings with the Old Order Mennonite ministry.

Friday morning Jon Stoltzfus took them to Fairhaven Christian School and Friday evening to Upper Conewago Church of the Brethren. A meeting had been announced for Johann to give his story at the Midway Reception Center on Saturday evening. A large group attended and showed great interest as he told of his early life, the war years and imprisonments, and the long hard journey back home after his release. I interpreted, and Amos B. Hoover conducted the questions and answers at the end.

On Sunday morning Jon took Johann along to Summitview Christian Fellowship and in the evening to his church, the Gap View Amish-Mennonite Church.

Sometimes when I had to work in the shop, I would lay out on a table my assortment of German books for Johann to read. I also laid out the book *Soviet Evangelicals Since World War II* by Walter Sawatsky, published in 1981 with many photos of believers. When I returned, he had the book open to page 314 and said, "Hier bin ich." ("Here am I.") And there was his picture. He also pointed out in the photos many others with whom he was acquainted.

A photo taken secretly in 1979 shows Johann in a seriously emaciated condition. He had written to his wife, 'My conditions cannot become worse than they are." (Photo by permission of Friedensstimme). From Walter Sawatsky, *Soviet Evangelicals Since World War II* (Scottdale, PA: Herald Press, 1981), 314.

Johann related a longing he had to visit with one of his old comrades who some years prior had moved from Russia to America and was living in Detroit, Michigan. How far is it to Detroit? Could they fly to Detroit on Monday, visit, and spend the night with their friends, and fly back Tuesday? I contacted Amos K. Martin, who in turn got CAM to get the tickets. We took Johann's to the Harrisburg Airport (PA); they departed 11:00 AM and arrived in Detroit at 1:37 PM. They had arranged for their friends to pick them up at the airport.

But their friends were not there! The Steffens were stranded and could talk no English. Just then a pilot from Lufthansa, a German airline, came by. Johann called to him and was glad to hear a German answer! The pilot was very helpful, and suggested they find a pay phone and call Johann's friend. This they tried but got no answer. The pilot said they're probably on their way, and that he must care for some paperwork and will check back later. And so they sat there and waited and waited. A half hour later, the Lufthansa pilot came back. "Was? Noch nicht da?" ("What, not here yet?") Just then Johann's friend walked up—right on time! Johann had not realized the difference in time zones! So they had a very nice visit, and the next day their plane brought them to Philadelphia Airport, where Laura and I picked them up, and we all went back home for supper.

Having returned home from Detroit the night before, Johann and Elfriede and we were to meet at the Jon Stoltzfus home at 3:00 AM, to leave for New York. Jon had given me directions to his house: two and a half miles south of Route 322 on Route 897, on the right in the woods. When my odometer showed two and a half miles, there were several lanes going to houses back in the woods. I tried to see the name and number on the mailbox . . . I should have brought a flashlight. Oh, I should have checked the location the day before. It was 3:00 AM. A car came up behind us. Suddenly blue and red flashers lit up—the police! I turned on the interior light and rolled down my window. As the policeman walked up, I said, "We need help; we are to meet at our friend's house at Box 1622, and we don't know which lane to take." He helped me check the mailbox with his flashlight and, sure enough, this was it. I thanked him and we were soon at Jon's house, loading up his van to head for New York.

Traveling with Johann and Elfriede as they told their story was

Frank, Johann, Elfriede, and Laura.

an enriching and inspirational experience. We maintained contact with them and rejoiced to receive their autobiography, written and published in German in 1996. We felt strongly that their story must be made available to English-speaking Christians, and we rejoice that, with the help of God, this goal has been fulfilled.

—*Frank Weaver*

Appendix D: Johann Visits his Former Home in Ukraine

As noted in Appendix A, Johann visited the United States in October 1992 as a result of Christian Aid Ministries' support for Christliches Hilfswerk TABEA e.V., a German relief organization that Johann worked for. In the Postscript, Johann has described his bus trip to Ukraine, taken five months later in March 1993 with a group organized by TABEA. To better understand where relief channeled through TABEA was being distributed, three CAM board member couples joined the group: Robert and Esther Bauman, Frank and Mabel Roth, and David A. and Ruth Miller. Our family was serving in Romania with Christian Aid Ministries at the time, and so I also joined the group, taking our two sons Japheth and Adrian along. Johann served as their "grandpa" for the trip, and they enjoyed some good-natured reciprocal teasing. The bus group did not see the sites Johann shows in the Postscript since he had left the rest of the group to visit his former home.

The Postscript shows a sketch of the Schönsee Mennonite Church, built in 1909, and a photo of the ruins Johann saw in 1993 (see pages 198–199). The *Mennonite Encyclopedia* article gives additional interesting and heartbreaking information about the church.[1] The large church served seven or more villages, including Johann's home village of Wernersdorf, "altogether about 1,500 souls." During Johann's lifetime, Alexander Ediger "was called to the ministry at an hour (1922) when the storms of the Russian Revolution and the civil war swept the country. He was a man of exceptional intellectual and spiritual power, whose influence extended far beyond . . . Molotschna." He was imprisoned in

---

1. Goerz, Heinrich. "Schönsee Mennonite Church (Molotschna Mennonite Settlement, Zaporizhia Oblast, Ukraine)." In *Global Anabaptist Mennonite Encyclopedia Online*, 2015. Accessed Dec. 6, 2020. https://gameo.org/index.php?title=Sch%C3%B6nsee_Mennonite_Church_(Molotschna_Mennonite_Settlement,_Zaporizhia_Oblast,_Ukraine)&oldid=162986.

Members of the bus tour are listening to a guide. Seated on the left is Johann Stefffen, then Robert Bauman, and all the way to the right is David A. Miller.

From the left in the front row, Johann is the first standing on the street, then Mabel Roth and Frank standing partly behind her. Japheth Nolt is in the center on the picture and Adrian between him and the flower picture.

This Schönsee Mennonite Church was turned into a granary and was later used as a Communist club. It fell into ruins which is how Johann found it in 1993 when he visited his childhood home (page 199).

In 2013, this former Mennonite church was refurbished as a Ukrainian Greek Catholic church.

1931 and later banished. His young successor, Johann Görz, held services in private homes until he also was banished.

"The church building was first turned into a granary and then into a Communist club," with a large stage with a curtain depicting the goddess of beauty and life-sized pictures of Lenin, Stalin, and other Communist leaders on the wall. "During the German occupation the building again for a short time was used as a church." In 2013, about twenty years after Johann's visit there in 1993, "the former Mennonite church was refurbished as a Ukrainian Greek Catholic church."

"And at that time there was a great persecution against the church which was at Jerusalem; and they were all scattered abroad throughout the regions of Judaea and Samaria, except the apostles. . . . Therefore they that were scattered abroad went every where preaching the word" (Acts 8:1, 4). Like the early church at Jerusalem, the Schönsee Mennonite Church experienced *"great persecution."* It came to a tragic end, but men with spiritual roots there, such as Johann Steffen, built the church of Jesus Christ in other places. *"And he [Jesus Christ] shall reign over the house of Jacob for ever; and of his kingdom there shall be no end"* (Luke 1:33).

—James K. Nolt

Appendix E: Johann Visits His Former Home in Kazakhstan

This letter and the following poems were sent to Frank Weaver by the Steffen family, and were not part of the original book, Im Schmelztiegel, *that was published in German.*

June 19, 1995

"It is good for me to draw near to God." Psalm 73:28

Dearly Beloved,

We wish you all God's blessing and peace, and health for each day. We are thankful to God that it goes well with us and our children. With God's grace we have been given two more little grandchildren. Our son, David and his wife Elsa, a third child, son Georg born April 4th. Willi and Elsa have a fifth child, a daughter Anika born May 24th. We are thankful for the healthy children.

We also have much to be thankful for in spiritual things. We have never had our own church building for our congregation; always we have rented a room. And now God has made it possible that our church could buy a small sewing factory, which needs to be remodeled inside for our use. We are thankful for this privilege.

Johann's long looked-for wish was to once again travel to Kazakhstan to the place where we lived from September 1959 until April 1988, near Alma-Ata in the little town of Issyk where we experienced so much. It was here that Johann was arrested four times. He served in this time a total of eleven years and two months, for the faith and because he was a leader in the church.

We also experienced much joy in that church. Through God's grace many were brought to the true faith, including our children. Many good memories have stayed. We thank the almighty God for His blessings.

On May 19, 1995, Johann and two other church brethren flew from Hanover to Alma-Ata. There they were picked up at the airport by believers from Issyk. On June 2 again back to Hanover then by train safely home to Ulm. Johann was granted many joys on this visit with the people at the church service and also in their homes. The joy was very great to be able to meet once again. There are very few Germans left in the church insomuch that the preaching and singing is all in the Russian language. There are forty-six members at this church. He also visited the cemetery where many of our friends rest in peace, also my mother and a grandchild.

Johann then visited several authorities of the local government that in earlier times had tried to destroy our church, had called in the brethren for questioning, had threatened them, and had them arrested. Now since religious freedom is here, some regret what they had done. Anyway, they greeted Johann with great joy, embraced him and were glad to see him again. They invited him for a meal and to have tea with them and talked of times past.

One of the women officers asked Johann to forgive her for what she had done, and to also ask forgiveness of the others whom she had mistreated, who now live in Germany. She was an Asian Moslem. In 1980, I had given her a Bible; now she talked to Johann about it, and she still has the Bible. Her husband was also a police officer at that time. But he had not known Johann earlier and was glad to meet him at their home.

During this time that we have been living in Germany, many changes have taken place there in our old community in Kazakhstan. Churches have been built, the old Orthodox churches which had been taken from them have been returned, a clock tower has been rebuilt over the church, and they hold services in the churches again. The Jehovah's Witnesses have built a church; the Turks and Kazaks have also built a mosque and there hold their service.

Everything is altogether different; yet people try to get along and do so. It is peaceful among the different nationalities living there. They even would be glad to have some Germans come back to help with their work.

The markets have much to offer, including imported items. All daily necessities are available; the only lack is money to buy them, because the pensioners and the workers often get their payments two or three months late. So each one has to make out the best he can.

Johann took some pictures of the church, inside and outside, which was built in 1987 while we still lived there. This church was near to our house, and Johann labored much in that church, even after many had moved to Germany. There were at that time about 170 members.

He also took a picture of the Issyk river, or canal, which flows down from the high snow-capped mountains, but is a dry streambed now. It is a very nice area, with pure air and good water. Here is a picture of our house, which Johann had built. The walls were constructed of cane and then stucco and white-washed. The people that we sold it to have overlaid it with brick walls since then.

The house which Johann built. (Compare with picture on page 101.)

I must close this letter; it is already so long. There would be much more to tell, but if God makes it possible and it is His will, perhaps we can meet again sometime.

Greetings to all of you,

From Johann and Elfriede Steffen

Issyker Reunion

We greet all those who at this place have gathered,
    Who at some time in Issyk had their home.
All glory be to Him, the God of heaven,
    For blessings heretofore, and yet to come.

How beautiful, when friends can meet each other
    Who long have waited, friends to meet again,
Who joyfully may now embrace each other,
    In tears they understand each other well.

These hours indeed are ones we find noteworthy,
    One feels quite overjoyed, yet also grieved,
For they are shorter than we had expected.
    Then comes the parting, which a heartache leaves.

Yet it is true: we will not stay together.
    Today we bid a wistful, sad farewell.
We'll sing the old, old songs we sang together:
    "My friend, where will we chance to meet again?"

We want to cherish memories now of Issyk,
    The city where our roots were once so firm.
I hope 'twill hinder no one if we ask him,
    "My friend, are we already now at home?"

Is this the land where there's eternal pleasure?
    Is this the land where we'll be free from sin?
Is this the land where shines the sun forever,
    Where it is never dark, where all is made as new?

This is the question I would like to ask you.
    Back to Kazakhstan, very far away,
Where we once lived, believed, with little privilege,
    Which many of us still remember now.

Issyk—a place enclosed by highest mountains,
    Green at their base; above, eternal ice.
The men below looked small, like dwarfs so little.
    Winters scenic; summers, often hot.

A river, strong, streams down from those high mountains;
    It separates, like fingers on a hand.
The evening frog sounds forth his lively singing.
    Many a wand'rer found his dwelling there.

Issyk, a place with many beautiful fruits:
    Bring here the largest apple in the world.
Oh, the taste of the lovely fruit dishes,
    That graced the tables of our mealtimes there!

Issyk—the dwelling of so many Christians,
    Who prayed much for the welfare of the place.
Yet God-mockers rewarded them with hatred;
    Many among us this could deeply feel.

Issyk—a city built with our own labor,
    'Most everyone built his own dwelling place.
We fled from it; howe'er, the walls still stand
    That we, with God's kind help, had put in place.

So will it be when life on earth is ended:
    We leave here, yet we something leave behind.
Who lived with God, did not in vain here battle,
    At the end, he eternal joy will find.

The question comes: "Are we at home already,
    Since out of Russia land we here have come?
Does one indeed here feel as much at home now,
    As feels a little child when safe at home?

"Do you feel altogether safe, concealed here,
    As if no evil now could mar your life?
Do you in life no more have any sorrows?
    Oh, have you ever seen yourself as such?

"I think not so! You have been disillusioned,
    If you have clothing, money, food enough.
Your life is still not safe, securely sheltered,
    Your riches only a deception are.

(Continued on next page)

"We were glad when Germany we entered,
　　And this is good, but this is still no home;
We are often asked (in search of where we trace from):
　　"Are you truly Germans? Where are your roots?"

There is a home there, where the saved ones gather,
　　In that fair city that is built by God,
There, at the end of time, those meet their brethren,
　　Who here in life did fully trust in God.

I wish that those who here did come to join us,
　　Who still are not the children of the Lord,
Would yet today be reconciled, with God united
　　Become as pure as any newborn child.

For the Elderly

Take a look at elderly people,
　　Ask them how it goes with them.
Count the wrinkles in their faces,
　　Can you learn something from them?

They were also young as you are,
　　Like the youth we see today;
They could see, not using glasses,
　　Firmly stand upon their feet.

They could walk, as well as run,
　　Very well, uphill and down,
Carried burdens, large and heavy;
　　Time removed it all from them.

As time lengthened, strength was waning,
　　Hair has also turned to gray,
Oh, the aged, how I notice:
　　They fade away; they seem to melt.

Steadily their steps grow shorter,
　　Which had once been lengthy strides,
Often shaky footsteps sliding,
　　Some fall often, like a child.

And the body shows great changes,
    Making many stooped and bent.
Character is also changing,
    And one asks, "For what?" and "Why?"

Why can I not stay exactly
    As I was in days gone by?
What's the reason for my parting
    With my youth, which long has flown?

Why must I grow ever older?
    No one asks if it's my will.
For what purpose all the burdens?
    Why do wheels of life stand still?

All life undergoes its changes,
    And there's nothing one can do.
All his thinking, all his striving,
    One must simply lay to rest.

Simply trust in God's own leading,
    As He leads, so it is good.
He our prayers is ever hearing,
    Courage grants in older years.

Not everyone is allowed to get old;
    God alone determines this.
Many live a short time only,
    Pass away, quite young and small.

By the Lord you've been selected
    To grow older, this is good.
Yet He also wants to notice
    That you still for Him do good.

So hold still a bit, dear people,
    Ponder now the matter well:
Why is it our Lord's desire
    That you're here, although you're weak?

(Continued on next page)

Weak in body, strong in faith?
　　Many foes you've overcome.
You have learned to trust the Father,
　　Since you loved the Word of God.

Thanks to those who've faithfully carried
　　God's blest Word in this our time,
Harm and mock'ry bore so meekly,
　　Endured much suffering besides.

God has seen your humble service,
　　And rewards you for each deed.
Everything will sometime perish,
　　But the reward remains preserved.

Therefore, rejoice, you aged ones,
　　Pain and sorrow soon will cease.
What can yet detain you here?
　　Jesus comes! And sets you free.

Storms and waves will soon subside here,
　　Jesus stands on yonder strand.
Have no fear, don't be discouraged,
　　God's Son brings you to the land.

　　　　　　　—Peter Redekop, August 28, 1993

Appendix F: German Poems

Following are the original German poems that were translated into English throughout the book.

"HARD WORK, SCANT FOOD," ON PAGE 31

> Schwere Arbeit, magere Kost,
>   Kleider ganz zerissen,
> Kalter Ofen, draußen Frost,
>   Brot oft keinen Bissen.
> Wenn ich mich zur Ruh' begab,
> Zog ich nicht die Kleider ab,
>   Schlief ohn' Deck' und Kissen.
>
> Wanzen, Läuse, Schmutz und Krätz,
>   Hatten mich umgeben.
> Hunger, Elend, Sünd' und Schmerz,
>   Nagten mir am Leben.
> Gott, der selbst die Liebe ist,
> Blickt mich an durch Jesus Christ;
>   Gnad' ward mir gegeben.

"LET ME GO, LET ME GO," ON PAGE 51

> Laßt mich gehn, laßt mich gehn,
> Daß ich Jesus möge sehn.
>   Meine Seel' ist voll Verlangen
>   Ihn auf ewig zu umfangen,
> Und vor seinem Thron zu stehn.

"HOW GREAT IS THE GRACE OF THE ALMIGHTY . . ." ON PAGE 53

> Wie groß ist des Allmächtigen Güte! . . .
>   Nein, seine Liebe zu ermessen,
> Sei ewig meine größte Pflicht.
>   Der Herr hat mein noch nie vergessen,
> Vergiß, mein Herz, auch seiner nicht!

"ON THE FIELD OF TAJIKISTAN" ON PAGE 54

Auf dem Feld Tadschikistan
   Sitzen wir und weinen:
Unser Seufzen Klageton
   Muß deswegs vereinen.

Auf dem Feld Tadschikistan
   Müh'n wir uns und klagen
Über diese schwere Lage:
   Jedes Lebens Glück entsagen.

Auf dem Feld Tadschikistan
   Seufzend wir am Boden kauern,
Wie einst der verlorene Sohn,
   In dem Schicksal unserer Tage.

Auf dem Feld Tadschikistan
   Kauernd wir am Boden liegen,
Scheltend ist der Arbeitslohn
   Den wir für die Arbeit kriegen.

Auf dem Feld Tadschikistan
   Flehend wir zum Himmel schauen,
Dann an uns der Spott und Hohn
   Will den Mut zum Boden hauen.

Auf dem Feld Tadschikistan
   Müssen wir die Baumwoll' pflegen:
Ach, viel lieber möcht man schon
   Seine lieben Kinder pflegen.

Denn vom frühen Margengrauen
   Bis zur Abenddämmerung
Darf man nicht die Kinder schauen,
   Die sind noch so zart und jung.

Schlafend ließ man sie zurücke,
   Schlafend findet man sie vor.
Diese lieben Kinderblicke,
   Schon so früh man sie verlor.

Ach, mein Herz erbebt vor Trauer
      Wenn ich an die Zukunft denk,
Eine ach, so hohe Mauer
      Zwischen Kind und mir sich stellt.

Wenn sie ohne Elternliebe
      In die Welt gestoßen sind,
Wenn sie in dem Weltgetriebe
      Ganz verkommen, ganz verirrt.

Wenn kein Vater ihnen kann raten,
      Wenn sie keine Mutter sehn,
Wenn dann in böser Buben Taten
      Gar so oft wird eingeübt.

Mein Gott, mein Gott wie lange,
      Hast Du uns vergessen doch?
Ach, wir bitten schon so lange,
      Hörst Du's nicht und zürnest noch?

Doch Du prüfest unser Leiden,
      Leiden, deren wir nicht wert.
Danken werden wir mit Freuden,
      Für den Weg, den Du geführt.

Herr, Du gibst Geduld zum Leiden.
      Gib uns Kraft und Mut dazu!
Mach uns fertig zu dem Scheiden
      Von der Erd' zur bess'ren Ruh.

Dir sei Dank für diesen Glauben,
      Du verläßt die Deinen nicht!
Alle, die auf Dich hier bauen
      Werden bei Dir sein im Licht.

—*Herman Wall, 1936*

"BE AFRAID NO LONGER," ON PAGE 61

Fürchte dich nicht länger,
Sieh' ich bin bei dir,
Daß ist meine Leuchte, auf dem Wegehier,
      Durch die Wolken funkelt der Verheißung Licht
      Siehe ich bin bei dir und ich verlasse dich nicht.

Nein, niemals allein, nein niemals allein,
So hat der Herr mir verheißen
Niemals läßt er mich allein.

"BE STILL, FEAR NOT; BRAVELY GO ON YOUR WAY!" ON PAGE 95

Nur still, ohne Zagen, zieh hin deine Bahn!
Denn Jesus geht mit dir, Er geht dir voran,
Nur Ihm mußt du trauen, Er bringt dich zum Ziel
Trotz Stürme und Wogen, sind ihrer auch viel.
O vertraue, O vertraue, O vertraue auf Gott.

"THE MOST BEAUTIFUL HYMN ON EARTH" ON PAGE 102

Das schönste Lied auf Erden
Bleibt mir mein Leben lang,
Das Lied, daß meine Mutter
In meiner Jugend sang.

Mein Mütterlein, mein Mütterlein,
Ich hör das Lied and denke dein.
Kein Gold und auch kein Edelstein
Ersetzt mein liebes Mütterlein.

"AND IF HE LEADS ON PATHS THAT ARE ROUGH AND STEEP," ON PAGE 104

Und führt Er durch Wege, die rauh und steil,
So sind sie doch weise und zu meinem Heil.
Durch Leiden zu Freuden, durch Dunkel zum Licht,
Führt Jesus die Seinen, drum zage nur nicht!
O vertraue, O vertraue auf Gott!

"WE NEED MOTHERS," ON PAGE 106

Wir brauchen Mütter,
Die den Schwachen Liebe entgegen tragen,
Die Verständniß, Geduld, und Sanftmut üben,
Die Geister prüfen, den Geist nicht betrüben.

Wir brauchen Mütter, die warten und trauen,
Die in Kampf und Bedrängniß nur aufwärts schauen,
    Denen nichts kann Glauben und Ziel verrücken.

Wir brauchen Mütter, die Wunden pflegen,
Und kranke Seelen dem Arzt hinlegen,
    Unter deren Händen mit Schmerzen und Lasten
    Sich Söhne und Töchter flüchten und rasten.

Die als Mütter verstehen mitzuleiden,
Das Echte vom Falschen zu unterscheiden.
    Die Mütter sind es, die auf Erden
    In den letzten Tagen stets nötiger werden.

Wenn du noch eine Mutter hast,
    So danke Gott und sei zufrieden.
Nicht jedem auf dem Erdenrund
    Ist dieses hohe Glück beschieden.

Wenn du noch eine Mutter hast,
    So sollst du sie von Herzen lieben,
Eh' dich des Lebens kalter Strom
    Ins fremde Land getrieben.

"HE KNOWS, MY FATHER ABOVE DOES KNOW" ON PAGE 137

Er weiß, mein Vater droben weiß,
Welch Sturm wird stören meine Reis';
    Doch Stürme stillen Er vermag:
    Und wandeln Finsternis im Tag.

"AND WHEN ONE DAY ON EARTH" ON PAGE 185

Und ist einst auf Erden
    Mein Pilgern hier aus,
Dann bin ich geborgen
    Auf ewig zu Haus'.

Im Lichte der Ewigkeit
    Werd ich verstehen,
Warum solche Wege
    Ich hier mußte gehn.

"AT HOME, IT WAS ONCE BEAUTIFUL;" ON PAGE 199

Zu Hause war es einst mal schön,
Die Felder, der Fluß und die Höh'n
An die denk ich besonders gern
Die Gärten, die Wiesen so fern,
Das Lied, das zu Hause so schallt,
Mir heut noch im Herzen widerhallt.

"VISIT TO WERNERSDORF" ON PAGE 200

Besuch zu Wernersdorf

In der alten Ukraine, dem zerstörten Wernersdorf,
Gleicht es gänzlich der Ruine, dem zerriss'nen Schaf vom Wolf.
Alles rings umher verödet, kaum was zu erkennen mehr,
Alle Wohnungen geplündert, und der Ort von Menschen leer.

Da, nach fünfzig langen Jahren, macht sich Johann auf den Weg,
Um genauer zu erfahren, wie es sieht und wie es steht.
Hoffnungsvoll wird nun betreten hier ein Bus aus fern und nah.
Deutsche, Schweizer und Kanadier, auch der Johann ist jetzt da.

Und, nach mühevollem Fahren über Berg und über Tal,
Könnte endlich man erblicken das geliebte Rosental.
Wernersdorf, so hieß es früher, wo die Kindheit man verbracht,
Wo man liebend bei den Eltern auf dem Schoße froh gelacht.

O, welch Schrecken, nur Banderren, die jetzt leben hier und da,
Nirgend wo ein trautest Lächeln, niergens freudiger Gesang.
Nur die alten grauen Steine, diese zwei bezeugen noch,
Daß nicht ferne einst gestanden unser Haus, das weiß ich noch.

Siehe da, dort ist der Brunnen, der uns immer hat getränkt,
Zwar nur kümmerlich und öde, unten doch das Wasser glänzt.
Leider könnte ich nicht laben an dem schönen Wasser mich,
Denn es gab dort keinen Eimer, um was hoch zu holen sich.

Und die Straße, zum Verzweifeln, hier und dort nur noch ein Haus,
Voller Sehnsucht hielt ich Ausschau. Was wird hier wohl
                                        kommen, raus?
Plötzlich, es war kaum zu glauben, sah ich den Moloschna Fluß,
Wo wir oft hingingen fischen und uns baden voll Genuß.

Auch noch ein'ge schöne Bäume, die uns gäben Schatten dort,
Stehen jetzt noch, welch ein Wunder, immer noch an ihrem Ort.
Heimat, wo bist du geblieben, Giebt's denn wirklich nichts
mehr hier,
Wo die Sehnsucht wird gestillet, für den Müden Ruhe mehr?

Gott sei Dank, es gibt 'ne Heimat, die bereitet ist von Gott,
Wo wird aller Not enthoben, nimmer kennen Hohn und Spott.
Dort im ew' gen Himmelsglanze, wo das Herze nicht beschwert,
Ist durch Jesus, unsern Retter eine Heimat uns beschert.

—Johann Braun

"ISSYKER REUNION" ON PAGE 230

Issykertreffen!

Wir grüßen alle, die hier heut erschienen,
Die aus Issyk mal hergekommen sind.
Wir wollen Gott, den Höchsten, dafür rühmen,
Daß wir bis da von Ihm gesegnet sind.

Wie schön ist es, wenn Freunde sich mal treffen,
Die so gewartet auf ein Wiederseh'n,
Die sich so fröhlich in die Arme werfen
And unter Tränen sich so gut versteh'n.

Des sind doch Stunden, die man wirklich achtet.
Man fühlt sich glücklich and zugleich betrübt;
Denn sie sind kürzer, als man es gedacht hat,
Und dann das Scheiden, daß das Herz betrübt.

Daß ist mal so, wir bleiben nicht zusammen.
Wir sagen heute noch Aufwiederseh'n.
Wir werden singen, was wir damals sangen:
"Mein Freund, wo werden wir uns wiederseh'n?

Nun wollen wir uns an Issyk erinnern,
Der Stadt aus welcher wir gekommen sind.
Ich hoffe, daß es keinem nicht wird hindern,
Zu fragen, ob wir schon zu Hause sind?

Ist dies das Land, wo ew'ge Freud und Wonne?
    Ist dies das Land, wo du von Sünden frei?
Ist dies das Land, wo immer scheint die Sonne?
    Wo's niemals dunkel ist, wo alles neu?"

Daß ist die Frage, die ich stellen möchte,
    Und nun zurück ins weite Kasachstan,
Wo wir gelebt, geglaubt, fast ohne Rechte,
    Das mancher unter uns sich denken kann.

Issyk, ein Ort umringt von hohen Bergen,
    Die unten grün und oben ew'ges Eis.
Die Menschen unten klein, wie kleine Zwerge.
    Im Winter schön, im Sommer manchmal heiß.

Ein starker Fluß strömt von den Bergen 'runter,
    Der sich dann teilt wie Finger an der Hand.
Der Abendfrosch singt seine Lieder munter.
    So manch ein Wandrer dort sein' Wohnort fand.

Issyk, ein Ort mit vielen schönen Früchten:
    Apport, der größte Apfel jener Welt.
Wie schmecken doch die schönen Obstgerichte,
    Die man zur Mahlzeit auf den Tische stellt.

Issyk 'ne Stadt, wo viele Christen wohnten,
    Die viel gebetet um das Wohl der Stadt.
Doch Gottesspötter sie mit Haß belohnten,
    Das mancher unter uns verspühret hat.

Issyk, 'ne Stadt erbaut mit unsern Händen,
    Fast jeder hatte sich sein Haus gebaut.
Wir floh'n davon, doch stehen dort die Wände,
    Die wir mit Gottes Hilfe aufgebaut,

So wird es sein am Ende unsres Lebens,
    Wir geh'n davon, doch etwas bleibt zurück.
Wer hier mit Gott gelebt, 's ist nicht vergebens,
    Der findet einst am Ende ew'ges Glück.

Nun ist die Frage: "Sind wir schon zu Hause?
    Weil wir aus Rußland hergekommen sind?"

Fühlt man sich wirklich hier so ganz zu Hause,
  Wie sich zuhause fühlt ein kleines Kind?

Fühlst du dich hier ganz sicher und geborgen,
  Als könnte dir im Leben nichts gescheh'n?
Hast du in deinem Leben keine Sorgen?
  Hast du dich schon als solchen mal geseh'n?

Ich glaube nicht ! Du bist enttäuscht geworden
  Wenn du auch Essen, Kleider, Geld genug.
Dein Leben ist dann doch noch nicht geborgen,
  Der ganze Reichtum ist ja nur Betrug.

Wir war'n wohl froh, als wir nach Deutschland kamen.
  Das ist auch gut, doch das ist noch kein Heim;
Wo viel gefragt, geforscht, von wo wir stammen:
  "Bist du auch wirklich Deutscher, oder nein?"

Ein Heim ist dort, wo sich die Sel'gen treffen
  In dessen Stadt, die von dem Herrn erbaut.
Das ist das le l te Mal, wo die sich treffen,
  Die hier im Leben ganz auf Gott vertraut.

Ich wünsche mir, daß die, die hier erschienen,
  Die noch kein Eigentum des Herren sind,
Daß die sich heute noch mit Gott versöhnen
  Und werden rein, wie ein gebornes Kind.

"FOR THE ELDERLY" ON PAGE 232

Für den Alten

Schaut mal hin auf unsre Alten,
  Fragt sie mal, wie's ihnen geht.
Zählt mal im Gesicht die Falten,
  Ob man daraus was versteht?

Sie sind auch mal Jung gewesen
  Wie die Jungen, die wir sehn;
Könnten ohne Brille sehen,
  Feste auf den Füßen stehn,

Könnten gehen, könnten laufen
  Ob Bergauf oder Bergab
Trugen Lasten ganze Haufen,
  Doch die Zeit nahm's ihnen ab.

Mit der Zeit verschwanden Kräfte,
  Auch die Haare wurden grau.
O die Alten, wie ich merke:
  Sie vergehn, als ob sie tauen.

Kürzer werden auch die Schritte
  Die mal lang gewesen sind,
Oftmals gleiten auch die Tritte,
  Mancher fällt oft, wie ein Kind,

Auch der Körper sich verändert
  Mit der Zeit geht mancher Krum.
Der Charakter, auch sich ändert
  Und man fragt: wozu, warum?

Warum durfte ich nicht bleiben
  Wie ich mal gewesen bin?
Wozu mußte ich mich scheiden
  Von der Jugend, die längst hin?

Warum muß ich älter werden?
  Keiner fragt mich, ob ich's will.
Wozu sind all die Beschwerden?
  Warum stehn die Räder still?

Alles ändert sich im Leben,
  Und man kann daran nichts tun.
Alles Denken, alles Streben,
  Muß man einfach lassen ruhn.

Einfach trau'n auf Gottes Führung,
  Wie Er führt, so ist es gut.
Er schenkt im Gebet Erhöhrung
  Und schenkt auch im Alter Mut.

Alt darf nicht ein jeder werden;
 Das bestimmt nur Gott allein.
Viele leben Kurz auf Erden,
 Sterben weg, ganz jung und klein.

Ihr seid von dem Herrn ersehen
 Alt zu werden; das ist gut.
Doch Er will von euch auch sehen
 Daß ihr noch für Ihn was tut.

Darum haltet einmal stille,
 Und denkt gut darüber nach,
Warum ist es Gottes Wille
Daß ihr da seid, wenn euch schwach?

Schwach am Körper, stark im Glauben?
 Manchen Feind habt ihr besiegt,
Habt gelernt auf Gott vertrauen,
 Weil ihr Gottes Wort geliebt.

Dank sei denen, die getragen
 Gottes Wort in unsre Zeit,
Die ertrugen Spott und Schaden,
 Die erdulden manches Leid.

Gott hat euren Dienst gesehen
 Und er lohnt für jede Tat;
Alles wird einmal vergehen
 Nicht der Lohn—der bleibt bewahrt.

Darum freuet euch, ihr Alten,
 Bald ist Schmerz und Leid vorbei.
Was kann euch hier noch aufhalten?
 Jesus kommt! und macht euch frei.

Bald sich Stürme, Wogen Legen,
 Jesus stehet schon am Strand.
Fürchtet nichts, seid nicht verlegen—
 Gottes Sohn bringt euch ans Land.

—Peter Redekop, August 28, 1993

Appendix G: Maps and Glossary of Place Names

Geographical names are a challenging aspect of this book. Johann wrote the location names in German as he knew them in his lifetime, but the names often differ from those used in Russian or local languages. Many names were altered through the political changes in the former Soviet Union. There are differing ways of transliterating these names into English.

The first map is taken from the original German book and gives the names as Johann originally wrote them. As much as practical, the names on the second map are current.

The entry words below are based on the words shown in the English text. We hope the footnotes, glossary, and maps help you to meaningfully travel with Johann and Elfriede.

Glossary

Ak-Mechet; Ak-Meschet **(German):** Elfriede's hometown; about eight miles from Khiva, Uzbekistan. Founded by Mennonites in 1884.

Aktyubinsk **(Russian name until 1999);** *Aktubinsk* **(German);** *Aktobe* **(current Kazakh name):** Located in northeastern Kazakhstan. Johann was imprisoned here.

Alma-Ata; Almaty **(current name):** A region and the largest city in Kazakhstan. Johann was tried and imprisoned here.

Arkalyk: A city in the Kostanay region of northern Kazakhstan. Johann was imprisoned here.

Chelyabinsk; Tscheljabinsk **(German):** East of the Ural Mountains.

Dushanbe; Duschanbe **(German):** The capital and largest city of Tajikistan.

Dzhambul; Dschambul **(German); in 1993, changed to** *Jambyl* **or** *Dzhambyl;* **in 1997, renamed** *Taraz:* City in southern Kazakhstan where Johann was imprisoned for a while.

Continued on page 252

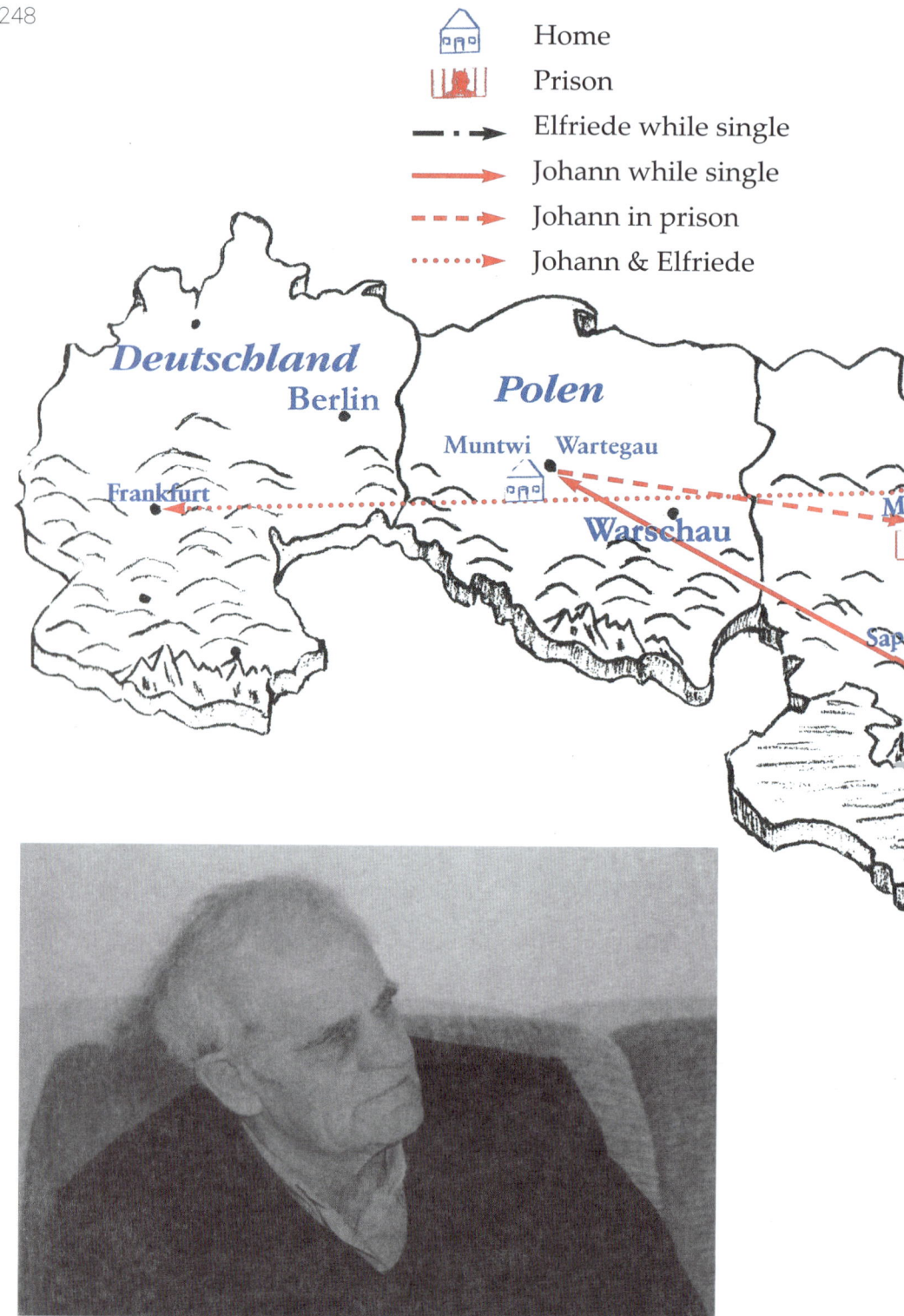

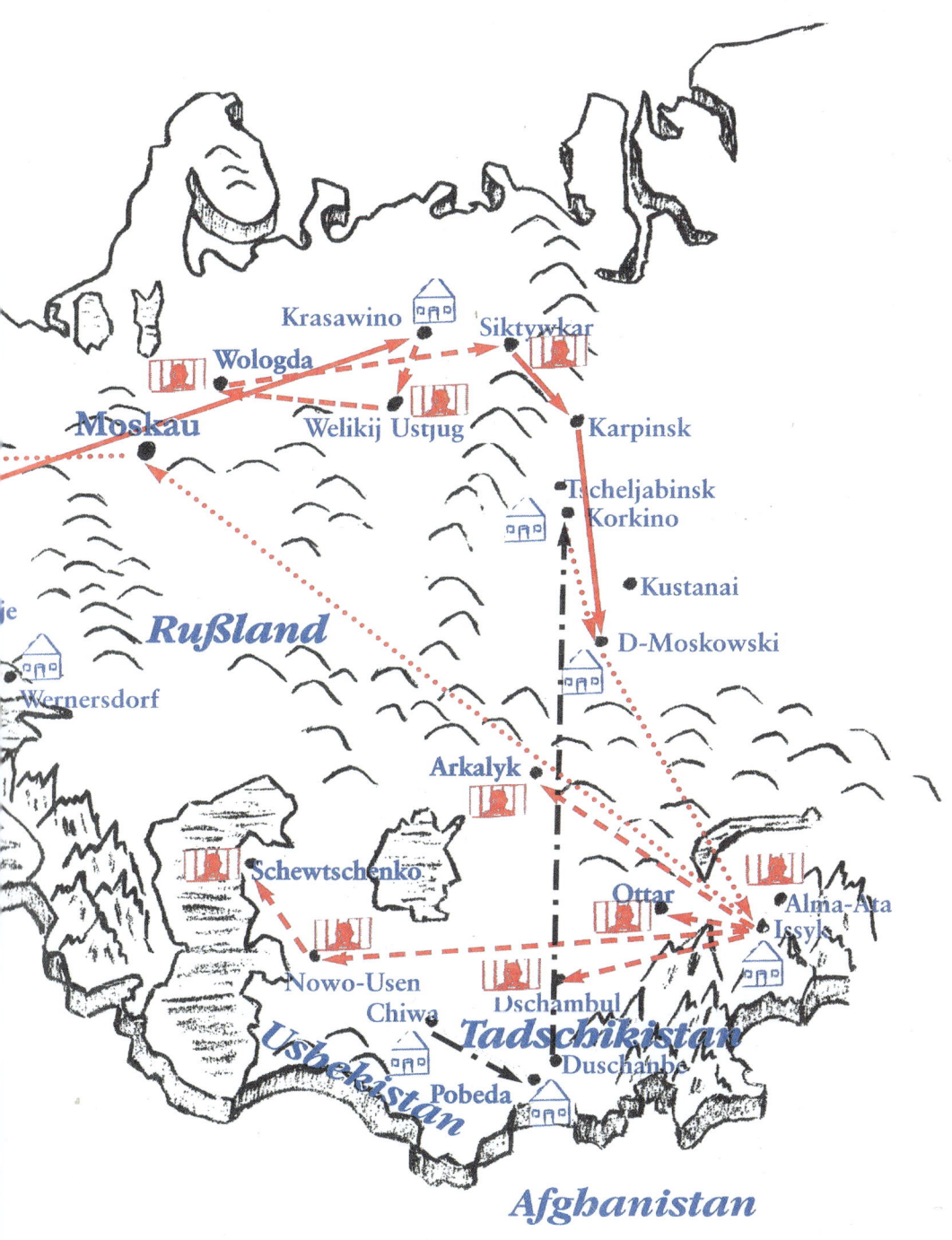

FINLAND

SWEDEN

NORWAY

Vologda •

ESTONIA

*North
Sea*

Volga

LATVIA

DENMARK

LITHUANIA

★ Moscov

POLAND

★ Minsk

NETHER-
LANDS

Berlin
★

Elbe

WARTHEGAU
★Warsaw

BELARUS

GERMANY

• Frankfurt

CZECH REPUBLIC

UKRAINE

D

FRANCE

SLOVAKIA

AUSTRIA

MOLDOVA

• Zaporizhzh

LIECHENSTEIN

HUNGARY

Snihurivka •
• Ostrykivk

SWITZERLAND

SLOVENIA
CROATIA

ROMANIA

Danube

BOSNIA &
HERZEGOVINA

SERBIA

Black Sea

ITALY

MONTENEGRO

KOSOVO

BULGARIA

ALBANIA

MACEDONIA

GREECE

TURKEY

ALGERIA

CYPRUS

SYRIA

TUNISIA

LEBANON

Mediterranean Sea

IRA

Issyk **or** *Esik:* a town in the Almaty Region of Kazakhstan. The Steffens moved here in 1959, raised their family, and served the church.

Karpinsk: Johann lived here for a few months after his Siberian imprisonment while still single.

Khiva; Chiwa **(German):** City in Uzbekistan near Mennonite village of Ak-Metchet.

Kirgizia **(older name);** *Kirgisia* **or** *Kirgisien* **(German);** *Kyrgyzstan* **(English):** Country in Central Asia. Home area of Elfriede's family.

Korkino: On the eastern slope of the Ural Mountains. Elfriede's home as a young adult. Johann and Elfriede were married here.

Kostanay, Kustanai **(German),** *Kustanay* **until 1997:** In northern Kazakhstan. Johann lived here right before and after his wedding.

Krasavino; Krasawina **(German in the text) or** *Krasawino* **(German on the map):** Johann's home in Russia while single, after leaving Minsk.

Leninabad; **currently** *Khujand:* The second-largest city of Tajikistan. Johann's father died here.

Minsk: Capital and largest city of Belarus. Johann spent time here in a work camp and prison.

Novy Uzen; Nowo Usen **(German); now called** *Zhanaozen:* East of the Caspian Sea. Johann was imprisoned here.

Ottar; Otar: In southern Kazakhstan. Johann was imprisoned here.

Schoensee; **now** *Snihurivka:* Johann attended a large Mennonite church here in his childhood.

Shevchenko; Schewtschenko **(German); now** *Aktau:* On the eastern shore of the Caspian Sea. Johann was imprisoned here.

Siktyvkar; Siktywkar **(German):** Map shows Johann was imprisoned here, but it is not mentioned in the text.

Sverdlovsk;   Swerdlowsk   (German);   Yekaterinburg   or Ekaterinburg: near the Ural Mountains.

Tajikistan; Tadschikistan **(German);** also *Tadzhikistan* **(English):** Small mountainous country of Central Asia.

Tashkent: The largest city and capital of Uzbekistan. Elfriede's grandfather died here.

Urgench; Urgentsch **(German):** City in western Uzbekistan where Mennonites were forcibly relocated; close to Khiva.

Uzen; Usen **(German):** Not shown on the map. Near the Caspian Sea, northeast of Novy Uzen or Zhanaozen; Johann was imprisoned here.

Veliky (Velikiy) Ustyug; Welikij Ustjug **(German):** Northern Russia: Johann was imprisoned here.

Vologda; Wologda **(German):** Northern Russia. Johann was imprisoned here.

Warthegau; (Wartegau **on German map);** *Wartheland* **(English):** Area of Poznań, Poland, where Johann and other Germans relocated.

Wernersdorf **(German);** also called *Rosental:* Johann's place of birth; a Mennonite village about four miles east of Schoensee, in the Zaporozhe district of Ukraine. In 1993 it was called Pribereschne (page 197). Its current name is Ostrykivka.

Zaporozhe;   Zaporoshje **(German);** also *Zaporizhia   or Zaporizhzhia:* City and region where Mennonites settled in Ukraine.

—James K. Nolt

Notes:

Helpful sources of information included *Wikipedia* articles, *Mennonite Encyclopedia* and *GAMEO* articles, Map Resources, and Google maps.

Schroeder, William, and Helmut T. Huebert. *Mennonite Historical Atlas*. Winnipeg, Canada: Springfield Publishers, 1990.

The Evening Draweth Near

Translated by John B. Martin

1. Life's morn - ing hour   is   al - most end - ed; The   sun   is sink - ing   in   the west.
2. Thou didst, when I   was young and ten - der, In   mer - cy guide   my   steps to Thee.
3. So man - y friends   and   dear - ly loved ones, Al - rea - dy left   this earth - ly shore.
4. And when in my   last days on earth here, This mor - tal bo - dy   weak - er grows,

To Thee, Lord, my   de - sire ex - tend - ed; I   in Thy bos - om   seek my rest.
A weak - ling I,   Thou, my   De - fen - der, Didst grant me peace,   from care set free.
Their part - ing, it   has deep - ly moved me; They are with Thee   for - ev - er more.
When eye and ear   no long - er serve me, The wheels of life   hum   to   a close,

Old age comes slow - ly   on   me creep-ing; Lord, hear my prayer,   my ear - nest weep-ing.
Oh Lord, I   owe Thee thanks and prais - es. Be with me still,   bear me in   pa - tience,
The cir - cle of   my friends grows tight - er; The bur - den of   my cares, not light - er.
Then let me, Lord,   to Thee as - cend - ing, In peace my walk   bring to   an end - ing.

Thou know'st my lack—what can   I   say?   For - get me not,   when old   and gray.
And judge me not,   dear Lord, I   pray.   For - sake me not,   when old   and gray.
Oh Lord, I seek   Thy face each day;   For - sake me not,   when old   and gray.
Be Thou, oh Lord,   my con - fi - dence;   For - sake me not,   when life doth end.

The German title of this hymn-prayer is "Mein Lebensmorgen ist vergangen." Although its author is unknown, the song is undoubtedly of Old World origin. Elfriede Steffen and her daughter, Maria, introduced this tune to Frank Weaver and others by singing it on a cassette. In January 2016, John B. Martin translated the German words into English.

In February 2022, the world watched in horror and anguish as Russia attacked Ukraine, resulting in unimaginable suffering. As we worked on this book, little did we know that Ukraine, Johann's homeland, would be experiencing this "fiery furnace" as this book is released.

In the Fiery Furnace is not only a history book but also a call for a Christian response to our suffering world—the millions of displaced Ukrainians, the potentially severe food shortages, and the spiritual needs in our world. With the songwriter we pray, "Let woe and waste of warfare cease," and with the psalmist we pray, "O send out thy light and thy truth" (Psalm 43:3a). This book goes forth with prayers for Christian brothers and sisters in Ukraine and Russia—comfort for the sorrowing, relief for the suffering, healing for the wounded, protection for those who are assisting, and light for those in darkness.

We pray, and we find comfort because "Hitherto hath the Lord helped us," and He will again. "When thou walkest through the fire, thou shalt not be burned" (Isaiah 43:2b). "Thou shalt guide me with thy counsel, and afterward receive me to glory" (Psalm 73:24).

—*James K. Nolt*

A primary value of this book is the reality check that it provides us Westerners, who go about our peaceful Western lives knowing very little of true stories like this that are transpiring at the same time. We really need more of such stories. We tend to think that peace and prosperity will always be our experience in the West. The Russian Mennonites thought the same before World War I. Most Mennonites in the West are unprepared for deprivation and persecution. The book is not fiction; it is a record of actual terrible events which have happened not all that long ago.

—*Chester Weaver, teacher and historian*